Understanding .NET

Independent Technology Guides

The Independent Technology Guides offer serious technical descriptions of important new software technologies of interest to enterprise developers and technical managers. These books focus on how that technology works and what it can be used for, taking an independent perspective rather than reflecting the position of any particular vendor. These are ideal first books for developers with a wide range of backgrounds, the perfect place to begin mastering a new area and laying a solid foundation for further study. They also go into enough depth to enable technical managers to make good decisions without delving too deeply into implementation details.

The books in this series cover a broad range of topics, from networking protocols to development platforms, and are written by experts in the field. They have a fresh design created to make learning a new technology easier. All titles in the series are guided by the principle that, in order to use a technology well, you must first understand how and why that technology works.

Understanding .NET

A Tutorial and Analysis

David Chappell

✦ Addison-Wesley

Boston ■ *San Francisco* ■ *New York* ■ *Toronto* ■ *Montreal*
London ■ *Munich* ■ *Paris* ■ *Madrid*
Capetown ■ *Sydney* ■ *Tokyo* ■ *Singapore* ■ *Mexico City*

The publisher offers discounts on this book when ordered in quantity for special sales. For more information, please contact:

Pearson Education Corporate Sales Division
201 W. 103rd Street
Indianapolis, IN 46290
(800) 428-5331
corpsales@pearsoned.com

Visit AW on the Web: www.awprofessional.com

Pearson Education, Inc.
Rights and Contracts Department
75 Arlington Street, Suite 300
Boston, MA 02116
Fax: (617) 848-7047

Text printed on recycled and acid-free paper.
ISBN 0201741628
4 5 6 7 8 9 CRS 05 04 03 02
4th Printing June 2002

Contents

Preface

There's no single way to write good software, and there's no perfect platform for it, either. Yet the people who create platforms keep striving for that unreachable ideal, and so they regularly give us new technology foundations to build on. With very few exceptions, each change is better than what it replaces. But with no exceptions at all, each innovation makes the current contents of our heads at least partially obsolete. Change is the essence of working with software.

.NET is the biggest single set of new technologies that Microsoft (or possibly any vendor) has ever presented to its technical customers. The tremendous changes wrought by .NET improve nearly every aspect of a developer's life, but they also present a massive amount of new technology to understand. The goal of this book is to help you make the move to this big new world.

Who This Book Is For

.NET is huge. There will be plenty of books that provide detailed examinations of each facet of this enormous technology crystal, plenty of books with hardcore, hands-on information. This isn't one of those books. I believe strongly that understanding .NET as a whole is essential before delving more deeply into any single part of the technology. Accordingly, my goal here is to provide a broad overview of the major .NET technologies. And because one of the greatest strengths of this family of software and services is the way one part exploits another, this book also tries to show how those technologies fit together.

If you're looking for a big-picture introduction and a perspective on the whole of .NET, this book is for you. Whether you're a developer just getting started with .NET, a technical manager who needs to make decisions about these technologies, or a student seeing some of these ideas for the first time, this book should be a useful guide. There is enough detail here to satisfy many people completely, while others will use this book as a stepping-stone to more specific knowledge. In any case, I hope the book's organization and content make it easier for you to come to grips with this mass of technology.

Fact and Opinion

Grasping a new technology requires learning the fundamentals. What are its main parts? How do they work? How do they fit together? But really understanding a technology requires more than this. You need to know not just how things work but also why they're important, how they compare with what's gone before, and what might happen next.

This book provides all of these things. In the text itself, I've tried hard to remain strictly tutorial, focusing solely on describing what .NET is. In the analysis boxes, I give some broader perspective on various aspects of this technology. In every case, the analysis expresses my view of why things are the way they are or what the future is likely to hold. By separating the objective and the subjective, I hope to make it easier for you to distinguish between the two. By providing opinion as well as fact, I hope to make this book both more interesting and more enlightening.

Acknowledgments

If you've ever written a book, you know how much help you get from other people. If you haven't, well, trust me: Without these people's assistance, this book would be substantially less than it is. I'd like to express my heartfelt thanks to Bob Beauchemin, Keith Brown, Cori Day, Ted Demopoulos, Bill Estrem, Jeannine Gailey, Kit George, Greg Hack, Rob Howard, Maxim Loukianov, Juval Löwy, Peter McKiernan, Yahya H. Mirza, John D. Mitchell, Christophe Nassare, Eric Newcomer, David Sceppa, Aaron Skonnard, and Mike Woodring for reading, commenting on, and often correcting various parts of this book. I'd like to single out Richard Monson-Haefel, a strong technologist and fine writer, who read and commented intelligently on every chapter.

The attendees in the many .NET seminars I've presented have also contributed mightily to making this book better. By letting me practice my explanations, they helped me figure out which paths to understanding .NET worked. By asking insightful questions, they provided the inspiration for many of the analysis boxes scattered throughout this book.

Many people at Addison-Wesley also deserve my profound thanks. Without Kristin Weinberger, neither the *Independent Technology Guide* series nor this book would exist. Without Stephane Thomas, I would never have finished this project. Without Cindy Kogut, my text would have been significantly less clear. And without Katie Noyes, the beautiful cover design wouldn't have been created.

I'd also like to thank my good friends Jim and Judy Moffitt for a hand-delivered care package of chocolate chip cookies that arrived just when I needed it most. And finally, I owe all manner of things to Diana Catignani, without whom my life would be so very much poorer.

David Chappell
www.davidchappell.com
December 2001

1

An Overview of .NET

The world of software development is a volatile place. New ideas appear and are quickly embodied in new technologies. Sometimes those new technologies can be absorbed incrementally, adding to what software professionals already know. Other times, the changes are too great to be introduced as gradual innovations in what already exists. In cases like this, software developers, architects, and managers all experience a fundamental tectonic shift, an earthquake, in their world.

Microsoft's .NET initiative is this kind of earthquake. It will affect everybody who works in the Windows environment, and it will generate aftershocks in the wider world, too. By giving us so much change to adapt to at once, Microsoft has made our lives more difficult in the short run—there's a lot to learn. Once we've absorbed this new set of tools and technologies, however, most Windows developers will find themselves capable of building more powerful, more useful software in less time.

.NET is a tectonic shift for Windows developers

1

Defining .NET

.NET is a brand applied to a range of technologies

Microsoft views .NET as a vision, a platform for the digital future. A more concrete and equally accurate way to think about this new initiative is to understand that .NET is a brand, one that Microsoft has applied to several different technologies. Some of these technologies are entirely new, providing new services and new possibilities. Others allow an updated approach to creating the kinds of Windows applications we know today. Still other parts of the .NET family are just new releases of existing technologies dressed up with the .NET brand.

Web services are a core technology in .NET

The most important new technology in .NET is *Web services.* As the name suggests, a Web service provides some function that can be invoked programmatically via the Web. Most technologies that carry the .NET brand have direct support for Web services in some way, yet .NET is more than just Web services. The technologies that Microsoft has placed under the .NET umbrella today include the following:

- **The .NET Framework:** Includes the *Common Language Runtime (CLR)* and the *.NET Framework class library.* The CLR is a standard foundation for building a range of new applications, while the .NET Framework class library provides standard implementations of many new services for CLR-based applications. Among the technologies in the library are *ASP.NET*, which is the next generation of Active Server Pages; *ADO.NET*, the next generation of ActiveX Data Objects; support for building and using Web services; and much more. Microsoft is also releasing a trimmed-down incarnation of the .NET Framework called the *.NET Compact Framework.* This version is intended for use in smaller devices, such as personal digital assistants (PDAs).

- **Visual Studio.NET:** Supports several programming languages that can be used with the .NET Framework. These languages include Visual Basic.NET, which is the next generation of Visual Basic; an enhanced version of C++; and a wholly new language called C#[1] designed explicitly for the .NET Framework.

- **.NET My Services:** A group of services that allow users to store and access personal information, such as a calendar and address book, on Internet-accessible servers. These services also provide more general features such as authentication, which allows a client to prove its identity, and a way to send alert messages to clients on various devices.

- **The .NET Enterprise Servers:** A family of software servers that includes BizTalk Server 2000, Application Center 2000, Commerce Server 2000, Host Integration Server 2000, SQL Server 2000, Exchange Server 2000, Mobile Information Server 2001, and Internet Security and Acceleration Server 2000. In their current releases, these products are largely independent from the other .NET technologies listed here. They don't, for example, make use of the .NET Framework, nor do they provide much direct support for Web services.

Understanding .NET requires understanding Web services. It also requires grasping at least the basics of each of the .NET technologies just listed. This chapter provides an overview of all of these topics.

Web Services

The World Wide Web has radically changed the way we access information, buy products, find jobs, and generally live our lives. It has done all of this through applications that interact directly with people through a graphical user interface (GUI).

Web applications today are typically accessed via a GUI

---

1. Pronounced "C sharp," as in the musical note.

It's no exaggeration to say that GUI-based applications have made the Web what it is today.

Web services allow programmatic access to Web applications

But GUI-based applications probably won't be the vehicle for the next phase of the Web. To understand why, think about the kinds of services we get from the Web today. Some of them, such as reading *The Economist* online, should be delivered through a GUI-based application—how else could we get them? Yet an important set of services could be used more easily and more effectively if the applications that provided them were accessible programmatically. Rather than a person sitting at a browser, the client for these services would be software running on a desktop computer, a mobile phone, or some other device. Rather than making requests using only the traditional Hypertext Transfer Protocol (HTTP) that return Hypertext Markup Language (HTML), this client software could invoke remote operations in those applications with some other protocol, returning the information using the Extensible Markup Language (XML). In other words, the applications' functions could be accessed as Web services.

Web services can be applied in many ways

This technology can be used in many ways. For example, Web services could be used to allow desktop or handheld clients to access applications on the Internet, such as reservations systems. Web services can also be used for business-to-business (B2B) integration, connecting applications run by different organizations over the Internet. Web services can potentially be used even for enterprise application integration (EAI), connecting applications run by a single organization over private networks. In all of these cases, the technologies of Web services provide the standard glue between diverse pieces of software.

Interfaces to Web services can be defined using WSDL

Making all of this work requires several technologies. First, there must be some way to define standard Web service interfaces. Each interface contains one or more operations, each with parameters, much like the interfaces defined by the Component Object Model (COM) or the Object Management

Group's Common Object Request Broker Architecture (CORBA).[2] In .NET, Web service interfaces are usually specified using the Web Services Description Language (WSDL). Defined using XML, WSDL provides a standardized way to specify the operations in an interface, the input and output parameters of those operations, and more. Although it looks quite different, WSDL is functionally similar to the Interface Definition Languages (IDLs) used by COM and CORBA.

Once an interface has been defined, some protocol must be used to invoke the operations in that interface and return any results. WSDL doesn't specify any particular protocol, and so various choices exist. By far the most common protocol for invoking Web services is the Simple Object Access Protocol (SOAP). SOAP, which is itself defined using XML, also relies on XML to define a standard format for the data this protocol conveys. Although SOAP messages are most commonly sent on top of HTTP, this isn't required. In fact, SOAP can be used to invoke operations over a message queuing technology such as Microsoft Message Queue (MSMQ), over e-mail systems, or with other protocols.

Web services are most commonly invoked using SOAP

Given a way to describe Web service interfaces and a protocol with which to invoke the operations in those interfaces, the next problem is to let clients find compatible Web services. Universal Description, Discovery, and Integration (UDDI) allows developers of Web service clients to locate the information they need, such as WSDL interfaces, to build clients that can use appropriate Web services. And rather than invent a new technology to access this information, clients use SOAP to read and write the contents of the UDDI database.

Web service interface definitions can be published and accessed via UDDI

---

2. To distinguish them from interfaces defined using these earlier technologies, the convention in this book is to show all Web service interfaces as a diamond.

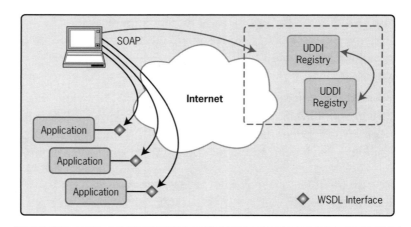

Figure 1-1   WSDL, SOAP, and UDDI are the core Web services technologies.

Windows application developers have long relied on Windows DNA

Figure 1-1 shows how the core Web services technologies fit together. As the figure shows, a client might access UDDI, which provides its services through a group of interconnected machines acting as UDDI *registries,* to learn about the Web services it wishes to use. It can then use SOAP to invoke operations in the interfaces those services provide, interfaces that were specified in WSDL. While other options are also possible—the client might invoke a Web service with a protocol other than SOAP, for example, or WSDL might not be used to describe all interfaces—this diagram shows the typical way in which these mainstream Web services technologies relate to one another.

Taken together, WSDL, SOAP, and UDDI allow building many kinds of applications. They can also make existing applications more useful by providing a standard approach to connecting them. Chapter 2 describes in more detail how these technologies work and how they can be used.

The .NET Framework

For most of the 1990s, application developers in the Microsoft environment relied on the technologies in Windows DNA.

Standards for Web Services

Web services are an unassailably good idea. Yet if these technologies were supported by Microsoft alone, they wouldn't be very interesting. Fortunately, Microsoft, IBM, Sun, Oracle, BEA, and many other vendors have all endorsed the core Web services technologies of SOAP, WSDL, and UDDI. Some of those technologies have been submitted to the World Wide Web Consortium (W3C) and so are on their way to becoming official standards. For example, the W3C has created an XML Protocol working group. This group now owns SOAP and is working to create the next version of this workhorse protocol for Web services. The key point is that while not all of these Web services technologies are official standards yet, all of them have broad vendor support.

Also, none of them contains dependencies on Microsoft-specific technologies such as the .NET Framework. This is a little surprising, given that Microsoft was a major player in the creation of each one. Despite the company's less than stellar reputation for conforming to multivendor standards, Microsoft seems to have realized that Web services cannot succeed without widespread endorsement. Accordingly, the Web services decision makers working with Redmond have thus far chosen to work with their competitors to make this new technology a multivendor reality.

Those technologies include COM and Distributed COM (DCOM), a larger group of COM-based technologies known collectively as COM+, Active Server Pages (ASP), ActiveX Data Objects (ADO), and others. The most commonly used languages for building Windows DNA applications have been Visual Basic and Visual C++, both provided as part of Microsoft's Visual Studio.

Tens of thousands of applications based on these technologies are in production today, providing solid evidence of Windows DNA's success. Yet at the start of a new century, Microsoft has introduced the .NET Framework, a new environment for creating applications. The technologies the Framework includes will

The .NET Framework is the successor to Windows DNA

change the way nearly every Windows application is created. They will also change the world of everyone who designs and develops Windows-based software or manages those who do.

For developers, the .NET Framework is the most important part of .NET

As this chapter illustrates, the .NET initiative encompasses a family of new technologies. For Windows developers, however, by far the most important is the .NET Framework. It's no exaggeration to say that the Framework is the most significant advance Microsoft has introduced for software developers since the release of Windows NT.

The Windows DNA technologies are a diverse lot

To understand the changes wrought by the .NET Framework, the place to start is Windows DNA. The technologies Windows DNA includes—COM, ASP, and others—were developed over time. Because of this, the integration among them wasn't as complete as it might have been. For example, one attractive aspect of the Windows DNA environment is that application developers can use various programming languages, including Visual Basic (VB) and VBScript, C++, and others. Yet each language has its own runtime libraries, its own data types, its own approach to building GUIs, as well as other differences.

Windows DNA applications vary in functionality depending on the language and environment they use

Applications written in different languages also access system services in different ways. C++ applications can make direct calls to the operating system through the Win32 interface, for instance, while Visual Basic applications typically access these services indirectly. These differences make life challenging for developers working in more than one language. Another example of diversity is the division between the scripting environment used in ASP pages and the compiled code in the COM components that those pages commonly use. Developers building ASP applications, one of the most popular Windows DNA technologies, must work in both environments using different languages and tools.

The CLR provides a common basis for all languages and environments

The lives of Windows developers would be simpler if there were a common foundation that could be used from all languages. This is exactly what the .NET Framework offers. Every application written using the Framework depends on a fundamental library called the Common Language Runtime (CLR). The CLR provides a common set of data types and other services that can be used by all languages that target the .NET Framework. Because the foundation is the same no matter which language they choose, developers now see a much more consistent environment.

Along with the CLR, the .NET Framework includes the .NET Framework class library, a large set of standard classes and other types that can be used by any .NET Framework application written in any language. All of those applications can now access system services in the same way—through the .NET Framework class library. The differences that complicate the Windows DNA world are gone.

The .NET Framework class library provides standard code for common functions

Among the most important technologies provided in the .NET Framework class library are the following:

- **ASP.NET:** The next generation of Active Server Pages for building Web-accessible applications. A key feature of this new technology is strong support for building applications that use and expose Web services.

- **ADO.NET:** The next generation of ActiveX Data Objects for accessing data stored in relational database management systems (DBMSs) and in other formats.

- **Windows Forms:** A standard set of classes for building Windows GUIs in any .NET Framework programming language.

- **Enterprise Services:** Standard classes for accessing COM+ services such as transactions and object pooling.

The .NET Framework class library contains much more than this short list indicates. Among the other services it provides are support for creating and working with XML documents, services for remote access, and mechanisms for interoperating with COM-based applications. Figure 1-2 illustrates the main components of the .NET Framework and how they relate to one another.

The .NET Framework supports various kinds of applications

As the figure shows, the .NET Framework can be used to create many different types of applications. The choices include browser-accessible applications, Web services applications, applications that display just a local Windows GUI, and others. Because all of the services in the .NET Framework class library are built on the CLR, applications can combine them as needed. A browser application built using ASP.NET, for example, might use ADO.NET to access stored data and Enterprise Services to perform distributed transactions.

A .NET Framework application consists of managed code

Software that uses the .NET Framework (and thus relies on the CLR) is referred to as *managed code.* That code is usually object-oriented, so the objects it creates and uses are known as *managed objects.* A managed object can use and even inherit from another managed object even if the two are written in different languages. This fact is a key part of what makes the .NET Framework class library an effective tool: Objects written in any CLR-based language can inherit and use the library's code.

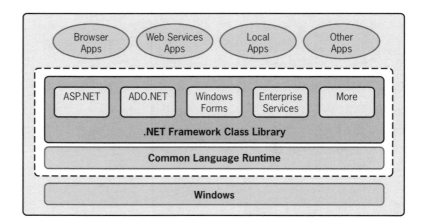

Figure 1-2   The .NET Framework consists of the Common Language Runtime and the .NET Framework class library.

Housing Windows Developers

Think of Windows DNA as a house. It's not a bad house, and a lot of people have lived in it quite happily. But *chez* DNA was built with no master plan—it just grew. Two languages with wildly different personalities, Visual Basic and C++, lived together uneasily beneath the same roof. Additions were constructed when required, and every effort was made to design these additions according to some common architecture. But because they were developed by different groups at different times to meet different needs, the additions didn't always fit together well. The duct tape of COM sometimes seemed like the main thing that kept the house standing.

Rather than trying to keep improving Windows DNA, Microsoft has chosen instead to buy a new lot and construct a completely new house. That house is the .NET Framework, and it's one that many people will one day find themselves living in. But unlike Windows DNA, the Framework has a clear, consistent architecture from its foundation on up to the skylights. There is a well-thought-out master plan, and just about everything in the Framework fits into it.

The lot on which the .NET Framework sits is right next door to the old Windows DNA place. This is good, because between the two there's a workable connection known as COM interoperability. People will still be living under the roof of Windows DNA for many years to come, so this close relationship is critically important. But Windows DNA won't gain many new residents. The future belongs to the .NET Framework.

The Common Language Runtime

The Common Language Runtime is the basis for everything else in the .NET Framework. It's used by every Framework application, regardless of the language in which that application is written, and it's the foundation for the .NET Framework class library as well. To understand the Framework, the CLR is the place to start.

What the CLR Defines

Think about how a programming language is defined today. Each language commonly has its own unique syntax, its own set of control structures, a unique set of data types, its own notions of how classes inherit from one another, and much more. The choices a language designer makes are driven by the target applications for the language, who its users are meant to be, and the designer's own sensibilities.

There's widespread agreement on the features a modern programming language should offer

Yet most people agree on much of what a modern programming language should provide. While opinions on syntax differ— some developers love curly braces, others abhor them—there's widespread agreement on what semantics a language should offer. Given this, why not define a standard implementation of those semantics, then allow different syntaxes to be used to express those semantics?

The CLR defines a common set of semantics that is used by multiple languages

The CLR provides this standard implementation. By providing a common set of data types such as integers, strings, classes, and interfaces, specifications for how inheritance works, and much more, it defines a common set of semantics for languages built on it. The CLR says nothing about syntax, however. How a language looks, whether it contains curly braces or semicolons or anything else, is entirely up to the language designer. While it is possible to implement languages with varying behaviors on top of the CLR, the CLR itself provides a consistent, modern set of semantics for a language designer to build on.

The CLR also provides other common services

Along with its standard types, the CLR provides other fundamental services. Those services include the following:

- **Garbage collection,** which automatically frees managed objects that are no longer referenced.

- **A standard format for metadata,** information about each type that's stored with the compiled code for that type. Unlike COM, there are no separate type libraries, nor is there any need for an IDL. Instead, interfaces and classes are defined directly using whatever programming language a developer is working in and then converted into a standard metadata format.

- **A common scheme for organizing compiled code, called *assemblies*.** An assembly can consist of one or more Dynamic Link Libraries (DLLs) and/or executables (EXEs), and it includes the metadata for the classes it contains. A single application might use code from one or more assemblies, and so each assembly can specify other assemblies on which it depends.

COM and the .NET Framework

Because it defines common conventions for interfaces, data types, and other aspects of interaction among different software, COM provides the glue that connects all of the components in a Windows DNA world. Since the introduction of COM in 1993, Windows developers (including those in Redmond) have used it more and more in creating new software. Given this technology's important role, it's worth saying a bit more about the place of COM in the .NET Framework environment.

Applications built on the .NET Framework don't face many of the problems that COM addresses. For example, .NET Framework applications all use the CLR, and the CLR defines a common approach to interfaces and other data types. As a result, the glue between different languages that COM provides is no longer necessary. This is why traditional COM technology isn't used in building pure .NET Framework applications. Instead, developers can build software that interacts in a more natural and substantially simpler way.

Does this mean that the arrival of the .NET Framework signals the death of COM? Certainly not. In a highly abstract sense, the CLR is the next generation of COM (in fact, Microsoft referred to it internally as COM+ 2.0 during its development). Also, as described later in this book, the CLR has a great deal of built-in support for interoperating with COM-based applications. Finally, for some new applications, developers will choose not to use the .NET Framework at all. The creators of a new DBMS, for instance, might decide to use straight C++ instead of building on the Framework. If so, they would likely also use COM to expose external services and define internal interfaces. While the role of COM gets much smaller in a .NET world, COM is not dead.

Using the CLR

The CLR supports many different programming languages

The CLR was not defined with any particular programming language in mind. Instead, its features are derived largely from popular existing languages, such as C++, Visual Basic, and Java. Yet it doesn't exactly match any of these languages. Accordingly, Microsoft has provided new languages built on the CLR for .NET Framework developers to use, including Visual Basic.NET and C#. C++ can also be used to write .NET Framework applications using a set of managed extensions. The result, commonly called *Managed C++*, allows the large number of developers familiar with C++ to access the services provided by the .NET Framework.

Managed code is always compiled first into MSIL

No matter what language it's written in, all managed code is compiled into Microsoft Intermediate Language (MSIL) rather than a machine-specific binary. MSIL is a set of CPU-independent instructions for performing typical operations such as loading and storing information and calling methods. Each DLL and EXE in an assembly contains MSIL rather than processor-specific code. Installing a .NET Framework application on your system really means copying to your disk files that contain MSIL rather than a machine-specific binary. When the application is executed, MSIL is transformed into native code before it's executed.

Each method is typically JIT compiled the first time it's invoked

Figure 1-3 illustrates the process of compiling and executing managed code. Source code written in VB.NET, C#, Managed C++, or another language that targets the CLR is first transformed into MSIL by the appropriate language compiler. As the figure shows, the compiler also produces metadata that's stored in the same file as the MSIL. Before execution, this MSIL is compiled into native code for the processor on which the code will run. By default, each method in a running application is compiled the first time that method is called. Because the method is compiled just in time to execute it, this approach is called *just-in-time (JIT) compilation*.

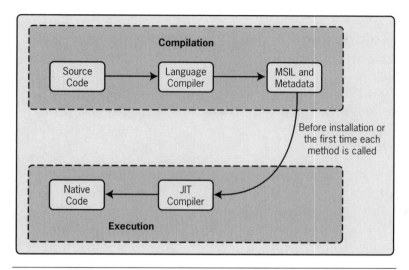

Figure 1-3   All managed code is compiled first to MSIL, then translated into native code before execution.

One point worth noting is that all languages targeting the CLR should exhibit roughly the same performance. Unlike the Windows DNA world, where the performance difference between VB and C++ is sometimes significant, .NET Framework applications written in C# are not noticeably faster than those written in VB.NET. While some compilers may produce better MSIL code than others, large variations in execution speed are unlikely.

All .NET Framework–based languages have about the same level of performance

The CLR is the foundation of everything else in the .NET Framework. All code in the .NET Framework class library depends on it, as do all Framework-based applications. Chapter 3 provides a more detailed look at the technology of the CLR.

CLR-Based Languages

One of the goals of the .NET Framework is to let developers work in the language of their choice. To allow this, the CLR can support many different programming languages. Those

Visual Studio.NET provides four languages for building .NET Framework applications

The .NET Framework and Existing Applications

The .NET Framework is a big change. It's so big, in fact, that most existing applications, especially those written in Visual Basic 6, won't run on the Framework without at least some modification. Releasing a new development environment that won't run existing applications is an unusual step for a vendor to take. How big a problem is it likely to cause?

For most organizations, the fact that existing applications won't run on the .NET Framework shouldn't be too much of an issue. To see why, it's important to realize that most existing applications won't *need* to run on the Framework. Installing the Framework doesn't break any code that's already running on a system, so Framework-based applications can run side by side with existing software, such as Windows DNA applications. In spite of the .NET Framework's benefits for developing new applications, there probably won't be compelling business reasons to modify most existing applications to run on top of it.

The core problem, then, is building new Framework-based code that either extends or interacts with existing non-Framework-based software. To make this possible, the CLR has built-in support that allows managed code to call existing DLLs, access and be accessed by COM objects, and interoperate in other ways with the current generation of software. Achieving this interoperability can be simple, but it can also get complicated in more involved situations. It is possible, however, so existing code does not need to be rewritten to work with new Framework-based code.

Transitioning to a wholly new environment still has its challenges, however. One of the most obvious is the cost of retraining. In the long run, avoiding the .NET Framework isn't possible for Windows-oriented organizations, so ponying up the cash for developer education is unavoidable. It's not fun, and time will be lost as developers come up to speed on this new technology. The .NET Framework really is substantially better than Windows DNA, however, so most organizations are likely to see productivity gains once developers have internalized this new environment.

Another concern is that organizations will need to have two development environments for some period of time. Maintaining Windows DNA applications will generally require Visual Studio 6, while new applications will require Visual Studio.NET. Both can be installed at once on a single machine, but still, maintaining parallel worlds is not a desirable thing. Also, Microsoft promises to support Visual Studio 6 for some time, but it's not yet clear exactly how long this will be. Microsoft is now an enterprise vendor—mission-critical applications rely on Windows DNA—so this period should be measured in years, perhaps even decades. If the people in Redmond fail to understand this and drop support for Visual Studio 6 too soon, they will demonstrate that Microsoft isn't really an enterprise vendor after all.

languages often have a good deal in common, since the CLR defines the core semantics for each one, but a developer can still choose the language that feels most natural to her. Visual Studio.NET, Microsoft's primary tool for building .NET Framework applications, supports four CLR-based languages: Visual Basic.NET, C#, C++, and JScript.NET. Third parties have demonstrated support for other languages built on the CLR, including Perl, Python, and COBOL. All of these languages use at least some of the services provided by the CLR, and some expose virtually everything the CLR has to offer. This section provides a short introduction to each of the CLR-based languages included in Visual Studio.NET.

Visual Basic.NET

From its humble beginnings at Dartmouth College in the 1960s, Basic has grown into perhaps the most widely used programming language in the world today. This success is due largely to the popularity of Microsoft's Visual Basic. Yet it's likely that the original creators of Basic wouldn't recognize their creation as it's implemented in the Microsoft tool. The price of success has been adaptation—sometimes radical—to new requirements.

Visual Basic is a very widely used environment

Visual Basic.NET is the next step in the evolution of Visual Basic. In addition to being enormously different from the original Basic language, it is a big leap from its immediate

VB.NET is a big change from VB 6

predecessor, Visual Basic 6. The primary reason for this substantial change is that VB.NET is built entirely on the CLR. In fact, it's not possible to create traditional standalone binary executables with VB.NET. Instead, every application built with this tool is compiled into MSIL and requires the .NET Framework to execute.

Because it's built on the CLR, VB.NET has a host of new features that this standard library provides, including the following:

- Support for implementation inheritance, allowing a new child class to inherit code from one parent class (this is sometimes referred to as *single inheritance*)

- The ability for a child class to override one or more methods in its parent

- Support for exception handling

- Full multithreading

- The ability to define explicitly interfaces directly in VB

- Support for properties and events

- Support for attributes, allowing features such as transaction support and Web services to be implemented by inserting keywords in source code

- Garbage collection, freeing developers from the need to destroy explicitly objects they have created

VBScript no longer exists as a separate technology

VB.NET also marks the end of Visual Basic, Scripting Edition (commonly called just VBScript) as a separate technology. Traditionally used in Active Server Pages, command scripts, and other places, this VB dialect is replaced by VB.NET. Among other things, this change allows using the full power of Visual Basic in ASP.NET applications. Yet it also replaces a simple tool with a more complex one, which may make life a bit more challenging for system administrators accustomed to the simplicity of VBScript.

C#

Modifying Visual Basic to work with the CLR required substantial changes to the language, but the result is still close enough to the original to warrant having the same name. The other dominant language in the pre-.NET Microsoft world has been C++. A large number of Windows developers know (and love) C++, so how can those developers be brought forward to use the .NET Framework? One answer is to extend C++, an option described in the next section. Another approach, one that will likely prove more appealing for most current C++ developers, is to create a new language based on the CLR but with a syntax derived from C++. This is exactly what Microsoft has done by creating C#.

C# is the natural language for .NET Framework developers who prefer a syntax derived from C

The only completely new language in Visual Studio.NET, C# will look familiar to anyone accustomed to programming in C++ or Java. Like those languages and like VB.NET, C# is object-oriented. C# is much like VB.NET in other ways, too, which shouldn't be surprising. Both are built on the CLR, and both expose the same core functionality from this standard foundation. In fact, the biggest difference between C# and VB.NET is in syntax; functionally, the two languages are very similar.

C# provides almost exactly the same features as Visual Basic.NET

The list of features provided by C# is nearly identical to the list just given for Visual Basic.NET. Among those features are the following:

- Support for single implementation inheritance

- Method overriding

- Support for exception handling

- Full multithreading

- The ability to define explicitly interfaces directly in C#

- Support for properties and events

- Support for attributes as in VB.NET

- Garbage collection

C# also provides a few features that aren't available in VB.NET, including the following:

- Operator overloading, allowing a class to define its own unique meaning for standard operators such as the plus sign

- The ability to write code that directly accesses specific memory addresses, sometimes referred to as *unsafe* code

Most Visual Basic programmers can safely ignore C# if they choose because VB.NET offers almost everything that's in C#. C++ or Java developers, who are accustomed to a C-like syntax, will likely prefer C# for writing .NET Framework applications.

C++

The semantics of C++ differ from those defined by the CLR

C++ presents a challenge in the world of .NET. To be used in building .NET Framework applications, this popular language must be modified to use the CLR. Yet some of the core semantics of C++, which allows such things as a child class inheriting directly from multiple parents (known as *multiple inheritance*), conflict with those of the CLR. At the same time, C++ is likely to remain the dominant language for creating non-Framework-based Windows applications, so modifying it to be purely Framework specific isn't possible. What's the solution?

.NET Framework applications can be created using Managed C++

In Visual Studio.NET, Microsoft's answer is to support standard C++ as always, leaving this powerful language able to create efficient processor-specific binaries as before (in fact, there are even quite a few enhancements in this area). To allow the use of C++ to create .NET Framework applications, Microsoft added a set of extensions to the language. The C++ dialect that includes these extensions is called *Managed C++*, and it provides access to all features of the CLR. Using Managed C++, for instance, a developer can write C++ code that takes advantage of garbage collection, defines interfaces, uses attributes, and more.

Because not all applications will use the .NET Framework, Visual Studio.NET still allows building traditional Windows applications in C++. Rather than using Managed C++, a developer can write standard C++ code and then compile it into processor-specific binaries. Unlike VB.NET, C#, and JScript.NET, C++ is not required to compile into MSIL.

Standard C++ can also be used to create non-Framework-based applications

JScript.NET

JScript, Microsoft's implementation of what's more commonly called JavaScript, is primarily used for two things in the Windows DNA world: writing code that's sent to and executed by browsers, and writing code for Active Server Pages. JScript.NET, the .NET world's successor to JScript, still can be used for both of these things. In fact, it is a superset of standard JScript, although one to which quite a bit has been added.

JScript.NET is the Visual Studio.NET implementation of JavaScript

Like the other languages in Visual Studio.NET, JScript.NET is now implemented on top of the CLR. Accordingly, it now includes several new features, among the most important of which are

JScript.NET is built on the CLR

- Support for classes, which can contain methods, variables, and properties; can implement interfaces; and can inherit from other classes.

- A variety of new data types, including Boolean, String, int, float, and more.

- Compiled rather than interpreted code.

Especially for developers accustomed to writing Active Server Pages in traditional JScript, JScript.NET should bring welcome enhancements. Creators of scripts sent to and executed by browsers, however, probably won't gain much from these new features. Unless the target browser is guaranteed to be a recent version of Internet Explorer, the extensions can't be used. Furthermore, because the Microsoft extensions aren't supported by Netscape's browser, embedding JScript.NET code in pages

ASP.NET developers will likely be the most common users of JScript.NET

sent to arbitrary browsers on the Internet is unlikely to lead to happy users. For these situations, applications will need to continue to use traditional JavaScript, an option that is still supported for .NET Framework applications.

Support for multiple programming languages is one of the most attractive things about the .NET Framework. Chapter 4 takes a closer look at C#, VB.NET, and Managed C++, the three languages likely to be most popular for building .NET Framework–based applications.

The .NET Framework Class Library

The .NET Framework class library can be used from any CLR-based language

The .NET Framework class library is exactly what its name suggests: a library of classes and other types that developers can use to make their lives easier. While these classes are written in C#, they can be used from any CLR-based language. Code written in VB.NET, C#, Managed C++, or any other language supported by the .NET Framework can create instances of these classes and call their methods. That code can also rely on the CLR's support for inheritance to inherit from the library's classes.

Surveying the Library

The .NET Framework class library is organized as a tree

The contents of the .NET Framework class library are organized into a tree of namespaces. Each namespace can contain types, such as classes and interfaces, and other namespaces. The root of the tree, the namespace that contains all other namespaces as well as many types of its own, is the System namespace. Figure 1-4 shows a very small part of the .NET Framework class library's namespace tree. The namespaces shown include the following:

- **System:** Along with all of the other namespaces in the .NET Framework class library, this namespace also contains the core data types used by the CLR (and thus by languages built on the CLR). These types include several varieties of integers, a string type, and many more.

- **System.Web:** The types in this namespace comprise ASP.NET. Types in the System.Web.UI namespace are used to build browser-accessible applications, while those in System.Web.Services are used to build Web services applications.

- **System.Data:** The types in this namespace comprise ADO.NET. For example, the Connection class is used to establish connections to a database management system (DBMS), while an instance of the DataSet class can be used to cache and examine the results of a query issued against that DBMS.

- **System.Windows.Forms:** The types in this namespace are used to build Windows GUIs. Rather than using language-specific mechanisms, such as Microsoft Foundation Classes (MFC) in C++, .NET Framework applications written in any programming language use this common set of types to build local GUIs.

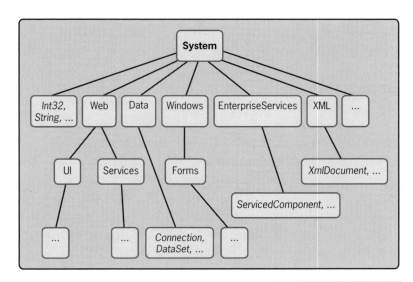

Figure 1-4   The .NET Framework class library is structured as a hierarchy of namespaces, with the System namespace at the root.

- **System.EnterpriseServices:** Services provided by COM+, such as distributed transactions, remain important in the .NET world. The types in this namespace allow managed code to access these services. Most important is the ServicedComponent class, from which every class that wishes to use COM+ services must inherit.

- **System.XML:** Types in this namespace provide support for creating and working with XML-defined data. The XmlDocument class, for instance, allows accessing an XML document using the Document Object Model (DOM). This namespace also includes support for newer technologies such as the XML Schema definition language (commonly referred to as XSD) and XPath.

Learning the .NET Framework class library will take time

Many more namespaces are defined, providing support for file access, serializing an object's state, remote access to objects, and much more. In fact, the biggest task facing developers who wish to build on the .NET Framework is learning to use the many services that the library provides. There's no requirement to learn everything, however, so a developer is free to focus on only those things relevant to his or her world. See Chapter 5 for a more complete description of this large library.

ADO.NET

ADO.NET lets applications access stored data

Because it contains the types that implement ADO.NET, System.Data is one of the most important namespaces in the .NET Framework class library. Like its predecessor ADO, ADO.NET lets applications work with data stored in a DBMS. Apart from this fundamental similarity, however, ADO and ADO.NET don't have much in common. Instead, ADO.NET focuses on allowing managed code to work with data in a way that makes sense for a world increasingly dominated by Web-based applications.

ADO.NET clients rely on a .NET data provider to access a DBMS

Figure 1-5 illustrates how an application can use ADO.NET to access stored information. As the figure shows, access to a

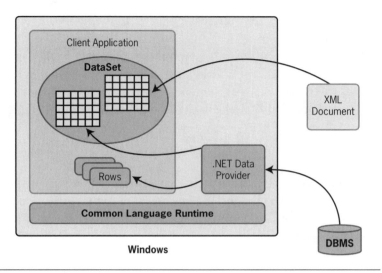

Figure 1-5   ADO.NET allows .NET Framework applications to access data stored in DBMSs and XML documents.

DBMS relies on a *.NET data provider,* written as managed code. .NET data providers that allow access to SQL Server, Oracle, and other DBMSs exist today, and they allow a client application to issue commands against the DBMS and examine any results those commands return. The result of a SQL query, for example, can be examined in two ways. Applications that need only read the result a row at a time can do this in a straightforward way, marching directly through what a query returns one record at a time. Applications that need to do more complex things with the result of a query, such as send it to a browser or store it on disk, can instead have the query's result packaged inside a DataSet object.

As Figure 1-5 illustrates, a DataSet can contain one or more tables. Each table can hold the result of a different query, so a single DataSet might potentially contain the results of two or more queries, perhaps from different DBMSs. In effect, a DataSet acts as an in-memory cache for data. As the figure shows, however, DataSets can hold more than just the result of a SQL query.

An ADO.NET DataSet acts as an in-memory cache for data

It's also possible to read an XML document directly into a table in a DataSet without relying on a .NET data provider. Data defined using XML has become much more important in the last few years, so ADO.NET allows accessing it directly. While not all .NET Framework applications will rely on ADO.NET for data access, a large percentage surely will. Given this importance, ADO.NET is described in more detail in Chapter 6.

ASP.NET

ASP.NET is the successor to Active Server Pages

Implemented in the System.Web namespace, ASP.NET is a major piece of the .NET Framework. The successor to the very popular Active Server Pages technology, ASP.NET brings a number of new features to ASP developers. Like traditional ASP applications, ASP.NET applications are built from one or more pages. Each page contains HTML and/or executable code. As Figure 1-6 shows, however, ASP.NET allows the creation of two types of applications: traditional browser applications accessible via HTTP and HTML, and Web services applications accessible via SOAP.

These two different kinds of applications use different kinds of pages. Applications that present traditional browser GUIs can

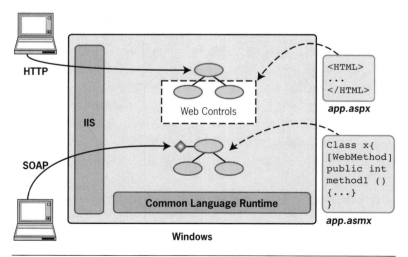

Figure 1-6   ASP.NET allows the creation of both browser applications and Web services applications.

be built by combining HTML and executable code in files with the extension *.aspx.* Applications that expose methods as Web services can be built from files with the extension *.asmx,* each of which contains only code. As Figure 1-6 shows, all that's . required to expose a method as a Web service from an .asmx page is to insert *WebMethod* before the method definition.

ASP.NET applica-tions can use .aspx pages and .asmx pages

ASP.NET also brings many other new features to the world of ASP development. Among the most important are the following:

ASP.NET changes ASP development in many ways

■ The code in ASP.NET applications is compiled rather than interpreted as in traditional Active Server Pages, so applications execute faster than in previous versions.

■ The distinction between script code and components is eliminated. Rather than deciding whether a function should be implemented as script code or as compiled but more complex COM components, all code in ASP.NET applications is managed code.

■ Web controls can be used to build browser-based GUIs more easily. Running on the server rather than the client, Web controls allow drag-and-drop construction of a user interface, just as in Visual Basic today.

■ ASP.NET applications are easier to install and remove than traditional ASP applications. An ASP.NET application is just a .NET Framework application, so it can be installed by simply copying files and removed by delet-ing those files. No registration entries are required (unless COM interoperability features are used).

Given the popularity of traditional ASP technology, ASP.NET may affect more developers than any other part of the .NET Framework class library. Although it's just one part of this large set of new technology, ASP.NET is likely to be very widely used. Chapter 7 provides more detail on this important part of the .NET Framework.

The .NET Framework and the Java Environment

Mainstream software development today has split cleanly into two camps. Microsoft, promoting the .NET Framework, is in one, while most other vendors, backing Sun's Java environment, are in the other. Both technologies have their fans and detractors, and I'm convinced that both have a good future.

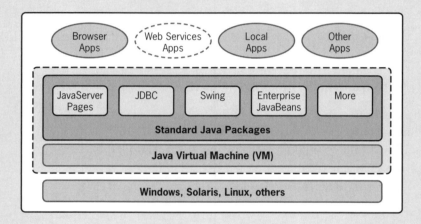

These competing worlds are strikingly similar. To see how similar, compare the figure above with Figure 1-2. Both environments are trying to support the same classes of applications (although the .NET Framework has significantly better support for Web services than is specified for the Java world today), and the Java virtual machine is similar to the .NET Framework's CLR. The large standard library that Java provides includes JavaServer Pages for Web scripting, JDBC for database access, Swing for building GUIs, Enterprise JavaBeans for building more scalable server applications, and other classes. These are quite analogous to the .NET Framework's ASP.NET, ADO.NET, Windows Forms, and Enterprise Services, respectively. Even the semantics of the dominant languages—Microsoft's C# and VB.NET versus Java—are quite similar.

There are also differences, of course. One obvious distinction between the two is that the Java environment runs on diverse operating systems, while the .NET Framework focuses on Windows. The trade-off here is clear: Portability is good, but it prevents tight integration with any one system, and integration is also good. You can't have everything, at least not all at the same time. Also, Java-based products are available from multiple vendors, while only Microsoft provides the .NET Framework. Java products commonly provide extensions to the core specifications, so developers tend to get somewhat locked into a single vendor. Still, portability across different Java platforms is possible, while the .NET Framework unambiguously ties your application to Microsoft.

This bifurcation and the competition it engenders are ultimately a good thing. Both camps have had good ideas, and each has borrowed from the other. Having one completely dominant technology, whether the .NET Framework or Java, would produce a stultifying monopoly. Having a dozen viable choices would produce something close to anarchy, an idea that should send shivers through anyone who lived through the chaos of the two-tier client/server era. Two strong competitors, each working to outdo the other, is just right.

The .NET Compact Framework

While the .NET Framework is useful for writing applications on desktops and server machines, it can also be used with smaller devices, such as mobile phones, PDAs, and set-top boxes. Small devices are becoming more and more important, and they're an important piece of Microsoft's overall .NET strategy. These devices typically have less memory, however, so they're unable to run the complete .NET Framework. The .NET Compact Framework addresses this issue. By eliminating some parts of the .NET Framework class library, it allows use of the Framework in smaller devices.

The .NET Compact Framework is a smaller version of the .NET Framework

The .NET Compact Framework first targets Windows CE, but Microsoft also plans to make it available in other environments. Because it's built on the same foundation used in larger systems, the .NET Compact Framework allows the use of Visual Studio.NET as its development environment. Organizations that must create software for a range of devices can now use the same languages and the same tools to target systems of all sizes.

Visual Studio.NET can be used to develop applications for the .NET Compact Framework

The .NET Framework on Non-Windows Systems

Applications written using the .NET Framework are compiled to a processor-in-dependent form—MSIL—and shield themselves from the vagaries of a specific operating system by writing to the .NET Framework class library. This is much like the Java world, where applications are compiled to bytecode and can rely on standard Java libraries rather than making direct calls to a specific operating system. Java was expressly designed to work on multiple processors and operating systems. Is the same thing true for .NET?

To some extent, the answer is clearly yes. Microsoft has said that the .NET Compact Framework will be available for multiple processors and operating systems, not just for devices running Windows CE. Microsoft has also announced a port of the Framework's fundamentals to the FreeBSD version of UNIX. Theoretically, the .NET Framework could become a cross-platform solution on a wide range of systems.

Yet some technical issues remain. While MSIL is clearly platform independent, some parts of the .NET Framework class library just as clearly are not. Enterprise Services, for example, providing support for scalable, transaction-oriented applications, is based on COM+. Accordingly, this part of the library runs only where COM+ is available. This leaves out not only UNIX, but also older versions of Windows, such as Windows 98. Other parts of the class library also betray their Windows origins in more or less obvious ways.

Just as important, Microsoft will face some challenges in making customers believe that it's serious about long-term support of the .NET Framework on non-Windows systems. The company's laserlike focus on its own operating systems has been a hallmark of its business, as well as a primary factor in its success. Customers may remember earlier promises about making COM available on other platforms. While partners such as Software AG and Compaq labored mightily to make cross-platform COM a reality, Microsoft appeared to lose interest in the idea quickly. Might the same thing happen with non-Windows versions of the .NET Framework?

It's too soon to know. If Microsoft wishes to make the .NET Framework a true multiplatform rival for Java, the technical potential is there. But it will be several years before a critical mass of customers believes that the company is serious about helping them build software on operating systems that don't come from Redmond.

The .NET Framework itself is scheduled to be generally available in early 2002. The .NET Compact Framework is not scheduled to ship until sometime after that, however. Given that the Compact Framework is a subset of its larger sibling, this is counterintuitive. Why should it ship later? A large part of the answer is that the version of the CLR provided with the .NET Compact Framework is not the same as that in the Framework itself. Instead, the Compact Framework's CLR was rewritten to work more effectively on smaller devices with less memory and less processing power. As a result, the .NET Compact Framework will come to market some number of months later than its big brother.

The .NET Compact Framework will ship after the .NET Framework

.NET My Services

New technologies frequently create wholly new kinds of applications. Web services, for instance, a new way to expose functionality over the Internet, are bound to engender some innovative ideas. .NET My Services, a set of Internet-accessible Web services provided by Microsoft, provides one good example of this innovation.

Rather than store a copy of information such as your calendar and address book on each device, why not instead make this information available via an Internet-accessible Web service? This would allow access to the same information from your desktop computer at work, your home machine, your wireless PDA, and perhaps even your mobile phone. And if this kind of information can be made available as Web services, why not provide other services as well, such as a place to store documents or a way to access e-mail? And why not build in other services such as notifications that can find you and inform you immediately of some event? Providing these kinds of services is the goal of .NET My Services.

The .NET My Services technology provides access to information across the Internet

As Figure 1-7 shows, all of these services are accessed via the Internet, and both client and server applications can potentially

.NET My Services includes an authentication service

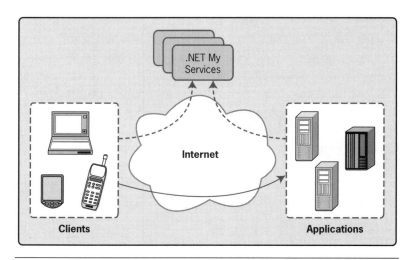

Figure 1-7   .NET My Services can be accessed by users and applications on the Internet.

use them. Along with these services, however, .NET My Services also provides a standard authentication service that allows clients to prove their identity. Based on Microsoft's Passport service, this authentication is required to ensure that only authorized users can access the information .NET My Services contains. The .NET My Services version of Passport will rely on Kerberos, a technology that in the last few years has become widely used to provide strong authentication.

Once a user has been authenticated, he can access other services provided by .NET My Services. These include the following:

- **.NET Alerts:** Allows sending alert messages to a .NET My Services user

- **.NET Calendar:** Maintains a user's personal calendar

- **.NET Contacts:** Provides a list of names, addresses, and other contact information for a user

- **.NET Inbox:** Allows access to a user's e-mail

- **.NET Documents:** Provides Internet-accessible storage for a user

- **.NET Wallet:** Contains payment information such as a user's credit card number and shipping address

- **.NET Lists:** Contains lists such as a to-do list or a shopping list

- **.NET Profile:** Contains information about an individual such as her name, address, and photograph

- **.NET Presence:** Contains electronic presence information for a user, such as when and where that user is reachable via instant messaging

With the exception of Passport, which uses Kerberos, all the information stored in .NET My Services is accessed via SOAP and defined using XML. Unlike the browser-accessible services offered on the Internet today for e-mail, calendaring, and so on, .NET My Services is meant to be accessed by applications. In a very real sense, .NET My Services is a platform for application development. It will succeed only if developers build .NET My Services–based applications that make their users' lives better.

.NET My Services is largely a group of SOAP-accessible Web services

Storing personal information on the Internet raises a number of issues, however. Can Microsoft keep this information secure? How can I control who is allowed to access information about me? And how can I keep Microsoft from selling this information once I've given it to them? Answering these questions in a way that pleases customers is an essential part of making .NET My Services succeed. For a more detailed look at the technology of .NET My Services and some of the larger issues it raises, see Chapter 8.

.NET My Services raises many security and privacy issues

The .NET Enterprise Servers

Building effective distributed applications requires a host of services. Windows DNA has provided many of those services, as does the .NET Framework. Whichever environment a developer uses, however, some potential problems aren't addressed. The goal of the .NET Enterprise Servers is to address a critical subset of these problems.

The .NET Enterprise Servers don't rely on the .NET Framework

It's important to realize that although the .NET Enterprise Servers carry the .NET brand, they don't use the .NET Framework. Instead, at least in their first releases, they are based entirely on traditional Windows DNA technologies, such as COM. While all of these servers can be used with .NET Framework applications through the interoperability features the Framework provides, they're not intrinsically tied to the Framework. Because of this, they're not discussed in this book beyond the short summaries in this section.

The .NET Enterprise Servers include the following products:

BizTalk Server 2000 can be used to integrate applications running on diverse platforms

- **BizTalk Server 2000:** One of the most challenging problems in enterprise computing today is the effective exchange of information among diverse applications running on a range of different systems. BizTalk Server 2000 is Microsoft's attempt at addressing this problem in a general way. Although the product has just one name, it includes two loosely related technologies: the Messaging Engine, which provides a way to define and transfer XML-based documents among applications, and the Orchestration Engine, offering a graphical interface for describing and then implementing business processes.

Application Center 2000 makes management of replicated server applications easier

- **Application Center 2000:** Scaling out—making a Windows DNA application able to handle more users by adding machines at all tiers—can be an effective way of making an application able to support more simultane-

Why Are the .NET Enterprise Servers Part of .NET?

It's not obvious why the .NET Enterprise Servers are considered part of .NET. Most of the .NET Enterprise Servers were released by the end of 2000, but the .NET Framework wasn't released until more than a year later. Furthermore, the .NET Enterprise Servers are based on Windows DNA technologies: COM, Active Server Pages, and more. Given that they don't require the .NET Framework, why view them as part of .NET?

The problem for Microsoft was that the .NET Enterprise Servers were already well under way by the time .NET was announced. Even though they are built on Windows DNA technology—in fact, they were once marketed under the name *Windows DNA 2000*—marketing people quite sensibly hate to promote a brand, such as Windows DNA, that's being replaced. Since all of the servers shipped after .NET was announced, it made sense from a marketing perspective to give them the .NET brand.

Doing this makes less sense from a technical perspective. It's easy to be confused, thinking that Microsoft's promised big changes with .NET can actually be found in the .NET Enterprise Servers. While this will eventually be true, it's not true today. Also, some customers have assumed that the .NET Enterprise Servers are useful only with applications based on the .NET Framework, which is certainly not correct. While I understand why Microsoft made the branding choice they did—in their shoes, I might well have done the same thing—the result was substantial confusion among their customers.

ous users. The problem with this approach is that it can also require complex, human-intensive, and expensive management of the machines involved. Application Center 2000 provides a set of management tools aimed at lowering both the cost and the complexity of deploying and managing Windows DNA applications on replicated servers.

Commerce Server 2000 provides packaged components for building e-commerce applications

- **Commerce Server 2000:** Most e-commerce Web sites have a great deal in common. Rather than reinventing the wheel for each new application, reusing existing code allows faster implementation with fewer defects. By providing a standard set of ASP pages, COM components, and other parts of an e-commerce application, Commerce Server 2000 allows creating e-commerce applications in less time and with less effort.

HIS 2000 helps integrate Windows applications with those running on other platforms

- **Host Integration Server (HIS) 2000:** Windows DNA applications must often interoperate with applications running in other environments. One of the most important examples of this is communicating with applications on IBM mainframes, but there are many others. HIS 2000 provides a set of standard services for connecting with non-Microsoft environments. These services include the COM Transaction Integrator (COM TI), which allows an IBM mainframe transaction to become part of a COM+ transaction; the OLE DB for DB2 Provider, which allows access to DB2 databases; and the MSMQ-MQSeries Bridge, which allows messages to be exchanged between MSMQ and IBM's MQSeries product.

SQL Server 2000 is the next generation of Microsoft's primary DBMS product

- **SQL Server 2000:** This product is the next release of Microsoft's flagship database management system. Among the enhancements in this release are XML integration, allowing a client to issue SQL queries that return XML-defined data and to pass XML documents directly to the DBMS; support for up to 32 processors and 64 gigabytes of memory; and new data types, such as bigint, which provides a 64-bit integer, and sql_variant, which allows storing values of different types in the same column.

Exchange Server 2000 is the next generation of Microsoft's core messaging product

- **Exchange Server 2000:** Microsoft Exchange has become a very popular product for e-mail and related applications. Exchange Server 2000 is the next release of this

messaging and collaboration services technology. It introduces the Microsoft Web storage system, a platform for
building and hosting native Web applications. Exchange
2000 Conferencing Server also provides a client/server
solution for voice, video, and data conferencing.

- **Mobile Information Server 2001:** Wireless networks are
  rapidly becoming an indispensable part of the computing infrastructure. Mobile Information Server 2001 provides a platform for wireless applications, enabling
  communication with PDAs, mobile phones, and other
  portable devices. The product comes in two versions:
  Enterprise Edition, designed for use on internal corporate networks, and Carrier Edition, designed for use by
  mobile operators.

  Mobile Information Server 2001 supports building applications for wireless devices

- **Internet Security and Acceleration Server (ISA) 2000:**
  Deploying applications on the Internet commonly raises
  two serious issues: security and performance. As its name
  suggests, ISA 2000 addresses both issues for Internet applications. To improve performance, the product provides a proxy service that caches frequently accessed
  pages near the client. The product also blocks access by
  inappropriate users and to inappropriate sites by providing a firewall service. This firewall works in both direc-
  tions: It can block outside access from clients that don't
  obey its configured rules, while also preventing intranet
  users from accessing specific sites.

  ISA 2000 provides firewall and proxy services

The .NET Enterprise Servers provide a useful set of services.
Organizations building Windows DNA applications today are
likely to use at least some of these products. And even though
none of them specifically targets .NET Framework applications
in their 2000 releases, it's likely that all of them will do so in
the not-too-distant future.

The .NET Enterprise Servers can be useful in building various kinds of applications

A .NET Scenario

An example can illustrate how various .NET technologies interact

Describing the parts of .NET separately can help in understanding the trees of this technology initiative. The best way to get a view of the forest, however, is to see how these parts work together. To do this, see Figure 1-8. It shows how various .NET technologies might be used to construct an e-commerce Web site.

This site is built around an ordering application that lets a user place an order from her browser. The site might sell books or CDs or toys or anything else that's available on the Internet. This site relies on Passport for authentication, so the user contacts this part of .NET My Services to obtain a way to identify herself reliably (step 1). (It's worth pointing out that using Passport authentication for a Web site built using the .NET Framework isn't required, but rather it is just one of several available options.) Next, she uses her browser to access the appropriate pages in the ordering application, a .NET

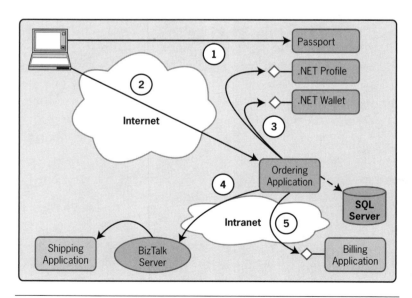

Figure 1-8   An e-commerce Web site might use many .NET technologies.

Framework application built, say, in C# using ASP.NET and relying on SQL Server for storage (step 2). If this customer allows it, the ordering application can access .NET My Services to acquire information about her, such as her credit card number and mailing address (step 3). Next, the ordering application communicates with a separate shipping application across an intranet. This shipping application might be built on a non-Windows system, such as Linux, so BizTalk Server provides the glue between these disparate applications (step 4). Finally, the ordering application uses SOAP to communicate with a billing application, also across the intranet (step 5). Given that Web services are supported by many different vendors, this billing application might be a .NET Framework application or something else, such as an application written using Java running on an IBM mainframe. In either case, the same technologies—SOAP and XML—can potentially be used to interact with it.

The broad set of technologies grouped under the .NET banner can be applied in many different ways. The e-commerce Web site shown here provides a good example of how they might be used, but there are plenty of other choices. Depending on the problem to be solved, different .NET technologies can be combined with one another and with other technologies as needed.

The .NET technologies address a broad set of problems

Conclusion

The .NET initiative is a big step for Microsoft. By providing a new foundation for building Windows applications, the company is all but forcing developers to begin climbing a long learning curve. Yet the benefits brought by Web services, the .NET Framework, .NET My Services, and the other aspects of .NET are significant. The new development environment is much more modern, and it provides many more services. Once developers have internalized at least the core .NET technologies, their productivity should improve significantly. And with the built-in support for Web services, whole new classes of

.NET provides a better, more powerful environment for developers

applications can be created. Ultimately, .NET is likely to be another step in the ladder toward the ultimate goal: producing the best possible software in the least amount of time.

The price of more power is accepting change

The downside of all of this power is that it comes at the price of substantial change. Windows developers must learn many new language features (and in the case of C#, perhaps even an entirely new language), at least parts of a large new standard library, and various new concepts, such as Web services. Even scarier for some developers, a large chunk of their existing knowledge is no longer useful. For example, COM isn't used in the .NET Framework, except for interoperability with existing code, and so the detailed COM knowledge that many Microsoft-oriented software professionals have painfully acquired isn't

The Pain of Change

During a .NET seminar I gave in Moscow, one of the participants raised his hand with a worried expression. "I'm an experienced Windows DNA developer," he said. "If I learn this .NET stuff, can you promise me that this is the last new technology Microsoft will ever make me learn?"

I couldn't, of course. I could promise him, however, that he was in the wrong profession. Even if my worried interlocutor sticks with Microsoft for the rest of his career, it's all but certain that new technologies that he'll need to get his mind around will appear. As long as the hardware we depend on keeps getting faster, smaller, and cheaper, new software technologies will continue to exploit those advances.

Fortunately, changes as large as .NET aren't common. Bringing out new languages, a large new library, and significant revisions to other core technologies all at once is almost too much to swallow. Yet bringing out those same changes piecemeal would likely have been worse, if only because the integration among them would certainly have suffered. The bottom line is simple: If you don't like change, get out of the software business.

needed to build Framework-based applications. With the introduction of the .NET Framework's Windows Forms, knowing how
to use existing GUI technologies is much less valuable. Even
data access is substantially different, with ADO replaced by
ADO.NET. There's no use complaining, however. The only real
choice for developers who wish to continue working in this
environment is to devote the time required to come to grips with
.NET. It's the future of application development on Windows.

2

Web Services

In the last ten years, nothing has had a bigger impact on the software world than the Internet and the World Wide Web. Browser-based applications have become the norm as organizations adapt to this new environment. Useful as they are, however, applications that expose their services to browsers aren't the only way to exploit Web technology. Why can't those applications also expose their services programmatically? Allowing software running on other systems to invoke operations over the Web directly would allow Web applications to provide richer services to more diverse clients.

Web services make this possible. Using this new technology, software running on desktops, servers, personal digital assistants (PDAs), mobile phones, or any other intelligent device can directly invoke operations exposed by Web applications. And while applications available on the Internet will be a large part of this new world, applications running on internal networks can also exploit Web services. This new technology is a key part of Microsoft's plans, playing an important role in the .NET initiative. This chapter looks at some of the ways Web services

Web services allow accessing software programmatically over the Web

can be used and then examines the core technologies that underlie this idea.

Describing Web Services

Web services rely on four fundamental technologies

The technology of Web services can be broken down into four separate areas, each addressing a particular aspect of the problem. Those areas are as follows:

- **Describing information sent over the network:** Invoking a remote operation commonly involves passing in parameters and getting back some kind of result. With Web services, this information is described using the Extensible Markup Language (XML). Universally accepted as the modern lingua franca for describing data, XML allows a variety of information to be described and exchanged.

- **Defining Web service capabilities:** Some mechanism must exist to allow the provider of a Web service to specify the technical details of exactly what services are offered. As with other types of services, it makes sense to group related operations into interfaces and then provide some way to describe each of those operations. For Web services, this can be done using the Web Services Description Language (WSDL).[1] Each WSDL-defined interface contains one or more operations, and WSDL itself is defined using XML.

- **Accessing Web services:** Once an interface has been defined, clients must use some protocol to invoke the operations in that interface. There's no single required protocol (in fact, WSDL explicitly allows specifying different protocols for invoking the operations in an inter-

---

1. Commonly pronounced "wizdel."

face). The most important choice, however, is the Simple Object Access Protocol (SOAP). SOAP provides a way to identify which operation to invoke, to convey that operation's inputs as XML-defined data, and to return any outputs, also as XML-defined data. SOAP itself defines only a simple envelope for conveying this information, one that can be carried in various ways. For example, SOAP calls can be carried on the Hypertext Transfer Protocol (HTTP), on a messaging technology such as the Simple Mail Transfer Protocol (SMTP), or in other ways.

- **Finding Web services:** For developers to create clients that use Web services, there must be some way for those developers to learn what services are available, what they provide, and what their interfaces look like. Given the existence of the Internet, it makes sense to create a standard registry for storing and accessing this kind of information. This is exactly what's done by the technology defined for Universal Description, Discovery, and Integration (UDDI). Using UDDI, providers of Web services can advertise their offerings in a standard way, allowing clients to learn what services each provider offers and letting creators of client software learn what they need to know to build those clients.

Each of these technologies was created by groups of vendors and users working together. XML, for instance, was created by a large group working under the auspices of the World Wide Web Consortium (W3C), while WSDL was created primarily by Microsoft and IBM. SOAP comes from a group somewhere in between in size, with Microsoft, IBM, UserLand Software, DevelopMentor, and several other organizations playing a role. UDDI was originally developed by Microsoft, IBM, and Ariba, although many more organizations have since joined the effort. The key point to notice about the origin of these Web services technologies is that none of them is a single-vendor solution. Instead, Web services based on XML, WSDL, SOAP, and UDDI

All of these technologies have broad vendor support

can be used across virtually all platforms, languages, and object models.

Applying Web Services

Web services can be applied in several different ways

There's no shortage of possible scenarios for using Web services. The most obvious choices fall into three categories:

- Allowing programmatic access to applications accessed via the Internet

- Business-to-business (B2B) integration, allowing applications from different organizations to communicate across the Internet

- Application-to-application (A2A) integration, allowing applications within a single organization to communicate across an intranet

A technology that addressed any one of these problems would be interesting. Web services, able to address all three, are certain to be important.

Access to Internet Applications

Some browser applications would work better as Web services applications

Suppose you'd like to make an appointment with your dentist, book a flight to Mumbai, or check the balance in your bank account. Today, you can do all of these things on the Web using traditional Web applications. Those applications provide their services through a conventional browser, however, and so they require a good bit of human interaction. Also, because they're so graphical, they're less appealing when the client is a handheld device such as a PDA or a mobile phone. All of these functions and many more could likely be done more effectively if they were exposed as Web services. Using an appropriate interface for the client device, you could express your wishes and then have them carried out on your behalf.

For example, your calendar program might have built-in access to an airline reservations application. You could perhaps enter your travel plans into your calendar and then rely on it to book the flight on your behalf. In fact, you could do many things in this way: schedule an appointment with your dentist, have flowers sent to your mother on Mother's Day, buy tickets to the Metropolitan Opera, and more. A world of interoperable Web services would be a much more convenient place to live, especially given the increasing popularity of handheld devices with wireless connections to the Internet.

Web services could make our lives more convenient

Using Web services in this way raises another possibility, too: Why can't some of those services generate revenue for the firms that provide them? Just as browser-based Web applications allowed new business models that gave rise to the Internet boom, Web services could also provide new ways for their providers to make money. Not all Web services fit this model, of course— your dentist is unlikely to charge you for scheduling an appointment—but some certainly do. A Web services–based airline reservations application will probably charge you something for using its services, as will a SOAP-accessible ticket broker. By increasing ways for customers to access services, today's e-commerce Web sites can also increase their profits.

Web services could make money for companies that provide them

B2B Integration

Another important application of Web services, one that also commonly depends on the Internet, is B2B integration, connecting software running in diverse organizations. To date, connecting applications at two different companies has often been done in specialized, idiosyncratic ways. Why not use a more standard approach? Web services are a straightforward, universally available technology that can be used to address this problem. Most important, they're a technology that has been embraced by every major vendor. Describing data using XML, defining interfaces with WSDL, finding available interfaces with

B2B integration will be an important application of Web services

UDDI, and invoking services via SOAP can provide a common glue across all kinds of diverse environments.

Another advantage of this approach is that since SOAP can run over HTTP, Web services can potentially be accessed through firewalls. The obvious security concerns this raises are discussed later in this chapter, but without some way to tunnel through firewalls, B2B integration over the Internet can't happen. SOAP plays an important part in making this solution possible.

A2A Integration

A2A integration is a major concern in many organizations

The hardest problem in many organizations is connecting together existing applications. Every company of any size has running on diverse systems a mix of software that was written at different times in different languages. Uniting this plethora of applications into a usable whole is one of the biggest challenges those companies face, especially when adding new applications to the mix. Web services offer a solution to this vexing problem of A2A integration.[2]

Web services can provide a common glue between applications

To see how, recall that the fundamental notion underlying Web services is to define an interface whose operations can potentially be accessed from any client. While new applications can easily include support for Web services interfaces, it's also possible to retrofit these interfaces onto existing applications. Because the core Web services technologies aren't tied to any particular environment and because they're supported by multiple vendors, they're an excellent choice for connecting diverse applications within an organization.

A Web Services Scenario

A single application might use Web services in several different ways

To get a sense of how Web services might be applied, imagine that you wished to book an airplane reservation from your PDA

---

2. This problem is also sometimes referred to as enterprise application integration (EAI).

The Role of ebXML

Effective B2B integration requires a higher level of agreement than WSDL, SOAP, and UDDI alone can provide. If one company wishes to send a purchase order to another, for example, what should that purchase order look like? Most kinds of business interactions depend on documents like this, and carrying out those interactions electronically requires agreement on what these documents look like. Standards for electronic data interchange (EDI) have long defined common formats for these kinds of business exchanges. Yet many people working in this area have come to believe that EDI is no longer sufficient. Instead, the rise of XML allows defining standard business documents in a more flexible and useful way.

As its name suggests, the goal of the ebXML initiative is to define XML-based standards for e-business. The group defines standard business documents, rules for exchanging those documents, and even entire business processes, all described using XML. A large number of vendors and users is involved in ebXML, and they've produced many documents so far.

The ebXML effort originally appeared to be competitive with SOAP-based Web services. The group defined its own protocol for conveying ebXML documents, for example, which competed with SOAP. Eventually, however, the ebXML group endorsed SOAP as an approved option for conveying their standard documents and UDDI as a way to locate Web services. What could have been a painful split in the Web services world was avoided.

Still, perhaps because of this initial conflict, Microsoft hasn't been much of an ebXML backer. Today, .NET doesn't offer direct support for this family of specifications. ebXML is likely to be important, though, at least in some areas, so it's probable that Microsoft will support it if and when its customers insist. If effective Web services–based B2B integration requires ebXML, as it very well might, Microsoft won't have much choice.

via a wireless Internet connection. Once you've entered the destination and dates you're interested in, Figure 2-1 illustrates how the system you use to book your trip might look. As shown in step 1, the process begins when the PDA contacts on the Internet

Creating Common Connections: Why COM and CORBA Couldn't

Wouldn't it be nice if all kinds of software on all kinds of systems could snap to-gether like LEGO blocks? The technical problems that stand in the way of this goal aren't hard, especially if we're willing to accept a fairly basic level of con-nectivity. What has stopped us in the past is will: Users have had it, but vendors haven't. And in this case, vendors rule.

Microsoft, for example, has been quite successful in creating snap-together soft-ware for Windows platforms. COM makes this possible even when that software is running on remote systems. But other major vendors haven't seriously sup-ported COM, and one could debate whether Microsoft ever really wanted them to. Similarly, the Object Management Group's CORBA was intended to connect all kinds of applications on all kinds of systems. Two problems doomed the OMG's efforts, though. First, their standards weren't complete enough, so orga-nizations were all but forced to stick with a single CORBA vendor to make their systems communicate. And second, Microsoft didn't support it.

At long last, however, something has appeared with both the right technical mer-its and, more important, vendor agreement. That something, of course, is Web services. After more than one false start with other technologies, we're likely to see SOAP and its fellow travelers emerge as the standard mechanism that all ap-plications use to expose their services to the outside world. Given that every ven-dor has endorsed these technologies, users should expect (and, if necessary, demand) that software providers make their products more interoperable by pro-viding Web services interfaces. While some problems remain, as discussed later in this chapter, Web services look like the best chance we've seen yet to create true standards for application interoperability.

a reservations application that provides a Web services interface. This application might be provided by an Internet travel service, and so it offers a common access point to the actual reservation systems provided by various airlines. Given this, step 2 in the diagram shows this application contacting a specific reservation

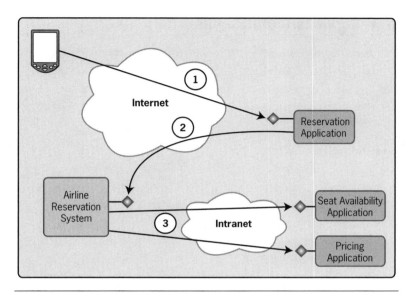

Figure 2-1   Web services can be applied in many different ways.

system provided by a particular airline. Once again, this happens over the Internet, which means that this airline must have chosen to expose its reservation system to the Internet travel service (although not necessarily to anyone else) as a Web service. Finally, as shown in step 3, the airline reservation system interacts with a seat availability application and a pricing application to make the actual reservation. These applications are available only on this airline's intranet, yet they may well run on different kinds of systems using different implementation technologies. Here, Web services provide the glue that unites diverse software.

Step 1 in Figure 2-1 is an example of a client directly accessing services across the Internet, the first use of Web services described earlier. Step 2 shows Internet-based B2B integration using Web services, while step 3 illustrates an A2A scenario that uses Web services to integrate in-house applications across an intranet. In every case, these useful technologies provide common interfaces and common ways to communicate among diverse applications on diverse systems over diverse networks.

Web Services Technologies

Understanding Web services requires understanding four technologies—XML, WSDL, SOAP, and UDDI—and how they relate to one another. This section provides an introduction to each of these four pillars.

Describing Information: XML

Every Web services technology relies on XML

Meaningful communication isn't possible without some agreement on how to represent what is being communicated. In the last few years, XML has emerged as the standard solution for describing information exchanged between heterogeneous systems. Not too surprisingly, then, XML is fundamental to Web services. Every other technology in the Web services family uses it in some way, and so understanding Web services requires understanding XML.[3] Providing a complete XML tutorial is beyond the scope of this book. Fortunately, grasping the basics of Web services requires knowing only a few core XML concepts. What follows is an informal description of those core ideas.

An XML document contains one or more elements

XML provides a way to describe information. That information is typically contained in an *XML document,* which is a set of characters that meets the basic syntactic requirements of XML. An XML document contains one or more *elements,* each of which is demarcated using *tags.* A tag is typically a word enclosed in angle brackets, such as <Account> or <Balance>. Tags are used in pairs, beginning and ending each element, and the end tag in an element is just the start tag with a slash in front of the word. Each element contains information that has some relationship to the word in the tags. For example, in the element

```
<Account>729-1269-4785</Account>
```

-----

3. In fact, Microsoft usually refers to Web services as "XML Web services," which is slightly redundant.

the text between the two tags probably represents the number of some account, such as a checking account at a bank. Similarly, in the element

```
<Balance>3,822.55</Balance>
```

the text between the tags might represent the amount of money currently available in an account. Given the right set of tags, it's possible to create an XML document containing elements that describe almost any information. You might, for example, create a simple document containing information about bank accounts and the balances they contain using only the two elements just described.

The start tag for an element can also contain one or more *attributes*. Each attribute describes some aspect of the element in which it appears. For example, in the element

Elements can contain attributes

```
<Account type="checking">729-0084-7823</Account>
```

the `type` attribute indicates that this is a checking account.

An optional simplification, one that's especially useful in elements with attributes, allows omitting the end tag from an element. To indicate that an element consists of only a single tag, a slash can appear before the closing bracket. For example, if a particular document lists the types of accounts a customer has, it might contain the element

```
<Account type="checking"/>
```

This is equivalent to, but simpler than, this:

```
<Account type="checking"></Account>
```

Elements are the core of an XML document. Yet how are these elements actually defined? There must be a way to specify a

An XML document can have an associated XML schema

group of elements (and thus tags) that will be used for a particular purpose. In the original incarnation of XML, elements were defined using *document type definitions (DTDs)*. DTDs had various limitations, however, so today a more flexible approach called the *XML Schema definition* (XSD) language is used. The XML Schema language is too complicated to illustrate here, but the basic idea is fairly simple. Each schema defines one or more elements, along with rules on how those elements can be used. For example, a schema might define an `Envelope` element demarcated with the tags <Envelope> and </Envelope> and then mandate that this element can contain within it one or more occurrences of a `Body` element, demarcated with the tags <Body> and </Body>. An XML document that conforms to a particular schema is said to be *valid*.

A namespace allows specifying a scope for element names

If a single document will use tags from only one schema, life is simple. It's common, however, to mix elements from two or more schemas in a single document. Since the schemas were created independently, it's entirely possible that the same tag is defined in each schema with a different meaning. For example, the <Account> tag in one schema might identify a checking account element, while the very same tag defined in some other schema might identify an element representing a brokerage account. To mix tags from different schemas in the same document, there must be a way to associate an element with the schema in which it's defined. Providing this association is the role of *namespaces*. A namespace provides a unique identifier for a group of names. Each namespace is assigned a uniform resource identifier (URI).[4] Note that even though the URI used to identify a namespace often looks like a URL you type into a browser, there's no requirement that a Web page actually exists with this name. Instead, a URI just provides a convenient format for creating a unique name for some namespace.

---

4. A URI can be either a Uniform Resource Locator (URL), identifying a resource on the Web, or a Uniform Resource Name (URN), which can be used to name pretty much anything.

Whatever its name, the namespace in which an element is defined can be specified using an attribute. For example, in the
element

*A namespace can
be specified using
an attribute*

```
<Account xmlns="http://www.qwickbank.com/bank">
729-1269-4785
</Account>
```

the xmlns attribute indicates that the Account element is defined in a namespace identified by the URI http://www.qwick-
bank.com/bank.

Finally, although not essential to its meaning, an XML document can contain comments. Comments allow including information intended for a human reader rather than for any
software that processes this document. XML comments look
like this:

```
<!-- This is an XML comment -->
```

XML contains much more than the relatively few ideas
described here. Still, a basic grasp of Web services doesn't require knowing much more than the fundamentals of this data
description language. Armed with these core concepts, we're
ready to examine the technologies of Web services.

Defining Web Services: WSDL

To invoke a Web service, client software must know several
things: It must know the name of the operation it wishes to invoke, for example, along with what kinds of input parameters
that operation expects and what results it will return. For the
developers of the client and server software to agree on these
things, there must exist some standard format in which this information—the interface between client and server—can be described. In both COM and CORBA, for example, interfaces and
the operations they contain can be described in an Interface
Definition Language (IDL). Web services need something similar.

*Clients and servers
must agree on the
interface between
them*

WSDL can be used to describe Web services interfaces

WSDL was created to address this problem. Unlike COM's IDL, whose syntax is derived from the C programming language, WSDL is defined using XML. WSDL isn't simple, and so completely understanding even a small interface definition expressed in WSDL requires a fairly good knowledge of XML. Despite this, however, the core elements of a WSDL definition can be understood in a straightforward way. Here's an example that illustrates the basic components of a very simple WSDL definition. Note that this example is neither legal WSDL nor legal XML, but rather a simplified illustration of the language's key aspects.

```
<definitions name="AccountAccess">
   <types>
      <element name="BalanceRequest">
         <!-- definition of input type, e.g.,
              Account, appears here -->
      </element>
      <element name="BalanceResult">
         <!-- definition of output type, e.g.,
              Balance, appears here -->
      </element>
   </types>
   <message name="GetBalanceInput">
      <part name="body" element="BalanceRequest"/>
   </message>
   <message name="GetBalanceOutput">
      <part name="body" element="BalanceResult"/>
   </message>
   <portType name="AccountAccessPortType">
      <operation name="GetBalance">
         <input message="GetBalanceInput"/>
         <output message="GetBalanceOutput"/>
      </operation>
   </portType>
   <binding name="AccountAccessSoapBinding"
            type="AccountAccessPortType">
      <soap:binding transport=
         "http://schemas.xmlsoap.org/soap/http"/>
      <operation name="GetBalance">
         <!-- definitions for input and output
              bindings appear here -->
      </operation>
   </binding>
   <service name="AccountAccessService">
      <port name="AccountAccessPort"
            binding="AccountAccessSoapBinding">
         <soap:address location=
```

```
        "http://www.qwickbank.com/accounts.asmx"/>
      </port>
   </service>
</definitions>
```

This definition has only a single operation, GetBalance, that takes an account number as its input and responds with the balance in that account. WSDL is a nontrivial language, and so even this simplified description of a simple interface isn't especially simple. Yet with a little effort, it's not hard to understand what the key parts of the definition are and what they're defining.

To see the definition's overall structure, note that like every WSDL interface, all of the elements in this example are contained within an outermost definitions element. The key elements within definitions are types, message, portType, binding, and service. How each of these is used will be described shortly, but first, it's important to understand that the contents of a WSDL interface can be thought of in two logical parts. First, operations are defined abstractly using the types, message, and portType elements. Once this is done, those abstract operations are then bound to a specific protocol using the binding and service elements. WSDL doesn't assume that any particular protocol is used to invoke the operations it describes, and so the same set of operations can have bindings defined for more than one protocol.

A WSDL interface defines operations, then binds them to one or more protocols

To get a sense of how operations are specified, look at the types, message, and portType elements in the example shown earlier. The types element is used to define basic types that will be needed later in the definition. In this example, those types are BalanceRequest, which specifies the account number, and BalanceResult, which defines the type of the returned information. The contents of these types are omitted in this simple example, but they are the parameters that are passed into and out of the operation this interface defines. The next elements use the message element to define the messages sent and received by the GetBalance operation, and they make use of the types just defined. The first, called GetBalanceInput, contains

The types, message, and portType elements are used to define operations

a value of the type `BalanceRequest`, while the second message, `GetBalanceOutput`, contains a value of the type `BalanceResponse`. Once the necessary messages and the types they contain have been defined, it's possible to define the `GetBalance` operation that uses those messages. Operations are specified within the `portType` element, and as shown earlier, each operation can define its input and output messages. In this case, those messages are `GetBalanceInput` and `GetBalanceOutput`, both defined earlier in this WSDL interface.

The `binding` and `service` elements are used to define a protocol binding

All three of the elements described so far have focused on defining the `GetBalance` operation. The last two elements in this example associate (that is, bind) that operation to a particular protocol, which in this case is SOAP. The `binding` element defines the `AccountAccessSoapBinding`, explicitly associating the `GetBalance` operation with the SOAP protocol. Finally, the `service` element explicitly defines a port, associating the `AccountAccessSoapBinding` with a particular URL at which this service, the `GetBalance` operation, can be found. In this example, the `GetBalance` operation is provided by the fictitious QwickBank, and so it can be accessed at the URL http://www.qwickbank.com/accounts.asmx.

People seldom need to use WSDL directly

All of this might seem like a lot of work (and remember, several details are omitted in this simplified example), but the result is a quite flexible approach to defining Web services interfaces. Given the diversity of uses for Web services, the flexibility WSDL provides is both necessary and useful. And fortunately, as described in more detail in Chapter 7, WSDL is typically produced and consumed by software tools such as Visual Studio.NET; people don't usually need to look at it.

Accessing Web Services: SOAP

SOAP defines an envelope and rules for representing information sent in that envelope

While WSDL doesn't require any particular protocol, it's fair to say that the most common choice for invoking Web services is SOAP. SOAP isn't especially complicated, and so even a brief description doesn't need to omit much detail. To begin, think about what's required to invoke a Web service. To convey any kind of request and return a response, it's useful to define an envelope that carries the information in those messages. A key part of SOAP, then, is the definition of a standard envelope format. Each envelope—that is, each message sent—usually contains some typed information. A call to the `GetBalance` operation described in the previous section, for example, contains a string representing an account number. To enable this, SOAP specifies a set of encoding rules for representing data while it's in transit. Finally, because it's common to express remote communications as a request followed by a response, SOAP defines a convention for representing remote procedure calls and responses. (SOAP can also be used for asynchronous communication; however, it's not limited purely to synchronous calls.) These three things—an envelope, a set of encoding rules, and an optional remote calling convention—are the heart of what SOAP defines.

As with WSDL, the clearest way to get a concrete feeling for SOAP is to look at an example. Suppose a client wished to access the `GetBalance` operation exposed by QwickBank and defined in the last section. Here's how the SOAP message for invoking that operation might look:

```
<soap:Envelope
    xmlns:soap=
        "http://schemas.xmlsoap.org/soap/envelope/">
    <soap:Body>
        <GetBalance
            xmlns="http://www.qwickbank.com/bank">
            <Account>729-1269-4785</Account>
        </GetBalance>
    </soap:Body>
</soap:Envelope>
```

Like all SOAP messages, this one consists of an `Envelope` element with an embedded `Body` element. The `Envelope` element identifies the standard XML namespace that defines the SOAP

Each SOAP envelope contains a body

envelope itself, while the `Body` element contains the primary
contents of the message and also illustrates the SOAP convention for making a remote request. In this example, the
`GetBalance` operation is being invoked, and it's defined in another XML namespace created by QwickBank. The operation
has one parameter, the number of the account whose balance
should be returned, which in this case is 729-1269-4785.

Here's how the response to this message might look:

```
<soap:Envelope
   xmlns:soap=
      "http://schemas.xmlsoap.org/soap/envelope/">
   <soap:Body>
      <GetBalanceResponse
         xmlns="http://www.qwickbank.com/bank">
         <Balance>3,822.55</Balance>
      </GetBalanceResponse>
   </soap:Body>
</soap:Envelope>
```

Once again, the message consists of an `Envelope` element containing a `Body` element, and the `Envelope` references the standard SOAP namespace. The `Body` contains the response
returned by the `GetBalance` operation, which is the amount of
money in this account. And as before, the XML namespace
containing the operation's definition is identified within the
message's `Body`.

*SOAP messages are
most commonly
conveyed using
HTTP*

These two messages provide very simple examples of all three
core aspects of SOAP: the envelope, the encoding rules, and
the convention for representing remote calls and responses.
There are many aspects of real communication that they don't
show, however. The most obvious of these is that there's no
way to tell from these examples how the messages are
conveyed between the parties involved in the communication.
The most common choice today is to send the request on an
HTTP POST message, with the response sent back on the standard HTTP response to a POST. For example, if we assume that

the messages shown earlier are exchanged using HTTP—a reasonable although not obligatory assumption—what gets sent initially might actually look like this:

```
POST /AccountAccess/Accounts.asmx HTTP/1.1
Host: www.qwickbank.com
Content-Type: text/xml; charset="utf-8"
Content-Length: 231
SOAPAction:

<soap:Envelope
   xmlns:soap=
      "http://schemas.xmlsoap.org/soap/envelope/">
   <soap:Body>
      <GetBalance
          xmlns="http://www.qwickbank.com/bank">
          <Account>729-1269-4785</Account>
      </GetBalance>
   </soap:Body>
</soap:Envelope>
```

The SOAP message in this example is just the same as before. What's different is that it's now preceded by an HTTP POST header. This header identifies the machine to which this message should be sent and the application that should handle it (which in this case is an .asmx page, indicating that the Web service is implemented using ASP.NET); it identifies the content type and includes everything else necessary to convey this message from sender to receiver using HTTP. As this example shows, the HTTP header must contain the SOAPAction field, which among other things can be used by a firewall to block SOAP traffic.

SOAP requests are commonly sent on an HTTP POST

The response would also likely be sent over HTTP and might look as follows:

```
HTTP/1.1 200 OK
Content-Type: text/xml; charset="utf-8"
Content-Length: 213

<soap:Envelope
   xmlns:soap=
      "http://schemas.xmlsoap.org/soap/envelope/">
```

```
<soap:Body>
   <GetBalanceResponse
      xmlns="http://www.qwickbank.com/bank">
         <Balance>3,822.55</Balance>
   </GetBalanceResponse>
</soap:Body>
</soap:Envelope>
```

As before, the message itself is no different from the earlier example. All that's new is the information added in front of the
message to allow it to be sent via HTTP. Once again, it's important to emphasize that, although it's very common, sending
SOAP messages over HTTP is not required—other protocols can
also be used. Also, the example shown here might seem to
imply that SOAP messages must always take the form of a request and a response. While this is also common, it too is not
required. SOAP defines a convention for specifying requests
and responses but doesn't require using it.

*The SOAP spec
doesn't define how
security should be
provided*

To be as broadly useful as possible and to avoid unnecessarily
reinventing existing technologies, there are several things that
the SOAP specification does not currently define. As already
mentioned, the spec doesn't define what protocol should be
used to convey SOAP-defined messages, and it also doesn't
define how to provide security services such as authentication
and data privacy. Instead, those services are currently provided
as necessary depending on the protocol used to carry SOAP
messages. When those messages are conveyed using HTTP, for
instance, one possibility is to use the Secure Sockets Layer (SSL)
protocol to provide a secure channel (although as described in
Chapter 8, .NET My Services takes another approach). SOAP
messages sent using some other protocol, such as a messaging
technology, might well use another mechanism to provide the
required security services.

*SOAP can pass
through firewalls
more easily than
protocols such as
DCOM or IIOP*

Because SOAP is commonly carried over HTTP, it can potentially pass through firewalls undetected. Firewalls typically
leave open port 80, the port used by HTTP, to allow access to

Web servers. Traditional protocols for remote access such as Distributed COM (DCOM) and the Object Management Group's Internet InterORB Protocol (IIOP) generally require opening a range of ports in the firewall, something network administrators are loath to do. By using port 80, SOAP avoids this problem. Administrators can still block SOAP calls if desired, however, by filtering out any HTTP request that contains SOAP content. If calls are not blocked, then the use of some reliable authentication mechanism for SOAP calls is critical for any organization that cares about security.

The SOAP specification also defines other useful components for SOAP messages. An envelope may contain a `Header` element, for example, that itself contains elements allowing various kinds of information to be sent. A header might contain information used to authenticate a client, for instance, or an indication of the path a message should take. While the initial SOAP specification leaves headers completely up to each application, work has begun on defining a few standard headers. (Microsoft's initial proposals in this area are described later in this chapter.) Each header can contain a `mustUnderstand` attribute that indicates whether it can be safely ignored. If this attribute is present and has the value 1, a receiving SOAP implementation either must be able to understand it or must not process the message that contains it at all.

A SOAP message can contain one or more headers

The specification also defines a standard `Fault` element for conveying error information. This element contains a fault code that identifies the error, a fault string that provides human-readable information about the error, and possibly other information. A few standard faults are defined, including the `MustUnderstand` fault that is sent when a header in a received message contains a `mustUnderstand` attribute with a value of 1 but the receiver doesn't understand this header.

A SOAP message can identify an error with a `Fault` element

Finally, notice once again that nothing about this messaging standard is connected to any particular operating system, programming language, or object model. This fact is one of the most important attributes of this technology. Ecumenical by design, SOAP can be adopted by all faiths in the software world today.

SOAP Interoperability

SOAP has been endorsed by Microsoft, IBM, Oracle, Sun, BEA, and many other vendors. Even the open source world has embraced SOAP, with the Apache Web server now providing strong support. As a result, several different implementations of SOAP exist. To fulfill the promise of this new technology, all of these implementations must interoperate seamlessly. Sadly, the reality today falls somewhat short of this ideal.

For example, SOAP allows adding proprietary headers, something that implementations quite commonly do. Knowing that two products each speak SOAP isn't enough to be confident that they will interoperate—one or both may send entirely legal but nonetheless proprietary headers. Another source of problems is that the SOAP 1.1 specification was completed before the XML Schema specification. As a result, SOAP's rules for expressing information in XML, defined in Section 5 of the SOAP spec, don't exactly match what's allowed in a standard XSD schema. Also, think about the problem of converting from the type system of a programming language, such as C# or VB.NET, into the XML types required by SOAP. The SOAP 1.1 specification doesn't define how this should be done in every case, so different implementations can make different choices. (In fact, ASP.NET provides several options for controlling this translation.) Add the problems of converting from, say, C#'s type system first into XML and then into the type system of another language, such as Java. The potential for introducing incompatibilities in this process is very real.

Tim Ewald, a principal scientist at DevelopMentor in Torrance, California, has raised the possibility of a "Web services winter," a time during which this promising technology lies cold and barren because interoperability problems make it impossible to use effectively. This vision may well come true in the short term, but over the long run, I'm optimistic. I think the interoperability problems we're seeing today are the natural growing pains of a new technology, and they'll eventually be fixed by SOAP's current owner, the W3C's XML Protocol group. Still, be aware that cross-vendor interoperability with SOAP isn't always a given—it may take some work.

Finding Web Services: UDDI

The technologies discussed so far focus on describing a Web service and then invoking it over a network. While these are crucial parts of the solution, some important problems still remain. For example, how can businesses find out what Web services are exposed by their partners? How can developers find the WSDL interface they need to implement for a client for a particular service? How can software that wishes to invoke a Web service determine whether that service is implemented in a compatible way? And how can this information about Web services be managed?

All of these problems are addressed by UDDI. An organization that wants to expose Web services can create a UDDI *business registration,* an XML document whose format is specified in a UDDI-defined schema. Once they've been created, these business registrations are stored in a replicated database known as the UDDI *business registry*. A copy of the business registry is maintained by each UDDI *operator site*. These sites communicate with one another as needed to maintain consistency among the information they store. To access the information in the UDDI registry, client software always uses SOAP over HTTP. This means that UDDI is itself a Web service, one that provides useful information to other Web services. Finally, UDDI also defines a standard application programming interface (API) that developers can use when writing software that accesses or modifies the information in the registry.

UDDI stores registrations describing Web services and more

Describing a Business Registration

The UDDI XML schema defines the common structure for all business registration documents. Each one contains a `businessEntity` element that can contain one or more `businessService` elements. Each of these, in turn, can contain one or more `bindingTemplate` elements, each of which identifies a particular `tModel`. As always, the easiest way to make sense out of this is to walk through a simple example. As with WSDL, a complete example of a `businessEntity` element

A registration can describe one or more Web services and other information

providing even a single Web service is beyond the scope of this chapter. The example that follows is intended to give some idea of how the information stored in the business registry might actually look for QwickBank's very simple `GetBalance` service. What follows is not a fully complete UDDI definition—it's just a simplified example.

```
<businessEntity businessKey=
  "E7CD0D00-1827-11CF-9946-444553540000">
  <name>QwickBank</name>
  <description>Internet bank</description>
  <contacts>
    <contact>
      <personName>Webmaster</personName>
      <email>Webmaster@qwickbank.com</email>
    </contact>
  </contacts>
  <businessServices>
    <businessService serviceKey=
        "15940A43-1956-63DC-0124-444553540000">
      <name>AccountAccess</name>
      <bindingTemplates>
        <bindingTemplate bindingKey=
            "9E43F20A-1963-22EC-1053-444553540000">
          <accessPoint>
           http://www.qwickbank.com/accounts.asmx
          </accessPoint>
          <tModelInstanceDetails>
            <tModelInstanceInfo tModelKey=
              "uuid:F7A90326-EB0D-40E0-9013-
              F55606BD4804">
              <description>
                QwickBank balance access
              </description>
            </tModelInstanceInfo>
            <tModelInstanceInfo tModelKey=
              "uuid:43CAC139-D822-40B5-A004-
              82DDDC0A12F2">
              <description>
                WSDL binding reference
              </description>
              <instanceDetails>
                <!-- More about the
                     WSDL interface -->
              </instanceDetails>
            </tModelInstanceInfo>
          </tModelInstanceDetails>
        </bindingTemplate>
```

```
        </bindingTemplates>
      </businessService>
    </businessServices>
  </businessEntity>
```

The businessEntity element, container for all the others, has
a businessKey attribute that provides a globally unique identifier for this particular business. To guarantee uniqueness, these
names are 16-byte universally unique identifiers (UUIDs).[5] A
businessEntity also typically contains information about the
organization described by this registry entry. In this example,
that information includes the organization's name, what it does,
and whom to contact for more information. Each of these
pieces of data appears in an appropriate element: name,
description, and contacts, respectively. Finally, each
businessEntity can contain a businessServices element
indicating what Web services this organization provides.

*UUIDs provide
unique names for
several elements in
a registration*

The businessServices element, in turn, contains one or
more businessService elements, each describing a particular
service. This example shows only a single businessService
describing QwickBank's very simple offering. Like a
businessEntity, the businessService element has a UUID
key that serves to identify this specific service definition. It
can also include a name for this service, which in this example is "AccountAccess," and a bindingTemplates element.
Each bindingTemplates element can contain one or more
bindingTemplate elements, each identified with a UUID key.
The single bindingTemplate in this example contains the
information needed for a client to connect to and use
QwickBank's Web service. This information includes the

*A bindingTemplate
contains the infor-
mation needed for a
client to use a Web
service*

---

5. A UUID consists of a 6-byte globally unique value such as the Ethernet
address of the machine on which it was created, a timestamp indicating
when it was created, and a few more fields. The combination of the
unique value and the timestamp provides uniqueness, since no other
machine could have produced this same UUID. UUIDs are also sometimes referred to as globally unique identifiers (GUIDs).

access point, expressed here as the URL at which QwickBank's account access service can be found, as well as information about this service.

A tModel can identify one or more characteristics of a Web service

The specifics of a Web service are defined using one or more tModels.[6] Each tModel element identifies some specific aspect of a service. This information can include defining what the service offers, identifying a particular WSDL interface, specifying what protocols can be used to access the service, mandating certain security requirements, and more. A typical UDDI registration will contain multiple tModels for each bindingTemplate. Note, however, that information identified by the tModel is not directly included in the bindingTemplate element. Instead, each tModel has a unique identifier (again, a UUID) that references the actual definition of this tModel. Although it's not shown in the example, this tModel definition can also be made accessible in the UDDI business registry.

The example here shows a typical use of tModels. The first tModel in the bindingTemplate indicates that this is an interface provided by QwickBank for the purpose of accessing account balances, while the second references the WSDL file that describes this interface. In general, a bindingTemplate can include as many tModel references as necessary to specify completely the service it defines.

The businessEntity in this example contains only a single businessService, which in turn contains only one bindingTemplate. A real business, of course, might well offer many different services, with multiple potential bindings for each one. Still, this simple example gives the flavor of the nested structure UDDI uses to store the information needed to access a Web service.

---

6. The *t* doesn't stand for anything in particular—it was just an initial letter that the UDDI committee was able to agree on.

The UDDI API

Storing information about Web services in UDDI's business registry wouldn't be very useful if there weren't some way to access that information. Various applications need to create, search, and modify this information, so to make life easier for the developers of those applications, UDDI also defines a standard API. This interface defines a relatively small set of calls that is divided into two logical parts.

UDDI defines a two-part API for applications accessing its services

The calls used by applications that must search the business registry make up the *Inquiry API.* These calls include the following:

The Inquiry API allows searching the registry

- **find_business:** Locates information about specific businesses in the registry

- **find_service:** Locates specific services within a particular businessEntity

- **find_binding:** Locates a specific binding within a particular businessService

- **find_tModel:** Locates information about a particular tModel

- **get_businessDetail:** Returns the businessEntity information for one or more businesses

- **get_serviceDetail:** Returns the businessService information within a particular businessEntity

- **get_bindingDetail:** Returns the bindingTemplate information for one or more bindings

- **get_tModelDetail:** Returns information about one or more tModels

While the Inquiry API allows access to the business registry, applications such as management tools must also be able to

The Publishing API allows creating and modifying information in the registry

create and modify this information. The calls used for this make up the *Publishing API.* These calls include the following:

- **save_business:** Creates or updates `businessEntity` information

- **save_service:** Creates or updates `businessService` information

- **save_binding:** Creates or updates `bindingTemplate` information

- **save_tModel:** Creates or updates `tModel` information

- **delete_business:** Deletes the information in a specific `businessEntity`

- **delete_service:** Deletes the information in a specific businessService

- **delete_binding:** Deletes the information in a specific `bindingTemplate`

- **delete_tModel:** Deletes information about a `tModel`

Remote requests to modify the registry use SSL

Accessing information in the UDDI business registry—that is, using the calls in the Inquiry API—requires no authentication. Any client can access anything. Changing that information, however, does require authentication. An application using any of the calls in the Publishing API must prove its identity to the operator site it's accessing. How it does this is up to that site, but all calls in this part of the UDDI API must use HTTPS, that is, HTTP over SSL.

UDDI provides a necessary service in a Web services world

UDDI is an important piece of the Web services puzzle. Without it, there would be no way for organizations providing Web services to let potential clients know what they have to offer, nor would there be a simple way for clients to learn the details they need to access those services. And although a primary goal of UDDI is to allow clients to locate Internet-based

UDDI and Disco

UDDI is clearly a good idea. Yet like most good ideas, it's not perfect. One problem is that it's a fairly complex solution to what should be a simple problem. For developers, at least, a primary function of UDDI is to let them find the information they need to build compatible Web services clients. Today, this means letting developers find WSDL definitions for those Web services. Yet UDDI isn't especially focused on addressing this problem. It's certainly possible to store WSDL definitions—UDDI's tModels are general enough to allow storing anything—but UDDI has been used first for storing business information. While this may be valuable at some point, if developers can't build compatible clients for Web services, those Web services will have no business value.

While Microsoft is clearly behind UDDI, the company also recognizes that UDDI isn't the complete answer today. As a result, the .NET Framework includes Disco, a much simpler technology for discovering Web services. Disco is focused on accessing what developers need to build compatible clients, especially clients that will access Web services within a single organization's environment. Visual Studio.NET has built-in support for UDDI, but it also supports Disco.

New technologies are seldom exactly right. It takes time to understand the real problems and to figure out how best to solve them. UDDI's chances of success are good, but in the short run, it's not the only answer.

services, it can also be useful inside a single organization. Web services are a significant advance, yet they couldn't achieve their full potential without a service like UDDI.

Future Directions for Web Services

The technologies of Web services are certainly usable today, but they're also not fully mature. Many useful features could be added, and it's a safe bet that, one way or another, these features will find their way into the W3C specifications. As mentioned

Microsoft's GXA defines additions to SOAP

earlier, for example, SOAP allows adding arbitrary headers. Yet effective, full-featured interoperability among different vendors' SOAP implementations requires agreement on how at least some of these headers should look. Toward this end, Microsoft in late 2001 announced a Global XML Web Services Architecture (GXA). Although initially a Microsoft-only proposal, the company's stated intent is to submit this work to the W3C, then to conform to the standards that ultimately emerge from that organization.

GXA addresses security and routing of SOAP messages

The GXA specification defines a set of SOAP headers for addressing common problems. These headers, and thus the services they provide, can be combined as needed for a specific application. The initial GXA specs define headers in four areas:

- **WS-Security:** Provides a way to pass security credentials, such as the identity of the client, and to indicate what options (if any) are being used to provide integrity and confidentiality for a SOAP message. An integrity service allows the message's receiver to be certain that the message wasn't modified in transit, while a confidentiality service typically encrypts a message so it can't be read in transit.

- **WS-License:** Provides a standard way to identify common kinds of credentials, which are referred to in the specification as *licenses*. Among the supported options are Kerberos tickets and X.509 certificates, each of which relies on strong cryptographic techniques to allow the receiver to verify a client's identity. WS-License is typically used together with WS-Security, as the example shown later in this section illustrates.

- **WS-Routing:** Defines header information that can be used to route messages across intermediate SOAP nodes. Note that this routing happens at the application level, and so is distinct from the service that network routers provide.

- **WS-Referral:** Defines header information that allows configuring SOAP implementations to route SOAP messages correctly. Unlike WS-Routing, which is used to specify what path a particular SOAP message should take, WS-Referral allows configuring the SOAP systems themselves to route messages correctly.

To give some sense of how these are used, here's an example of how the simple SOAP message shown earlier might look if it used some of the headers defined by WS-Security and WS-License:

```
<soap:Envelope
    xmlns:soap=
        "http://schemas.xmlsoap.org/soap/envelope/"
    xmlns:xsd=
        "http://www.w3.org/2001/XMLSchema"
    xmlns:xsi=
        "http://www.w3.org/2001/XMLSchema-instance">
    <soap:Header>
      <wssec:credentials
          xmlns:wssec=
              "http://schemas.xmlsoap.org/ws/2001/10/
              security">
          <wslic:binaryLicense
              xmlns:wslic=
                  "http://schemas.xmlsoap.org/ws/2001/
                  10/licenses"
              wslic:valueType="wslic:kerberos"
              xsi:type="xsd:base64Binary">
                  eMrrI4GIEBAgIiIOgay52ZXJpc2lnbi5j …
          </wslic:binaryLicense>
      </wssec:credentials>
    </soap:Header>
    <soap:Body>
        <GetBalance
            xmlns="http://www.qwickbank.com/bank">
            <Account>729-1269-4785</Account>
        </GetBalance>
    </soap:Body>
</soap:Envelope>
```

Like the earlier example, this message contains a Body element wrapped in an Envelope element. While the message body is just the same as before, the envelope defines some extra namespaces and also contains a `Header` element. Inside this element is a `credentials` element, complete with an attribute defining a namespace. Inside the `credentials` element is a `binaryLicense` element, which also includes an attribute identifying an appropriate namespace. This `binaryLicense` element contains other attributes as well, indicating that the license supplied is a Kerberos ticket and specifying how the ticket is encoded. The ticket itself follows, although only part of its binary value is shown here.

DIME allows mapping SOAP messages directly to TCP

Defining standard headers for common functions is important. There are other enhancements that can also make Web services technology more effective, however. One of these is a mapping of SOAP directly to TCP, an option known as Direct Internet Message Encapsulation (DIME). Doing this makes getting through firewalls a bit more challenging, but it also allows better performance than sending SOAP messages over HTTP. Other likely enhancements include a standard way to identify transactions in SOAP messages and a way to guarantee reliable delivery of those messages. More additions are sure to come, as Web services continue to work their way into the fabric of modern computing.

Conclusion

Web services have a promising future

Web services are unquestionably a good idea. Providing a multivendor way to expose services running on all kinds of platforms across both intranets and the Internet has the potential to open up the world in a new way. The technologies underlying Web services—XML, WSDL, SOAP, and UDDI—are all relatively new. Yet despite their recent genesis, all are supported by multiple vendors, and all look likely to play important roles in the future of distributed computing. While browser-based applications have made the Web what it is today, Web services will likely make it what it will be tomorrow.

3

The Common Language Runtime

The Common Language Runtime (CLR) is the foundation for everything else in the .NET Framework. To understand .NET languages such as C# and Visual Basic.NET, you must understand the CLR. To understand the .NET Framework class library—ASP.NET, ADO.NET, and the rest—you must understand the CLR. And since the .NET Framework has become Microsoft's default foundation for new software, anybody who plans to work in the Microsoft environment needs to come to grips with the CLR.

Everything in the .NET Framework depends on the CLR

Software built on the CLR is referred to as *managed code,* and the CLR provides several things to support creating and running this code. Perhaps the most fundamental is a standard set of types that are used by languages built on the CLR, along with a standard format for metadata, which is information about software built using those types. The CLR also provides technologies for packaging managed code and a runtime environment for executing managed code. As the most important part of the

The CLR supports the creation and execution of managed code

.NET Framework, the CLR is unquestionably the place to start in understanding what the Framework offers.

Building Managed Code: The Common Type System

A programming language usually defines both syntax and semantics

What is a programming language? One way to think about it is as a specific syntax with a set of keywords that can be used to define data and express operations on that data. While language syntaxes differ, the underlying abstractions of most popular languages today are very similar. All of them support various data types such as integers and strings, all allow packaging code into methods, and all provide a way to group data and methods into classes. When a new programming language is defined, the usual approach is to define underlying abstractions such as these—key aspects of the language's semantics—concomitantly with the language's syntax.

The Common Type System defines core semantics but not syntax

Yet there are other possibilities. Suppose you choose to define the core abstractions for a programming model without mapping them to any particular syntax. If the abstractions were general enough, they could then be used in many different programming languages. Rather than inextricably mingling syntax and semantics, they could be kept separate, allowing different languages to be used with the same set of underlying abstractions. This is exactly what's done in the CLR's Common Type System (CTS). The CTS specifies no particular syntax or keywords, but instead defines a common set of types that can be used with many different language syntaxes. Each language is free to define any syntax it wishes, but if that language is built on the CLR, it will use at least some of the types defined by the CTS.

Types are an important part of a programming language

Types are fundamental to any programming language. One very concrete way to think of a type is as a set of rules for interpreting the value stored in some memory location, such as the value of a variable. If that variable has an integer type, for example, the bits stored in it are interpreted as an integer. If the variable has a string type, the bits stored in it are interpreted as characters. To a compiler, of course, a type is more than this. Compilers must also understand the rules that define what kinds of values are allowed for each type and what kinds of operations are legal on these values. Among other things, this knowledge allows a compiler to determine whether a value of a particular type is being used correctly.

The set of types defined by the CTS is at the core of the CLR. Programming languages built on the CLR expose these types in a language-dependent way. (For examples of this, see the descriptions of C# and Visual Basic.NET in the next chapter.) While the creator of a CLR-based language is free to implement only a subset of the types defined by the CTS, and even to add types of his own to his language, most languages built on the CLR make extensive use of the CTS-defined types.

CLR-based languages expose CTS types in different ways

Introducing the Common Type System

A substantial subset of the types defined by the CTS is shown in Figure 3-1. The first thing to note is that every type inherits either directly or indirectly from a type called Object. (All of these types are actually contained in the System namespace, as mentioned in Chapter 1, so the complete name for this most fundamental type is System.Object.) The second thing to note is that every type defined by the CTS is either a *reference* type or a *value* type. As their names suggest, an instance of a reference type always contains a reference to a value of that type, while an instance of a value type contains the value itself. Reference types inherit directly from Object, while all value types inherit directly from a type called ValueType, which in turn inherits from Object.

The CTS defines reference and value types

Value types tend to be simple. The types in this category include Byte, Char, signed integers of various lengths, unsigned integers of various lengths, single- and double-precision floating

Value types are simpler than reference types

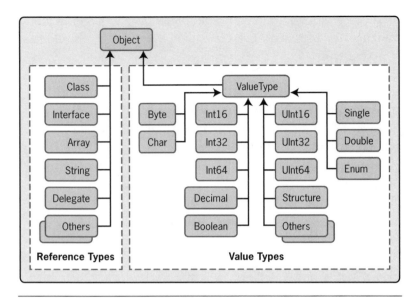

Figure 3-1   The CTS defines reference and value types, all of which inherit from a common Object type.

point, Decimal, Boolean, and more. Reference types, by contrast, are typically more complex. As shown in the figure, for instance, Class, Interface, Array, and String are reference types. Yet to understand the difference between value types and reference types—a fundamental distinction in the CTS—you must first understand how memory is allocated for instances of each type. In managed code, values can have their memory allocated in one of two[1] ways: on the *stack* managed by the CLR or on the CLR-managed *heap*. Variables allocated on the stack are typically created when a method is called or when a running method creates them. In either case, the memory used by stack variables is automatically freed when the method in which they were created returns. Variables allocated on the heap, however, don't have their memory freed when the method that created

---

1. In fact, there are three ways: Global variables and statics are allocated in a separate area.

them ends. Instead, the memory used by these variables is freed via a process called *garbage collection,* a topic that's described in more detail later in this chapter.

A basic difference between value types and reference types is that a standalone instance of a value type is allocated on the stack, while an instance of a reference type has only a reference to its actual value allocated on the stack. The value itself is allocated on the heap. Figure 3-2 shows an abstract picture of how this looks. In the case shown here, three instances of value types—Int16, Char, and Int32—have been created on the managed stack, while one instance of the reference type String exists on the managed heap. Note that even the reference type instance has an entry on the stack—it's a reference to the memory on the heap—but the instance's contents are stored on the heap. Understanding the distinction between value types and reference types is essential in understanding the CTS type system and, ultimately, the types used by CLR-based languages.

Value types live on the stack, while reference types typically live on the heap

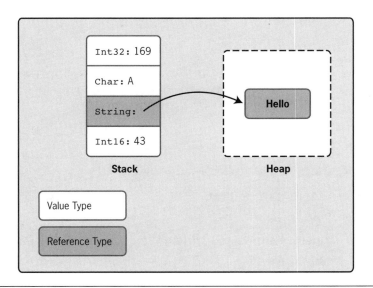

Figure 3-2   Instances of value types are allocated on the managed stack, while instances of reference types are allocated on the managed heap.

A Closer Look at CTS Types

The root Object type provides methods that are inherited by every other type

The CTS defines a large set of types. As already described, the most fundamental of these is Object, from which every CTS type inherits directly or indirectly. In the object-oriented world of the CLR, having a common base for all types is useful. For one thing, since everything inherits from the same root type, an instance of this type can potentially contain any value. (In this sense, Object is analogous to the Variant type in COM.) Object also implements several methods, and since every CTS type inherits from Object, these methods can be called on an instance of any type. Among the methods Object provides are Equals, which determines whether two objects are identical, and GetType, which returns the type of the object it's called on.

Value Types

The ValueType type provides methods that are inherited by every value type

All value types inherit from ValueType. Like Object, ValueType provides an Equals method (in fact, it overrides the method defined in Object). Value types cannot act as a parent type for inheritance, however, so it's not possible to, say, define a new type that inherits from Int32. In the jargon of the CLR, value types are said to be *sealed*.

Value types include Byte, Int32, Structure, and more

Many of the value types defined by the CTS were shown in Figure 3-1. Defined a bit more completely, those types are as follows:

- **Byte:** An 8-bit unsigned integer.

- **Char:** A 16-bit Unicode character.

- **Int16, Int32, and Int64:** 16-, 32-, and 64-bit signed integers.

- **UInt16, UInt32, and UInt64:** 16-, 32-, and 64-bit unsigned integers.

- **Single and Double:** Single-precision (32-bit) and double-precision (64-bit) floating-point numbers.

- **Decimal:** 96-bit decimal numbers.

- **Enum:** A way to name a group of values of some integer type. Enumerated types inherit from System.Enum and are used to define types whose values have meaningful names rather than just numbers.

- **Boolean:** True or false.

- **Structure:** A collection of elements of various types. A CTS structure is actually much like a CTS class, described in the next section. Like a class, it can contain methods, implement interfaces, and more. The biggest difference between a structure and a class is that structures are value types while classes are reference types. This makes structures somewhat more efficient to use since they're not allocated on the heap. Also, as mentioned earlier, it's not possible to inherit from a value type, so while a class can act as the parent for another class, nothing can inherit from a structure.

Reference Types

Compared with value types, the reference types defined by the CTS are relatively complicated. Before describing some of the more important reference types, it's useful to look first at a few elements, officially known as *type members,* that are common to several types. Those elements are as follows:

Many CTS types have common type members

- **Methods:** Executable code that carries out some kind of operation. Methods can be *overloaded,* which means that a single type can define two or more methods with the same name. To distinguish among them, each of these identically named methods must differ somehow in its parameter list. Another way to say this is to state that each method must have a unique *signature.* If a method encounters an error, it can throw an *exception,* which provides some indication of what has gone wrong.

- **Fields:** A value of some CTS type.

- **Events:** A mechanism for communicating with other types. Each event includes methods for subscribing and unsubscribing and for sending (often referred to as *firing*) the event to subscribers.

- **Properties:** In effect, a value together with specified methods to read and/or write that value.

- **Nested types:** A type defined inside another type. A common example of this is defining a class that is nested inside another class.

Type members have characteristics

Type members can be assigned various characteristics. For example, methods, events, and properties can be labeled as *abstract,* which means that no implementation is supplied; as *final,* which means that the method, event, or property can't be overridden; or as *virtual,* which means that exactly which implementation is used can be determined at runtime rather than at compilation. Methods, events, properties, and fields can all be defined as *static,* which means they are associated with the type itself rather than with any particular instance of that type. (For example, a static method can be invoked on a class without first creating an instance of that class.) Members can also be assigned different *accessibilities.* For example, a *private* method can be accessed only from within the type it's defined in or from another type nested in that type. A method whose accessibility is *family,* however, can be accessed from within the type it's defined in and from types that inherit from that type, while one whose accessibility is *public* can be accessed from any other type.

Reference types include Class, Interface, Array, and String

Given this basic understanding of type members, we can now look at reference types themselves. Among the most important are the following:

- **Class:** A CTS class can have methods, events, and properties; it can maintain its state in one or more fields; and it can contain nested types. A class's visibility can be *public,* which means it's available to any other type, or *assembly,* which means it's available only to other classes in the same assembly (assemblies are described later in this chapter). Classes have one or more *constructors,* which are initialization methods that execute when a new instance of this class is created. A class can directly inherit from at most one other class and can act as the direct parent for at most one inheriting child class. In other words, a CTS class supports single but not multiple implementation inheritance. If a class is marked as *sealed,* however, no other class can inherit from it. A class marked as *abstract,* by contrast, can't be instantiated but can serve only as the base class (that is, the parent) for another class that inherits from it. A class can also have one or more members marked as abstract, which means the class itself is abstract. If a class inherits from another class, it may *override* one or more methods, properties, and other type members in its parent by providing an implementation with the same signature. A class can also implement one or more interfaces, described as follows:

- **Interface:** An interface can include methods, properties, and events. Unlike classes, interfaces do support multiple inheritance, so an interface can inherit from one or more other interfaces simultaneously.

- **Array:** An array is a group of values of the same type. Arrays can have one or more dimensions, and their upper and lower bounds can be set more or less arbitrarily. All arrays inherit from a common System.Array type.

- **String:** A group of Unicode characters. Once created, a value of this type cannot be changed. In other words, Strings are immutable. (The .NET Framework class library provides a StringBuilder class that can be used for modifying character strings if necessary.)

- **Delegate:** A delegate is effectively a pointer to a method. All delegates inherit from a common System.Delegate type, and they're commonly used for event handling and callbacks. Each delegate has a set of associated members called an *invocation list*. When the delegate is invoked, each member on this list gets called, with each one passed the parameters that the delegate received.

The core types are the same in CLR-based languages such as C# and VB.NET

As the next chapter shows, CLR-based programming languages such as C# and Visual Basic.NET construct their own type system on top of the CTS types. Despite their different representations, however, the semantics of these types are essentially the same in C#, Visual Basic.NET, and many other CLR-based languages. In fact, providing this foundation of common programming language types is one of the CLR's most important roles.

Converting Value Types to Reference Types: Boxing

Boxing transforms an instance of a value type into an instance of a reference type

There are cases when an instance of a value type needs to be treated as an instance of a reference type. For example, suppose you'd like to pass an instance of a value type as a parameter to some method, but that parameter is defined to be a reference to a value rather than the value itself. For situations like this, a value type instance can be converted into a reference type instance through a process called *boxing*.

Boxing a value type instance moves its value to the heap

When a value type instance is boxed, storage is allocated on the heap, and the instance's value is copied into that space. A reference to this storage is placed on the stack, as shown in Figure 3-3. The boxed value is an object, a reference type, that contains the contents of the value type instance. In the figure, the Int32 value 169 shown in Figure 3-2 has been converted to a value of type Object, and its contents have been placed on the heap. A boxed value type instance can also be converted back to its original form, a process called *unboxing*.

CLR-based languages can make boxing invisible

Languages built on the CLR commonly hide the process of boxing, so developers may not need to request this transformation explicitly. (Not all of them do, however, as the discussion of Managed C++ in the next chapter will show.) Still, boxing has

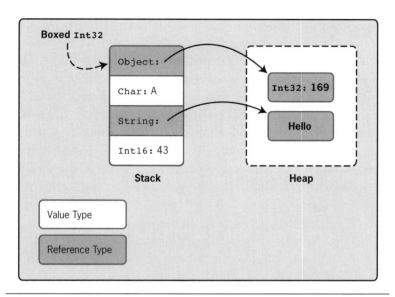

Figure 3-3   Boxing converts a value type instance into an instance of an analogous reference type.

performance implications—doing it takes time, and references to boxed values are a bit slower than references to unboxed values—and boxed values behave somewhat differently than unboxed values. Even though the process usually happens silently, it's worth understanding what's going on.

The Common Language Specification

The CTS defines a large and fairly complex set of types. Not all of them make sense for all languages. Yet one of the key goals of the CLR is to allow creating code in one language, then calling that code from another. Unless both languages support the same types in the same way, doing this is problematic. Still, requiring every language to implement every CTS type would be burdensome to language developers.

The solution to this conundrum is a compromise called the Common Language Specification (CLS). The CLS defines a (large) subset of the CTS that a language must obey if it wishes

The CLS defines a subset of the CTS to enable cross-language interoperability

to interoperate with other CLS-compliant languages. For example, the CLS requires support for most CTS value types, including Boolean, Byte, Char, Decimal, Int16, Int32, Int64, Single, Double, and more. It does not require support, however, for UInt16, UInt32, or UInt64. Similarly, a CTS array is allowed to have its lower bound set at an arbitrary value, while a CLS-compliant array must have a lower bound of zero. There are many more restrictions in the CLS, all of them defined with the same end in mind: allowing effective interoperability among code written in CLR-based languages.

One important thing to note about the rules laid down by the CLS is that they apply only to externally visible aspects of a type. A language is free to do anything it wants within its own world, but whatever it exposes to the outside world—and thus potentially to other languages—is constrained by the CLS. Given the goal of cross-language interoperability, this distinction makes perfect sense.

Compiling Managed Code

Compiling managed code generates MSIL and metadata

When managed code is compiled, two things are produced: instructions expressed in *Microsoft Intermediate Language (MSIL),* and *metadata,* information about those instructions and the data they manipulate. Whether the managed code is initially written in C#, Visual Basic.NET, or some other CLR-based language, the compiler transforms all of the types it contains—classes, structs, integers, delegates, and all the rest—into MSIL and metadata.

MSIL and metadata are contained in a DLL or EXE

Figure 3-4 illustrates this process. In this example, the code being compiled contains three CTS types, all of them classes. When this code is compiled using whatever compiler is appropriate for the language it's written in, the result is an equivalent set of MSIL code for each class along with metadata describing

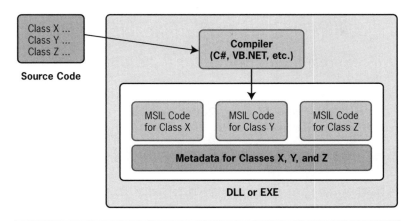

Figure 3-4   Compiling managed code written in any language produces MSIL and metadata describing that MSIL.

those classes. Both the MSIL and the metadata are stored in a standard Windows portable executable (PE) file. This file can be either a DLL or an EXE, with the general term *module* sometimes used to mean either of these. This section takes a closer look at MSIL and metadata.

Microsoft Intermediate Language (MSIL)

MSIL is quite similar to a processor's native instruction set. However, no hardware that actually executes these instructions (today, at least) is available. Instead, MSIL code is always translated into native code for whatever processor this code is running on before it's executed. It's probably fair to say that a developer working in the .NET Framework environment need never fully understand MSIL. Nevertheless, it's worth knowing at least a little bit about what a compiler produces from code written in C# or Visual Basic.NET or any other CLR-based language.

MSIL defines a virtual instruction set

As implied earlier in this chapter, the abstract machine defined by the CLR is stack based, which means that many MSIL

The CLR defines a stack-based virtual machine

Why Use MSIL?

The idea of compiling from a high-level language into a common intermediate language is a staple of modern compiler technology. The compilers in Visual Studio 6, for example, transform various programming languages into the same intermediate language and then use a common back end to compile this into a machine-specific binary. Prior to the .NET Framework, it was this binary that a user of the application would install.

For .NET Framework applications, however, what gets copied to the disk when an application is installed is not a machine-specific binary. Instead, it's the MSIL for this application, code that's analogous to the intermediate language that formerly remained hidden inside the compiler. Why make this change? What's the benefit of distributing code as MSIL?

The most obvious answer is the potential for portability. As discussed in Chapter 1, at least the core of the .NET Framework is available on systems that use non-Windows operating systems and non-Intel processors. While making the complete .NET Framework a truly multi-operating system technology would be challenging in many ways, Microsoft clearly wants at least the .NET Compact Framework to be available on many devices.

Portability isn't the only advantage of using an intermediate language. Unlike binary code, which can contain references to arbitrary memory addresses, MSIL code can be verified for type safety when it is loaded into memory. This allows better security and higher reliability, since some kinds of errors and a large set of possible attacks can be made impossible. Verification in the CLR is described later in this chapter.

One potential drawback of this approach is that it can lead to slower code. Microsoft actually admits that some .NET Framework applications are likely to run more slowly than those written with the earlier Windows DNA technologies. The right question to ask, however, is not how fast these applications will run, but whether they will be fast enough to meet customer requirements. There is a large body of evidence that suggests they will, evidence provided by the success of Java. Java developers have been using this approach for several years, and while Java code is typically slower than native code, it is fast enough that many organizations use it quite successfully. And unlike Java, which is often interpreted, MSIL is always compiled before execution, as described later in this chapter.

Relying heavily on an intermediate language could be unworkably slow five years ago. Today, though, it's fine: The hardware has gotten much faster. It's great working in software, isn't it? If things are too slow today, just wait a little while. They'll probably be fast enough in a year or two.

operations are defined in terms of this stack. Here are a few example MSIL instructions and what they're used for:

- **add:** Adds the top two values on the stack and pushes the result back onto the stack.

- **box:** Converts a value type to a reference type; that is, it boxes the value.

- **br:** Transfers control (branches) to a specified location in memory.

- **call:** Calls a specified method.

- **ldfld:** Loads a specified field of an object onto the stack.

- **ldobj:** Copies the value of a specified value type onto the stack.

- **newobj:** Creates a new object or a new instance of a value type.

- **stfld:** Stores a value from the stack into a specified field of an object.

- **stobj:** Stores a value on the stack into a specified value type.

- **unbox:** Converts a boxed value type back to its ordinary form.

MSIL reflects the CTS

In effect, MSIL is the assembly language of the CLR. One interesting thing to notice about this tiny sample of the MSIL instruction set is how closely it maps to the abstractions of the CLR's Common Type System. Objects, value types, even boxing and unboxing all have direct support. Also, some operations, such as the newobj used to create new instances, are analogous to operators more commonly found in high-level languages than they are to typical machine instructions.

For developers who wish to work directly in this low-level argot, the .NET Framework provides an MSIL assembler called *Ilasm*. Only the most masochistic developers are likely to use this tool, however. Why write in MSIL when you can use a simpler, more powerful language such as Visual Basic.NET or C# and get the same result?

Metadata

Compiled managed code always has associated metadata

Compiling managed code always produces MSIL. Compiling managed code also always produces metadata describing that code. Metadata is information about the types defined in the managed code it's associated with, and it's stored in the same file as the MSIL generated from those types. If you're familiar with COM, metadata serves much the same purpose as a COM type library.

Figure 3-5 shows an abstract view of a module produced by a CLR-based compiler. The file contains the MSIL code generated from the types in the original program, which once again are the three classes X, Y, and Z. Along with the code for the methods in each class, the file contains metadata describing these classes and any other types defined in this file. This information is loaded into memory when the file itself is loaded, making the metadata accessible at runtime. Metadata can also be read directly from the file that contains it, making information available even when code isn't loaded into memory. The process of

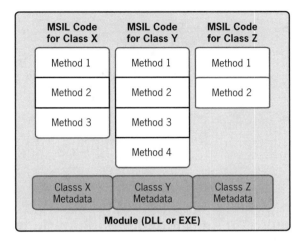

Figure 3-5   A module contains metadata for each type in the file.

reading metadata is known as *reflection,* and it's described in more detail in Chapter 5.

What Metadata Contains

Metadata describes the types contained in a module. Among the information it stores for a type are the following:

- The type's name
- The type's visibility, which can be *public* or *assembly*
- What type this type inherits from, if any
- Any interfaces the type implements
- Any methods the type implements
- Any properties the type exposes
- Any events the type provides

Metadata provides detailed information about each type

More detailed information is also available. For example, the description of each method includes the method's parameters and their types, along with the type of the method's return value.

MSIL Versus Java Bytecode

The concept of MSIL is similar to what Java calls bytecode. Java fans might point out, with some justice, that Microsoft has copied an approach first made popular by their technology. Microsoft sometimes responds to this claim, again with some justice, by observing that the idea of an intermediate language predates both Java bytecode and MSIL, with antecedents stretching back to UCSD Pascal's p-code and beyond.

In any case, it's interesting to compare the two technologies. The broad outlines are similar, with both the Java virtual machine and the CLR defining a stack-based virtual environment. One obvious difference is that Java bytecode was specifically designed to support the Java language, while MSIL was defined to support multiple languages. Still, a substantial amount of language semantics is embedded in MSIL, so while it is somewhat broader than Java bytecode, MSIL isn't completely general. Concepts defined by the CTS, such as the distinction between reference and value types, are fundamental to MSIL. This distinction is part of both C# and Visual Basic.NET, and it will likely appear in most CLR-based languages. Another difference is that the Java virtual machine was designed to allow bytecode to be interpreted as well as compiled, while MSIL's designers explicitly targeted JIT compilation. While interpreting MSIL is probably possible, it appears that it would be significantly less efficient than interpreting Java bytecode.

As is usually the case when a widely used model exists, Microsoft was probably able to learn from the experiences of the Java world in designing the CLR. As Moore's Law continues to make more processing power available for less money, both the Java and Microsoft camps have decided that the advantages of an intermediate language outweigh the potential performance penalty.

For a more detailed comparison of MSIL and Java bytecode, see K. John Gough's *Stacking Them Up: A Comparison of Virtual Machines,* available at http://sky.fit.qut.edu.au/~gough/publications.html.

The Evolution of Metadata

The idea of providing information about compiled code—metadata—has been around for quite a while. Even standard Windows DLLs offer a simple form of metadata by providing a list of the functions they export. But most Windows developers first encountered metadata in a serious way with the arrival of COM's type libraries. A COM component's type library allows tools and other software to learn about the COM classes a component supports, discover what interfaces each of those classes implements, and more.

Yet while a type library provides useful information about the COM classes it describes, the information it provides is limited. A developer can't determine what other COM classes this one depends on, for instance, nor can he be certain that the type library accurately describes every externally visible aspect of a COM class. COM's Interface Definition Language (IDL) allows expressing things that can't be represented in a type library, while type libraries can contain information that can't be expressed in IDL. Most developers don't suffer much from this mismatch, since the differences are fairly exotic. Still, while COM provides metadata, it does so in a needlessly idiosyncratic way.

The designers of the .NET Framework's metadata avoided these problems. For one thing, a module's metadata is full fidelity, which means that it completely and accurately describes the code it's associated with. Also, every module always contains metadata, unlike COM's optional type libraries. While the current form of a module's metadata probably isn't the last word on the subject—new ideas always appear—it is clearly a long step forward from what COM provided.

Because metadata is always present, tools can rely on it always being available. Visual Studio.NET, for example, uses metadata to show a developer what methods are available for the class name she's just typed. A module's metadata can also be examined using a tool called *Ildasm*. This tool is the reverse of the Ilasm tool mentioned earlier in this chapter—it's a disassembler for MSIL—and it can also provide a detailed display of the metadata contained in a particular module.

Tools can use metadata

Attributes

Attributes contain values stored with metadata

Metadata also includes *attributes*. Attributes are values that are stored in the metadata and can be read and used to control various aspects of how this code executes. Attributes can be added to types, such as classes, and to fields, methods, and properties of those types. As described later in this book, the .NET Framework class library relies on attributes for many things, including specifying transaction requirements, indicating which methods should be exposed as SOAP-callable Web services, and describing security requirements. These attributes have standard names and functions defined by the various parts of the .NET Framework class library that use them.

Developers can create custom attributes

Developers can also create custom attributes used to control behavior in an application-specific way. To create a custom attribute, a developer using a CLR-based programming language such as C# or Visual Basic.NET can define a class that inherits from System.Attribute. An instance of the resulting class will automatically have its value stored in metadata when it is compiled.

Organizing Managed Code: Assemblies

An assembly is one or more files that comprise a logical unit

A complete application often consists of many different files. Some files are modules—DLLs or EXEs—that contain code, while others might contain various kinds of resources such as image files. In .NET Framework applications, files that make up a logical unit of functionality are grouped into an *assembly*. Assemblies, described in this section, are fundamental to developing, deploying, and running .NET Framework applications.

Metadata for Assemblies: Manifests

Each assembly has a manifest

Assemblies are a logical construct; there's no single über-file that wraps all of the files in an assembly. In fact, it's not possible to tell what files belong to the same assembly just by looking at a directory listing. Instead, determining which files comprise a particular assembly requires examining that assembly's *manifest*. As just described, the metadata in a module, such as a DLL, contains information about the types in that module. An assembly's manifest, by contrast, contains information about all of the modules and other files in an assembly. In other words, a manifest is metadata about an assembly. The manifest is contained in one of the assembly's files, and it includes information about the assembly and the files that comprise it. Just as a tool such as Visual Studio.NET generates metadata for each module it compiles, so too it generates an assembly with an appropriate manifest.

As Figure 3-6 shows, an assembly can be built from a single file or a group of files. With a single-file assembly, the manifest is

An assembly's manifest contains the assembly's name, its version number, and more

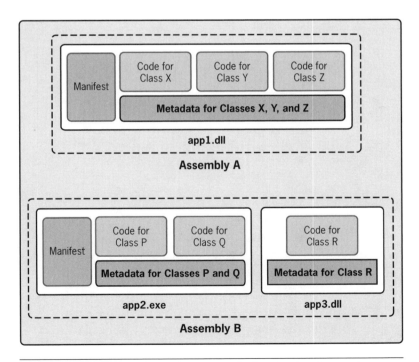

Figure 3-6   An assembly is often just a single DLL, but it can also include more than one file.

stored in the file itself. With a multifile assembly, the manifest is stored in one of the files in the assembly. In either case, two kinds of metadata exist: The manifest describes the entire assembly, while the metadata in each module defines the types in that module. Among the things an assembly's manifest includes are the following.

- The name of the assembly. All assemblies have a text name and can optionally have a strong name as well, as described in the next section.

- The assembly's version number. This number has the form <major version>.<minor version>.<build number>.<revision>. For example, the version number for an assembly that's part of a released application might be 1.2.1397.0. Note that versioning is per assembly, not per module.

- The assembly's culture, indicating the culture or language an assembly supports.

- A list of all files contained in this assembly, together with a hash value that's been computed from those files.

- What other assemblies this one depends on, and the version number of each of those dependent assemblies.

Assemblies define a scope for types

Most assemblies consist of just a single DLL. Whether it contains one file or multiple files, however, an assembly is logically an indivisible unit. For example, assemblies define a boundary for scoping types. To the CLR, a type name really consists of the name of the type together with the name of the assembly in which the type is defined. Note, however, that the notion of a namespace used in the .NET Framework class library and elsewhere is not directly reflected in assemblies. Namespaces are a useful way of grouping types in a CLR-based programming language, but they are not visible to the CLR itself.

One important corollary of the way assemblies are structured is that unlike COM classes, CLR classes don't have associated registry entries (unless they are also accessible as COM classes for backward compatibility, an option described in Chapter 5). When the CLR needs to find a class in some other assembly, it does not look up the class in the registry. Instead, it searches according to a well-defined (although slightly complex) algorithm that's described later in this chapter.

Assemblies don't require registry entries

Requiring no registry entries also has another benefit. Installing a typical assembly entails simply copying its constituent files to an appropriate directory on the target machine's disk. Similarly, an assembly can usually be uninstalled by simply deleting its files. Unlike COM-based applications, software built on the .NET Framework doesn't need to modify the system registry.

Installing a .NET Framework application typically requires just copying its assemblies

Categorizing Assemblies

There are various ways to categorize assemblies. One distinction is between *static* and *dynamic* assemblies. Static assemblies are produced by a tool such as Visual Studio.NET, and their contents are stored on disk. Most developers will create static assemblies, since the goal is usually to build an application that can be installed on one or more machines and then executed. It's also possible to create dynamic assemblies, however. The code (and metadata) for a dynamic assembly is created directly in memory and can be executed immediately upon creation. Once it's been created, a dynamic assembly can be saved to disk, then loaded and executed again. Probably the most common examples of dynamic assemblies are those created by ASP.NET when it processes .aspx pages, a topic covered in Chapter 7.

Both static and dynamic assemblies exist

Another way to categorize assemblies is by how they are named. Completely naming any assembly requires specifying three things: the assembly's name; its version number; and, if

An assembly can have a strong name

one is provided, the culture it supports. All assemblies have simple text names, such as "AccountAccess," but an assembly can also have a *strong name*. A strong name includes the usual three parts of an assembly name, but it also includes a digital signature computed on the assembly and the public key that corresponds to the private key used to create that signature.[2] Strong names are unique and so can be used to identify a particular assembly unambiguously.

The CLR performs version checking on assemblies with strong names

Strong-named assemblies have their version numbers automatically checked by the CLR when they're loaded. Version control for assemblies without strong names, however, is the responsibility of the developer creating and using those assemblies. Because assemblies have version numbers, it's possible for multiple versions of the same assembly to be installed on the same machine at the same time. And because an assembly can specify exactly which version it requires of every other assembly it depends on, the pain that has resulted from DLL conflicts in the past can be eliminated.

Assemblies can eliminate DLL hell

A more succinct way to say this is that the versioning the CLR enforces for strong-named assemblies means the end of DLL hell. Traditionally, installing a new version of a DLL required by one application could break another application that relied on that same DLL. With strong-named assemblies, however, a CLR-based application can insist on a particular version of each assembly it depends on without restricting other applications' use of new versions. Developers must still pay attention, however, or conflicts might arise. For example, suppose two ver-

---

2. A digital signature is a hash—a checksum—computed on some set of bytes, such as an assembly, that is then encrypted using the private key of a public/private key pair. To verify an assembly's digital signature, the same hash can be computed on the files in the assembly, and the public key in the key pair can be used to decrypt the digital signature. If the newly computed hash matches the decrypted signature, the assembly has not been modified since the signature was created.

sions of an assembly each write to the same temp file. Unless they agree on how this file should be shared, running both versions at once will lead to problems.

Executing Managed Code

Assemblies provide a way to package modules containing MSIL and metadata into units for deployment. The goal of writing code is not to package and deploy it, however; it's to run it. The final section of this chapter looks at the most important aspects of running managed code.

Loading Assemblies

When an application built using the .NET Framework is executed, the assemblies that make up that application must be found and loaded into memory. Assemblies aren't loaded until they're needed, so if an application never calls any methods in a particular assembly, that assembly won't be loaded. (In fact, it need not even be present on the machine where the application is running.) Before any code in an assembly can be loaded, however, it must be found. How is this done?

Assemblies are loaded into memory only when needed

The answer is not simple. In fact, the process the CLR uses to find assemblies is too complex to describe completely here. The broad outlines of the process are fairly straightforward, however. First, the CLR determines what version of a particular assembly it's looking for. By default, it will look only for the exact version specified for this assembly in the manifest of the assembly from which the call originated. This default can be changed by settings in various configuration files, so the CLR examines these files before it commences its search.

The CLR follows well-defined but involved rules to locate an assembly

Once it has determined exactly which version it needs, the CLR checks whether the desired assembly is already loaded. If it is, the search is over; this loaded version will be used. If the

The CLR looks first in the global assembly cache

desired assembly is not already loaded, the CLR will begin searching in various places to find it. The first place the CLR looks is usually the *global assembly cache (GAC),* a special directory intended to hold assemblies that are used by more than one application. Installing assemblies in this global assembly cache requires a process slightly more complex than just copying the assembly, and the cache can contain only assemblies with strong names.

The CLR can next look in the location referenced by a codebase element

If the assembly it's hunting for isn't in the global assembly cache, the CLR continues its search by checking for a *codebase* element in one of the configuration files for this application. If one is found, the CLR looks in the location this element specifies, such as a directory, for the desired assembly. Finding the right assembly in this location means the search is over, and this assembly will be loaded and used. Even if the location pointed to by a codebase element does not contain the desired assembly, however, the search is nevertheless over. A codebase element is meant to specify exactly where the assembly can be found. If the assembly is not at that location, something has gone wrong, the CLR gives up, and the attempt to load the new assembly fails.

If no codebase element exists, the CLR searches in other places

If there is no codebase element, however, the CLR will begin its search for the desired assembly in what's known as the *application base.* This can be either the root directory in which the application is installed or a URL, perhaps on some other machine. (It's worth pointing out that the CLR does not assume that all necessary assemblies for an application are installed on the same machine; they can also be located and installed across an internal network or the Internet.) If the elusive assembly isn't found here, the CLR continues searching in several other directories based on the name of the assembly, its culture, and more.

Despite the apparent complexity of this process, this description is not complete. There are other alternatives and even more options. For developers working with the .NET Framework, it's probably worth spending some time understanding this process in detail. Putting in the effort up front is likely to save time later when applications don't behave as expected.

Compiling MSIL

A compiler that produces managed code always generates MSIL. Yet MSIL can't be executed by any real processor. Before it can be run, MSIL code must be compiled yet again into native code that targets the processor on which it will execute. Two options exist for doing this: MSIL code can be compiled one method at a time during execution, or it can be compiled into native code all at once before an assembly is executed. This section describes both of these approaches.

JIT Compilation

The most common way to compile MSIL into native code is to let the CLR load an assembly and then compile each method the first time that method is invoked. Because each method is compiled only when it's first called, the process is called *just-in-time (JIT) compilation*.

MSIL code is typically JIT compiled before it's executed.

Figures 3-7, 3-8, and 3-9 illustrate how the code in an assembly gets JIT compiled. This simple example shows just three classes, once again called X, Y, and Z, each containing some number of methods. In Figure 3-7, only method 1 of class Y has been compiled. All other code in all other methods of the three classes is still in MSIL, the form in which it was loaded. When class Y's method 1 calls class Z's method 1, the CLR notices that this newly called method is not in an executable form. The CLR invokes the JIT compiler, which compiles class Z's method 1 and redirects calls made to that method to this compiled native code. The method can now execute.

A method is JIT compiled the first time it is called

Similarly, in Figure 3-8, class Y's method 1 calls its own method 4. As before, this method is still in MSIL, so the JIT

A method always executes as native code

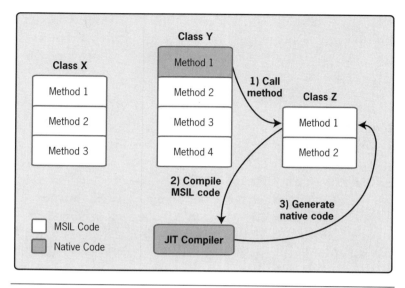

Figure 3-7   The first time class Z's method 1 is called, the JIT compiler is invoked to translate the method's MSIL into native code.

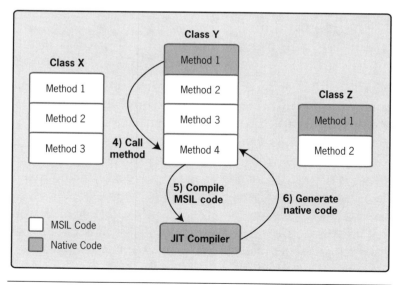

Figure 3-8   When class Y's method 4 is called, the JIT compiler is once again used to translate the method's MSIL into native code.

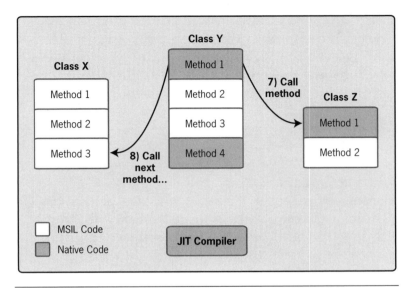

Figure 3-9   When class Z's method 1 is called again, no compilation is necessary.

compiler is automatically invoked and the method is compiled. Once again, a reference to the MSIL code for the method is replaced with one to the newly created native code, and the method executes.

Figure 3-9 shows what happens when class Y's method 1 again calls method 1 in class Z. This method has already been JIT compiled, so there's no need to do any more work. The native code has been saved in memory, so it just executes. The JIT compiler isn't involved. The process continues in this same way, with each method compiled the first time it is invoked.

When a method is JIT compiled, it's also checked for type safety. This process, called *verification,* examines the method's MSIL and metadata to ensure that the code makes no illegal accesses. The CLR's built-in security features, described in the next section, depend on this, as do other aspects of managed code behavior. Still, a system administrator can turn off verification—it's

Methods can be verified when they're JIT compiled

not required—which means that the CLR can execute managed code that is not type safe. This can be useful, since some compilers such as Visual Studio's Visual C++ can't generate type-safe code. In general, however, verification should be used whenever possible with .NET Framework applications.

Compiled code is not saved on disk

With JIT compilation, only those methods that get called will be compiled. If a method in an assembly is loaded but never used, it will stay in its MSIL form. Also, note that compiled native code is not saved back to disk. Instead, the process of JIT compilation is carried out each time an assembly is loaded. Finally, it's important to emphasize that the .NET Framework does not include an interpreter for MSIL. Executed code is either JIT compiled or compiled all at once, as described next.

Creating a Native Image: NGEN

NGEN allows compiling an assembly into native code before the assembly is loaded

Instead of JIT compiling, an assembly's MSIL code can be translated into native code for a particular processor all at once using the Native Image Generator (NGEN). Contained in the file Ngen.exe, this command-line tool can be run on an assembly to produce a directly executable image. Rather than being JIT compiled one method at a time, the assembly will now be loaded as native code. This makes the initial phase of the application faster, since there's no need to pay the penalty of JIT compilation on the first call to each method. Using NGEN doesn't make the overall speed of the application any better, however, since JIT compilation slows down only the first call to a method. In general, JIT compilation should suffice for most .NET Framework applications.

Securing Assemblies

An assembly defines a scope for types, a unit of versioning, and a logical deployment unit. An assembly also defines a security boundary. The CLR implements two different types of security for assemblies: *code access* security and *role-based* security. This section describes both.

Code Access Security

Think about what happens when you run a traditional Windows executable on your machine. You can decide whether that code is allowed to execute, but if you let it run, you can't control exactly what the code is allowed to do. This was a barely acceptable approach when all of the code loaded on your machine came from disks you or your system administrator installed. When most machines are connected to a global network, however, this all-or-nothing approach is no longer sufficient. It's often useful to download code from the Internet and run it locally, but the potential security risks in doing this can be huge. A malicious developer can create an application that looks useful but in fact erases your files or floods your friends with e-mail or performs some other destructive act. What's needed is some way to limit what code, especially downloaded code, is allowed to do. The code access security built into the CLR is intended to provide this.

Code access security can limit what running code is allowed to do

Unlike today's typical Windows solution for controlling whether downloaded code can run—asking the user—the .NET Framework's code security doesn't rely on the user knowing what to do. Instead, what CLR-based code is allowed to do depends on the intersection of two things: what permissions that code requests and what permissions are granted to that code by the *security policy* in effect when the code executes. To indicate what kinds of access it needs, an assembly can specify exactly what permissions it requires from the environment in which it's running. Some examples of permissions an assembly can request are the following:

Code access security compares requested permissions with a security policy

- **UIPermission:** Allows access to the user interface

- **FileIOPermission:** Allows access to files or directories

- **FileDialogPermission:** Allows access only to files or directories that the user opens in a dialog box

- **PrintingPermission:** Allows access to printers

- **EnvironmentPermission:** Allows access to environment variables

- **RegistryPermission:** Allows access to the system registry on the machine

- **ReflectionPermission:** Allows access to an assembly's metadata

- **SecurityPermission:** Allows granting a group of permissions, including the right to call unmanaged code

- **WebPermission:** Allows establishing or receiving connections over the Web

Fine-grained permissions are possible

Within these general and other permissions (more are defined), finer-grained options can also be used. For example, FileIOPermission can specify read-only permission, write/delete/overwrite permission, append-only permission, or some combination of these. An assembly can also indicate whether the permissions it requests are absolutely necessary for it to run, or whether they would just be nice to have but aren't essential. An assembly can even indicate that it should never be granted certain permissions or demand that its callers have a specific set.

An assembly can use declarative or imperative security

There are two different ways for a developer to specify the permissions he'd like for an assembly. One option, called *declarative security,* lets the developer insert attributes into his code. (How attributes look in various CLR-based languages is shown in the next chapter.) Those attributes then become part of the metadata stored with that code, where they can be read by the CLR. The second approach, known as *imperative security,* allows the developer to specify permissions dynamically within his source code. This approach can't be used to request new permissions on the fly, but it can be used to demand that any callers have specific permissions.

The Perils of Mobile Code

Nobody knows better than Microsoft how dangerous code downloaded from the Internet can be. The company has received a large share of criticism in this area over the last few years.

One of the first lightning rods for attack was Microsoft's support for downloading ActiveX controls from Web servers. An ActiveX control is just a binary, so if the user allows it to run, it can do pretty much anything that user is allowed to do. Microsoft's Authenticode technology allows a publisher to sign an ActiveX control digitally, but it's still up to the user to decide whether to trust that publisher and run the control. In practice, only ActiveX controls produced by large organizations (such as Microsoft itself) have seen much use on the Internet. Most people think, quite correctly, that it's too dangerous to run even signed code from any but the most trusted sources.

Microsoft has received even more criticism and much more adverse publicity for e-mail-borne attacks. Various viruses have cost many organizations a lot of money, providing a very visible example of the dangers of running code received from a stranger. Yet educating the enormous number of nontechnical Windows users about these dangers is effectively impossible. Relying on the user not to run potentially dangerous code won't work. And even if we could educate every user, there would still be unintentional bugs that could be exploited by attackers.

The Java world addressed this problem from the beginning. Because Java focused early on mobile code in the form of applets and because Java has always been built on a virtual machine, software written in Java could be downloaded with less risk. With the advent of the CLR, Microsoft has the opportunity to provide the same kind of "sandboxing" that Java offers. Both camps now offer more fine-grained control over what downloaded code is allowed to do; an all-or-nothing decision is no longer required.

Administrators establish security policy

The creator of an assembly is free to request whatever permissions he wishes. The permissions actually granted to the assembly when it runs, however, depend on the security policy established for the machine on which the assembly is running. This security policy is defined by the machine's system administrator, and it specifies exactly which permissions should be granted to assemblies based on their identity and origin.

An assembly provides evidence of its origins

Each assembly provides *evidence* that the CLR can use to determine who created this assembly and where it came from. Evidence can consist of

- The identity of an assembly's publisher, indicated by the publisher's digital signature on the assembly.

- The identity of the assembly itself, represented by the assembly's strong name.

- The Web site from which an assembly was downloaded, such as www.qwickbank.com.

- The exact URL from which an assembly was downloaded, such as http://www.qwickbank.com/downloads/accounts.exe.

- The zone, as defined by Microsoft Internet Explorer, from which an assembly was downloaded. Possible zones include the local intranet, the Internet, and others.

The CLR determines what an assembly is allowed to do

When an assembly is loaded, the CLR examines the evidence it provides. It also looks at the permissions this assembly requests and compares them with the security policy established for the machine on which the assembly is being loaded. The assembly is granted any requested permissions that are allowed by the security policy. For example, suppose an assembly downloaded from the Web site www.qwickbank.com carries the digital signature of QwickBank as its publisher and requests FileIOPermission and UIPermission. If the security policy on this machine is defined to allow only UIPermission to assemblies published by QwickBank and downloaded from QwickBank's Web site, the assembly will not be able to access any files. It will still be allowed to run and interact with a user, but any attempts to access files will fail.

As this simple example illustrates, permissions are checked at runtime, and an exception is generated if the code in an assembly attempts an operation for which it does not have permission. These runtime checks can also prevent an assembly with limited permissions from duping an assembly with broader permissions into performing tasks that shouldn't be allowed. An assembly can even demand that any code calling into it has a specific digital signature. Finally, note that all of the mechanisms used for code security depend on the verification process that's part of JIT compilation. If verification has been bypassed, these mechanisms can't be guaranteed to work.

An assembly's permissions are checked at runtime

While fully understanding the .NET Framework's code security takes some effort, two things should be clear. First, this mechanism is quite flexible, offering options that address a wide range of needs. Second, in a world of global networks and mobile code, providing an enforceable way to limit what code can do is essential.

Role-Based Security

Code access security allows the CLR to limit what a particular assembly is allowed to do based on the assembly's name, who published it, and where it came from. But code access security provides no way to control what an assembly is allowed to do based on the identity of the user on whose behalf the assembly is running. Providing this kind of control is the goal of role-based security.

The foundation for role-based security is a *principal* object. This object contains both the identity of a user and the roles to which she belongs. A user's identity is indicated by an *identity* object, which contains both the user's identity, expressed as a

A user can belong to one or more roles

name or an account, and an indication of how that identity has been authenticated. In a Windows 2000 domain, for example, authentication might be done with Kerberos, while some other mechanism might be used on the Internet. The user's role typically identifies some kind of group the user belongs to that is useful for deciding what that user is allowed to access. For example, the fictitious QwickBank might have roles such as loan officer, teller, clerk, and others, each of which is likely to be allowed different levels of access.

An assembly can use roles to limit what its users are allowed to do

Code in an assembly can demand that only users with a specific identity or a specific role be allowed to access it. This demand can be made for a class as a whole or for a specific method, property, or event. Whatever granularity is chosen, the demand can be made either imperatively or declaratively. For *imperative demands,* the code must make an explicit call to cause a check, while in *declarative demands,* the code contains attributes that are stored in metadata and then used by the CLR to check the user's identity automatically. In either case, the result is the same: The user will be granted access to this class, method, property, or event only if her identity or role matches what the assembly specifies.[3]

Garbage Collection

Garbage collection frees unused objects

The managed heap plays an important role in the execution of a .NET Framework application. Every instance of a reference type—every class, every string, and more—is allocated on the heap. As the application runs, the memory allotted to the heap fills up. Before new instances can be created, more space must be made available. The process of doing this is called *garbage collection.*

---

3. If you're familiar with roles in COM+, the CLR's role-based security will look familiar. In fact, it's possible (although a little complex) to use both in the same application.

Describing Garbage Collection

When the CLR notices that the heap is full, it will automatically run the garbage collector. (An application can also explicitly request that the garbage collector be run, but this isn't an especially common thing to do.) To understand how garbage collection works, think once again about the way reference types are allocated. As Figure 3-10 shows, each instance of a reference type has an entry on the stack that points to its actual value on the heap. In the figure, the stack contains the decimal value 32.4, a reference to the string "Hello," the integer value 14, and a reference to the boxed integer value 169. The two reference types—the string and the boxed integer—have their values stored on the heap.

Garbage collection happens automatically

But notice that the heap also contains information for an object of class X. The figure isn't drawn to scale—this object would likely take up much more space than either the string or the boxed integer—but it's entirely possible that the chunk of heap

Garbage objects can appear anywhere in the heap

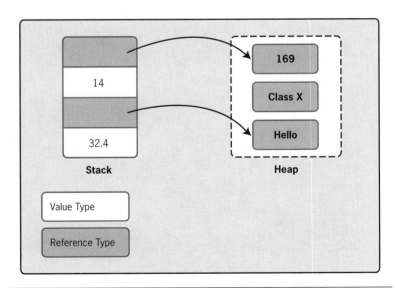

Figure 3-10   The space occupied on the heap by the object of class X is garbage.

memory allocated for the object would be in between the other two types. Maybe this object was created by a method that has completed execution, for example, so the reference that pointed to it from the stack is now gone. Whatever the situation, this object is just taking up space that could be used for something else. In other words, it's garbage.

Garbage collection can reposition the contents of the heap

When the garbage collector runs, it scans the heap looking for this kind of garbage. Once it knows which parts of the heap are garbage, it rearranges the heap's contents, packing more closely together those values that are still being used. For example, after garbage collection, the very simple case shown earlier would now look as illustrated in Figure 3-11. The garbage from the object of class X is gone, and the space it formerly occupied has been reused to store other information that's still in use.

The garbage collector views objects in generations

As this example suggests, longer-lived objects will migrate toward one end of the heap over time. In real software, it's typical

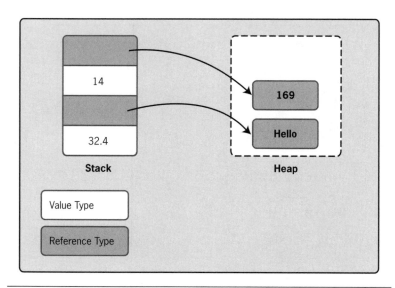

Figure 3-11   The garbage collector rearranges data on the heap to free more memory.

for the most recently allocated objects also to be the ones that most quickly become garbage. When looking for garbage, it makes sense to look first at the part of the heap where the most recently allocated objects will be. The CLR's garbage collector does exactly this, examining first this most recent generation of objects and reclaiming any unused space occupied by garbage. If this doesn't free up sufficient memory, the garbage collector will examine the next generation of objects, those that were allocated somewhat less recently. If this still doesn't free up enough space to meet current needs, the collector will examine all remaining objects in the managed heap, freeing anything that's no longer being used.

Finalizers

Every object on the heap has a special method called a *finalizer*. When an object has been garbage collected, it is placed on the finalize list. Eventually, each object on this list will have its finalizer run. By default, however, this method does nothing. If a type needs to perform some final clean-up operations before it is destroyed, the developer creating it can override the default finalizer, adding code to do whatever is required.

An object's finalizer runs just before the object is destroyed

Note that a finalizer is not the same thing as the notion of a destructor provided in languages like C++. You can't be sure when the finalizer will run, or even if it will run (the program could crash before this happens). If an object needs deterministic finalization behavior, guaranteeing that a particular method will run at a specific time before the object is destroyed, it should implement its own method to do this and then require its users to call this method when they're finished using the object.

Finalizers are non-deterministic

Application Domains

The CLR is implemented as a DLL, which allows it to be used in a quite general way. It also means, however, that there must typically be an EXE provided to host the CLR and the DLLs in

A runtime host is an EXE that hosts the CLR

any assemblies it loads. A *runtime host* can provide this function. The runtime host loads and initializes the CLR and then typically transfers control to managed code. ASP.NET provides a runtime host, as does Internet Explorer. The Windows shell also acts as a runtime host for loading standalone executables that use managed code.

An app domain isolates the assemblies it contains

A runtime host creates one or more *application domains* within its process. Each process contains a default application domain, and each assembly is loaded into some application domain within a particular process. Application domains are commonly called *app domains,* and they're quite a bit like a traditional operating system process. Like a process, an app domain isolates the applications it contains from those in all other app domains. But because multiple app domains can exist inside a single process, communication between them can be much more efficient than communication between different processes.

App domain isolation depends on verification

Yet how can app domains guarantee isolation? Without the built-in support for processes provided by an operating system, what guarantee is there that applications running in two separate app domains in the same process won't interfere with each other? The answer is, once again, verification. Because managed code is checked for type safety when it's JIT compiled, the system can be certain that no assembly will directly access anything outside its own boundaries.

An app domain provides the benefits of a process without the over-head

App domains can be used in a variety of ways. For example, ASP.NET runs each Web application in its own app domain. This allows the applications to remain isolated from each other, yet it doesn't incur the overhead of running many different processes. The most recent versions of Internet Explorer, another runtime host, can download Windows Forms controls from the Internet and then run each one in its own app domain. Once again, the benefit is isolation without the expense of cross-process communication. And because applications can be started and stopped independently in different app domains in the same process, this approach also avoids the overhead of starting a new process for each application.

Figure 3-12 shows how this looks. App domain 1, the default app domain, contains assemblies A, B, and C. Assemblies D and E have been loaded into app domain 2, while assembly F is running in app domain 3. Even though all of these assemblies are running in a single process, each app domain's assemblies are completely independent from those in the other app domains.

App domains also serve another purpose. Recall that the .NET Framework is intended to run on Windows and at least potentially on other operating systems. Different systems have quite different process models, especially systems used on small devices. By defining its own "process" model with app domains, the .NET Framework can provide a consistent environment across all of these platforms.

App domains provide a consistent environment on multiple platforms

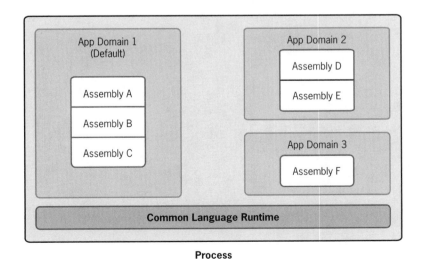

Figure 3-12   A process can contain one or more application domains.

Conclusion

The CLR introduces many new ideas for Windows developers. To help tie together the concepts described in this chapter, Figure 3-13 shows a process running a CLR-based application. The process includes a runtime host, a single app domain, and the CLR itself. Some of the CLR's more important components are shown, including the loader, the JIT compiler, and the garbage collector. Within the app domain, there's a single loaded assembly containing the three classes X, Y, and Z along with their metadata. Some methods in the classes have already been JIT-compiled, while others have not. And as the figure shows, variables of various value and reference types are in use

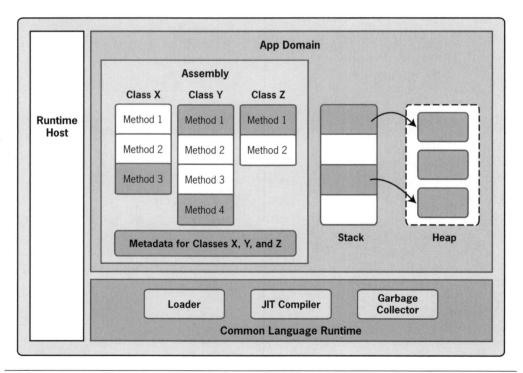

Figure 3-13   Managed code, software built on the .NET Framework, relies on the CLR to provide many different services.

by this running code. There's even some garbage on the heap waiting to be collected.

Creating software on the .NET Framework requires using the CLR, but it doesn't really require understanding how the CLR provides all of its services. Still, having a good conceptual model of what's going on will help in understanding how .NET Framework applications work. This understanding will help you make better choices and so build better applications using the .NET Framework.

Understanding the CLR is important

4

.NET Languages

The Common Language Runtime is explicitly designed to support multiple languages. In general, though, languages built on the CLR tend to have a good deal in common. By defining a large set of core semantics, the CLR also defines a large part of a typical programming language built using it. For example, a substantial chunk of learning any CLR-based language is seeing how the standard types defined by the CLR are mapped into that language. You must also learn the language's syntax, of course, including the control structures the language provides. Yet once you know what the CLR offers, you're a long way down the path to learning any language built on top of it.

Understanding a CLR-based language starts with understanding the CLR

This chapter describes C# and Visual Basic.NET, the most important CLR-based languages. It also takes a brief look at the Managed Extensions for C++ that allow C++ developers to write CLR-based code. The goal is not to provide exhaustive coverage of every language feature—that would require three more books—but rather to give you a sense of how these languages look and how they express the core functionality provided by the CLR.

What About Java for the .NET Framework?

In the fall of 2001, Microsoft announced Visual J#.NET, an implementation of the Java language built on the CLR. Despite this, I doubt that Java will ever be a viable choice for the .NET Framework. The reason is that even if a Java aficionado chooses to use a CLR-based Java compiler, such as Visual J#.NET, she's unlikely to be truly happy. Java implies a group of libraries and interfaces such as Swing and Enterprise JavaBeans. The .NET Framework provides its own equivalent technologies, so most of these won't be available. As a result, a developer using the Java language on the .NET Framework won't feel like she's working in a true Java environment because the familiar libraries won't be there.

The real target market for Visual J#.NET is Microsoft's existing Visual J++ customers. By providing a migration path to the .NET Framework, Microsoft is helping them move away from a dying product to one with a long future ahead of it. People who believe that Microsoft is truly interested in creating a first-class environment for building new Java applications might also wish to examine their beliefs about Santa Claus.

The battle lines are clear: It's .NET versus the Java world. This is unquestionably a good thing. Those who think everyone should implement Java forget both the dangers of monopoly and the sloth that comes with having no competition. Having two powerful technology camps, each with a strong position, is the ideal world. Each has innovations that the other can learn from, and each provides examples of things to avoid. In the end, the competition benefits everyone.

C#

C# is an object-oriented language with a C-like syntax

As its name suggests, C# is a member of the C family of programming languages. Unlike C, C# is explicitly object-oriented. Unlike C++, however, which is the most widely used object-oriented language in this family, C# isn't fiendishly complicated. Instead, C# was designed to be easily approachable by anyone with a background in C++ or Java.

The most popular tool today for creating C# code is Microsoft's Visual Studio.NET. It's not the only choice, however. Microsoft also provides a command-line compiler with the .NET Framework called csc.exe, and the open source world has also created a C# compiler. Visual Studio.NET provides a rich environment for building CLR-based applications in C#, however, so it's hard to imagine that other alternatives will attract a large share of developers.

Microsoft provides the dominant C# compilers but not the only ones

Standardizing C# and the CLR

Microsoft submitted C# and a subset of the CLR called the Common Language Infrastructure (CLI) to the international standards body ECMA, and they have now become ECMA standards. Along with C#, the things that were submitted for standardization include the syntax and semantics for metadata, MSIL (rechristened the Common Intermediate Language, or CIL), and parts of the .NET Framework class library. For more details on exactly what was submitted and its current status, see http://msdn.microsoft.com/net/ecma.

Sun came close to doing something similar with its Java technology but backed away at the last minute. Will Microsoft's efforts be more successful? Sun resisted this step in large part because they were unwilling to give up control of Java. Control of Java is a valuable thing, and since Sun is a for-profit company, its reluctance to relinquish this control makes perfect sense. Microsoft is also a for-profit company. Will they really wait until ECMA has approved, say, an enhancement to C# before including it in their next release? And if they do, is this a good thing? Standards bodies aren't known for their speed.

I'd be surprised if Microsoft lets ECMA control the rate at which innovations appear in future releases of .NET technologies. Still, making C# and the CLI standards does give others a way to build them. Somewhat surprisingly, given its traditional antipathy toward Microsoft, the open source world has spawned various efforts to build parts of .NET. The most visible of these is the Mono project. (*Mono* means "monkey" in Spanish, which may be an oblique commentary on the Mono team's view of Microsoft.) Mono's ambitious goal is to implement at least a large part of what Microsoft has given to ECMA, including a C# compiler and the CLI and perhaps more. Mono's creators say that they were attracted to the CLR for technical reasons, which must please Microsoft. In fact, from Mono's perspective, the CLI is the specification of a system while .NET's CLR is just the Microsoft implementation of this specification. Mono is certainly an interesting undertaking; to learn more about it, see http://www.go-mono.com.

Microsoft itself, together with Corel, has announced plans to make an implementation of C# and the CLI available for BSD UNIX. As discussed in Chapter 1, Microsoft faces substantial credibility problems in porting the .NET Framework to non-Windows platforms. Still, it's early in the game, and anything is possible. Whatever happens, having public standards and an open source implementation for their core technologies will certainly be a new experience for Microsoft.

A C# Example

Like most programming languages, C# defines data types, control structures, and more. Unlike older languages, however, C# does this by building on the CLR. Understanding the CLR therefore takes one a long way toward understanding C#. To illustrate this, here's a simple C# example:

```csharp
// A C# example
interface IMath
{
        int Factorial(int f);
        double SquareRoot(double s);
}

class Compute : IMath
{
        public int Factorial(int f)
        {
                int i;
                int result = 1;
                for (i=2; i<=f; i++)
                    result = result * i;
            return result;
        }
```

```
    public double SquareRoot(double s)
    {
        return System.Math.Sqrt(s);
    }
}

class DisplayValues
{
    static void Main()
    {
        Compute c = new Compute();
        int v;
        v = 5;
        System.Console.WriteLine(
            "{0} factorial: {1}",
            v, c.Factorial(v));
        System.Console.WriteLine(
            "Square root of {0}: {1:f4}",
            v, c.SquareRoot(v));
    }
}
```

The program begins with a comment, indicated by two slashes, giving a brief description of the program's purpose. The body of the program consists of three types: an interface named IMath and the two classes Compute and DisplayValues. All C# programs consist of some number of types, the outermost of which must be classes, interfaces, structures, enums, or delegates. (Namespaces, discussed later, can also appear here.) All methods, fields, and other type members must belong to one of these types, which means that C# doesn't allow either global variables or global methods.

Every C# program is made up of one or more types

The IMath interface, which is a C# incarnation of the Common Type System (CTS) interface type described in Chapter 3, defines the methods Factorial and SquareRoot. Each of these methods takes one parameter and returns a numeric result. These parameters are passed by value, the default in C#. This means that changes made to the parameter's value within the method won't be seen by the caller once the method returns. Placing the keyword ref in front of a parameter causes a parameter to be passed by reference, so any changes made within the method will be reflected back to the caller.

A C# interface is an expression of a CTS interface

A C# class is an expression of a CTS class

Each class in this example is also a C# incarnation of the underlying CTS type. C# classes can implement one or more interfaces, inherit from at most one other class, and do all of the other things defined for a CTS class. The first class shown here, Compute, implements the IMath interface, as indicated by the colon between Compute and IMath. Accordingly, this class must contain implementations for both of the interface's methods. The body of the Factorial method declares a pair of integer variables, initializes the second of them to 1, then uses a simple for loop to calculate the factorial of its parameter (and doesn't bother to check for overflow, which is admittedly bad programming practice). Compute's second method, SquareRoot, is even simpler. It relies on the .NET Framework class library, calling the Sqrt function provided by the Math class in the System namespace.

Execution of a C# program begins with the method named Main

The last type in this simple example, the class DisplayValues, contains only a single method named Main. Much like C and C++, a C# program begins executing with this method in whatever type it appears. Although it's not shown here, Main can take arguments passed in when the program is started, and it must be declared as static. In this example, Main returns void, which is C#'s way of saying that the method has no return value. The type void cannot be used for parameters as in C and C++, however. Instead, its only purpose is to indicate that a method returns no value.

In this example, Main creates an instance of the Compute class using C#'s *new* operator. When this program is executed, new will be translated into the MSIL instruction newobj described in Chapter 3. Main next declares an int variable and sets its value to 5. This value is then passed as a parameter into calls to the Factorial and SquareRoot methods provided by the Compute instance. Factorial expects an int, which is exactly what's passed in this call, but SquareRoot expects a double. The int will automatically be converted into a double, since this conversion can be done with no loss of information. C# calls this an *implicit* conversion, distinguishing it from type conversions that are marked explicitly in the code.

The results are written out using the WriteLine method of the Console class, another standard part of the .NET Framework's System namespace. This method uses numbers that are wrapped in curly braces and that correspond to the variables to be output. Note that in the second call to WriteLine, the number in braces is followed by ":f4". This formatting directive means that the value should be written as a fixed-point number with four places to the right of the decimal. Accordingly, the output of this simple program is

The Console class's WriteLine method writes formatted output to the console

```
5 factorial: 120
Square root of 5:  2.2361
```

The goal of this example is to give you a feeling for the general structure and style of C#. There's much more to the language, as the next sections illustrate.

C# Types

Each type defined by C# is built on an analogous CTS type provided by the CLR. Table 4-1 shows most of the CTS types and their C# equivalents. As mentioned earlier in this book, all of these data types are defined in the System namespace. The C# equivalents shown here are in fact just shorthand synonyms for these alternative definitions. In the example just shown, for instance, the line

C# types are built on CTS types

```
int i;
```

could have been replaced with

```
System.Int32 i;
```

Both work, and both produce exactly the same results.

Table 4-1   Some CTS Types and Their C# Equivalents

CTS	C#
Byte	byte
Char	char
Int16	short
Int32	int
Int64	long
UInt16	ushort
UInt32	uint
UInt64	ulong
Single	float
Double	double
Decimal	decimal
Boolean	bool
Structure	struct
String	string
Class	class
Interface	interface
Delegate	delegate

Note that C# is case sensitive. Declaring a variable as "Double" rather than "double" will result in a compiler error. For people accustomed to languages derived from C, this will seem normal. To others, however, it might take a little getting used to.

Classes

Like a CTS class, a C# class can inherit directly from only one other class

C# classes expose the behaviors of a CTS class using a C-derived syntax. For example, CTS classes can implement one or more interfaces but inherit directly from at most one other class. A C# class Calculator that implements the interfaces IAlgebra and ITrig and inherits from the class MathBasics would be declared as

```
class Calculator : MathBasics, IAlgebra, ITrig { ... }
```

Note that the class must come first in this list. C# classes can also be labeled as sealed or abstract, as defined in Chapter 3, and can be assigned public or internal visibility. These translate into the CTS-defined visibilities public and assembly, respectively. The default is internal. All of this information is stored in the metadata for this class once it has been compiled.

A C# class can contain fields, methods, and properties, all of which are defined for any CTS class. Each of these has an accessibility, which is indicated in C# by an appropriate access modifier such as public or private. It can also contain one or more constructors, called when an instance of this class is created, and at most one destructor, which is actually the name C# uses for a finalizer, a concept described in Chapter 3. If the class inherits from another class, it can potentially override one or more of the type members, such as a method, in its parent. To do this, the member being overridden must be declared as virtual.

A C# class can include fields, methods, properties, constructors, destructors, and more

A class can also define overloaded operators. An overloaded operator is one that has been redefined to have a special meaning when used with instances of this class. For example, a class representing workgroups in an organization might redefine the + operator to mean combining two workgroups into one.

C# supports operator overloading

Interfaces

Interfaces are relatively simple things, and the basic C# syntax for describing an interface was shown in the earlier example. Not shown there was how C# expresses multiple interface inheritance, that is, one interface that inherits from more than one parent. If, for example, the interface ITrig inherits from the

A C# interface can inherit directly from one or more other interfaces

three interfaces, ISine, ICosine, and ITangent, it could be declared as

```
Interface ITrig: ISine, ICosine, ITangent { ... }
```

ITrig will contain all the methods, properties, and other type members defined in its three parent interfaces as well as anything it defines on its own.

Structures

C# structures are like slightly simplified C# classes

Reflecting their definition in the CTS, structures in C# are much like classes. They can contain methods, fields, and properties and implement interfaces and more. They are value types rather than reference types, however, which means they're allocated on the stack. Value types also are prohibited from participating in inheritance. Unlike a class, a structure can't inherit from another type, and it's also not possible to define a type that inherits from a structure.

Here's a simple example of a C# structure:

```
struct employee
{
        string name;
        int age;
}
```

In this example, the structure contains only fields, much like a traditional C-style structure. Yet a structure can be much more complex. The Compute class shown earlier, for instance, could be converted to a structure, methods and all, by just changing the word *class* in its definition to *struct*. The program would function in just the same way.

Delegates

Passing a reference to a method as a parameter is often useful

Passing a reference to a method is a reasonably common thing to do. For example, suppose you need to tell some chunk of code what method in your code should be called when a specific event occurs. You need some way to pass in the identity of this callback function at runtime. In C and C++, you can do this by passing the address of the method, that is, a pointer to the code you want to be called. In the type-safe world of the .NET Framework, however, passing raw addresses isn't allowed. Yet the problem doesn't go away. A type-safe way to pass a reference to a method is still useful.

As described briefly in Chapter 3, the CTS defines the reference type *delegate* for this purpose. A delegate is an object that contains a reference to a method with a specific signature. Once it has been created and initialized, it can be passed as a parameter into some other method and then invoked. Here's a simple example of creating and using a delegate in C#:

A C# delegate provides a type-safe way to pass a reference to a method

```
delegate void SDelegate(string s);

class DelegateExample
{
    public static void Main()
    {
        SDelegate del = new SDelegate(WriteString);
        CallDelegate(del);
    }
    public static void CallDelegate(SDelegate Write)
    {
        System.Console.WriteLine("In CallDelegate");
        Write("A delegated hello");
    }
    public static void WriteString(string s)
    {
        System.Console.WriteLine("In WriteString:
            {0}", s);
    }
}
```

The example begins by defining SDelegate as a delegate type. This definition specifies that SDelegate objects can contain references only to methods that take a single string parameter. In the example's Main method, a variable del of type SDelegate is declared and then initialized to contain a reference to the WriteString method. This method is defined later in the class, and as required, has a single parameter of type string. Main then invokes the CallDelegate method, passing in `del` as a parameter.

CallDelegate is defined to take an SDelegate as its parameter. In other words, what gets passed to this method is a delegate object that contains the address of some method. Because it's an SDelegate, that method must have a single parameter of type string. Inside CallDelegate, the method identified by the passed-in parameter is referred to as Write, and after printing a simple message, CallDelegate invokes this Write method. Because Write is actually a delegate, however, what really gets called is the method this delegate references, WriteString. The output of this simple example is

```
In CallDelegate
In WriteString: A delegated hello
```

Note that the CallDelegate method executes first, followed by WriteString.

A delegate can be combined with other delegates

Delegates can be significantly more complicated than this. They can be combined, for example, so that calling a single delegate results in calls to the two or more other delegates it contains. Yet even simple delegates can be useful. By providing a type-safe way to pass a reference to a method, they offer this important feature of C and C++ in a much less risky way.

Arrays

Like CTS arrays, C# arrays are reference types

As in other languages, C# arrays are ordered groups of elements of the same type. Unlike many other languages, however, C# arrays are objects. In fact, as described in Chapter 3, they are reference types, which means they get allocated on the heap. Here's an example that declares a single-dimensional array of integers:

```
int[] ages;
```

Since ages is an object, no instance exists until one is explicitly created. This can be done with

```
ages = new int[10];
```

which allocates space for ten integers on the heap. As this example shows, a C# array has no fixed size until an instance of that array type is created. It's also possible to both declare and create an array instance in a single statement, such as

```
int[] ages = new int[10];
```

Arrays of any type can be declared, but exactly how an array gets allocated depends on whether it's an array of value types or reference types. The example just shown allocates space for ten integers on the heap, while

```
string[] names = new string[10];
```

allocates space for ten references to strings on the heap. An array of value types, such as ints, actually contains the values, but an array of reference types, such as the strings in this example, contains only references to values.

Arrays can also have multiple dimensions. For example, the statement

C# arrays can be multidimensional

```
int[,] points = new int[10,20];
```

creates a two-dimensional array of integers. The first dimension has 10 elements, while the second has 20. Regardless of the number of dimensions in an array, however, the lower bound of each one is always zero.

C#'s array type is built on the core array support provided by the CLR. Recall from the previous chapter that all CLR-based

Standard methods and properties can be accessed on all C# arrays

arrays, including all C# arrays, inherit from System.Array. This base type provides various methods and properties that can be accessed on any instance of an array type. For example, the GetLength method can be used to determine the number of elements in a particular dimension of an array, while the CopyTo method can be used to copy all of the elements in a one-dimensional array to another one-dimensional array.

C# Control Structures

The control structures in C# are typical of a modern high-level language

C# provides the traditional set of control structures. Among the most commonly used of these is the if statement, which looks like this:

```
if (x > y)
    p = true;
else
    p = false;
```

Note that the condition for the if must be a value of type bool. It can't be an integer, as in C and C++.

C# also has a switch statement. Here's an example:

```
switch (x)
{
    case 1:
        y = 100;
        break;
    case 2:
        y = 200;
        break;
    default:
        y = 300;
        break;
}
```

Depending on the value of x, y will be set to 100, 200, or 300. The break statements cause control to jump to whatever statement follows this switch. Unlike C and C++, these (or similar) statements are mandatory in C#, even for the default case. Omitting them will produce a compiler error.

C# also includes various kinds of loops. In a while loop, the condition must evaluate to a bool rather than an integer value, which again is different from C and C++. There's also a do/while combination that puts the test at the bottom rather than at the top and a for loop, which was illustrated in the earlier example. Finally, C# includes a foreach statement, which allows iterating through all the elements in a value of a *collection* type. There are various ways a type can qualify as a collection type, the most straightforward of which is to implement the standard interface System.IEnumerable. A common example of a collection type is an array, and so one use of a foreach loop is to examine or manipulate each element in an array.

C# includes while, do/while, for, and foreach loops

C# also includes a goto statement, which jumps to a particular labeled point in the program, and a continue statement, which immediately returns to the top of whatever loop it's contained in and starts the next iteration. In general, the control structures in this new language are not very new, so they will be familiar to anybody who knows another high-level language.

Other C# Features

The fundamentals of a programming language are in its types and control structures. There are many more interesting things in C#, however—too many to cover in detail in this short survey. This section provides brief looks at some of the more interesting additional aspects of this new language.

Working with Namespaces

Because the underlying class libraries are so fundamental, namespaces are a critical part of programming with the .NET Framework. One way to invoke a method in the class libraries is by giving its fully qualified name. In the example shown earlier, for instance, the WriteLine method was invoked with

C#'s using statement makes it easier to reference the contents of a namespace

```
System.Console.WriteLine(...);
```

To lessen the amount of typing required, C# provides the *using* statement. This allows the contents of a namespace to be referenced with shorter names. It's common, for example, to start each C# program with the statement

```
using System;
```

If the example shown earlier had included this line, the WriteLine method could have been invoked with just

```
Console.WriteLine(...);
```

A program can also contain several using statements if necessary, as some of the examples later in this book will illustrate. It's also possible to define your own namespaces directly in C# containing types or even other namespaces. The types they contain can then also be referenced either with fully qualified names or through appropriate using statements.

Handling Exceptions

Exceptions provide a consistent way to handle errors across all CLR-based languages

Errors are a fact of life, at least for developers. In the .NET Framework, errors that occur at runtime are handled in a consistent way through exceptions. As in so much else, C# provides a syntax for working with exceptions, but the fundamental mechanisms are embedded in the CLR itself. This not only provides a consistent approach to error handling for all C# developers, but also means that all CLR-based languages will deal with this potentially tricky area in the same way. Errors can even be propagated across language boundaries as long as those languages are built on the .NET Framework.

An exception can be raised when an error occurs

An exception is an object that represents some unusual event, such as an error. The .NET Framework defines a large set of exceptions, and it's also possible to create custom exceptions. An exception is automatically raised by the runtime when errors occur. For example, in the code fragment

```
x = y/z;
```

what happens if z is zero? The answer is that the CLR raises the System.DivideByZeroException. If no exception handling is being used, the program will terminate.

C# makes it possible to catch exceptions, however, using try/catch blocks. The code above can be changed to look like this:

Exceptions can be handled using try/catch blocks

```
try
{
    x = y/z;
}
catch
{
    System.Console.WriteLine("Exception caught");
}
```

The code within the braces of the try statement will now be monitored for exceptions. If none occurs, execution will skip the catch statement and continue. If an exception occurs, however, the code in the catch statement will be executed, in this case printing out a warning, and execution will continue with whatever statement follows the catch.

It's also possible to have different catch statements for different exceptions and to learn exactly which exception occurred. Here's another example:

Different exceptions can be handled differently

```
try
{
    x = y/z;
}
catch (System.DivideByZeroException)
{
    System.Console.WriteLine("z is zero");
}
catch (System.Exception e)
{
    System.Console.WriteLine("Exception: {0}",
        e.Message);
}
```

In this case, if no exceptions occur, x will be assigned the value of y divided by z, and the code in both catch statements will be skipped. If z is zero, however, the first catch statement will be executed, printing a message to this effect. Execution will then skip the next catch statement and continue with whatever follows this try/catch block. If any other exception occurs, the second catch statement will be executed. This statement declares an object e of type System.Exception and then accesses this object's Message property to retrieve a printable string indicating what exception has occurred.

Custom exceptions can also be defined

Since CLR-based languages such as C# use exceptions consistently for error handling, why not define your own exceptions for handling your own errors? This can be done by defining a class that inherits from System.Exception and then using the throw statement to raise this custom exception. These exceptions can be caught with a try/catch block, just like those defined by the system.

Although it's not shown here, it's also possible to end a try/catch block with a finally statement. The code in this statement gets executed whether or not an exception occurs. This option is useful when some final cleanup must take place no matter what happens.

Using Attributes

A C# program can contain attributes

Once it's compiled, every C# type has associated metadata stored with it in the same file. Most of this metadata describes the type itself. As described in the previous chapter, however, metadata can also include attributes specified with this type. Given that the CLR provides a way to store attributes, it follows that C# must have some way to define attributes and their values. As described later in this book, attributes are used extensively by the .NET Framework class library. They can be applied to classes, interfaces, structures, methods, fields, parameters, and more. It's even possible to specify attributes that are applied to an entire assembly.

For example, suppose the Factorial method shown earlier had been declared with the WebMethod attribute applied to it. Assuming the appropriate using statements were in place to identify the correct namespace for this attribute, the declaration would look like this in C#:

```
[WebMethod] public int Factorial(int f) {...}
```

This attribute is used by ASP.NET, part of the .NET Framework class library, to indicate that a method should be exposed as a SOAP-callable Web service. (For more on how this attribute is used, see Chapter 7.) Similarly, including the attribute

```
[assembly:AssemblyCompanyAttribute("QwickBank")]
```

in a C# file will set the value of an assembly-wide attribute, one that gets stored in the assembly's manifest, containing the name of the company creating this assembly. This example also shows how attributes can have parameters, allowing their user to specify particular values for the attribute.

Developers can also create their own attributes. For example, you might wish to define an attribute that can be used to identify the date a particular C# type was modified. To do this, you can define a class that inherits from System.Attribute, then define the information you'd like that class to contain, such as a date. You can then apply this new attribute to types in your program and have the information it includes be automatically placed into the metadata for those types. Once they've been created, custom attributes can be read using the GetCustomAttributes method defined by the Attribute class, part of the System.Reflection namespace in the .NET Framework class library. Whether standard or custom, however, attributes are a commonly used feature in CLR-based software.

Custom attributes can also be defined

Writing Unsafe Code

C# developers typically rely on the CLR's garbage collection for memory management

C# normally relies on the CLR for memory management. When an instance of a reference type is no longer in use, for example, the CLR's garbage collector will eventually free the memory occupied by that type. As described in Chapter 3, the garbage collection process also rearranges the elements that are on the managed heap and currently in use, compacting them to free more space.

Pointers and garbage collection don't mix well

What would happen if traditional C/C++ pointers were used in this environment? A pointer contains a direct memory address, so a pointer into the managed heap would reference a specific location in the heap's memory. When the garbage collector rearranged the contents of the heap to create more free space, whatever the pointer pointed to could change. Blindly mixing pointers and garbage collection is a recipe for disaster.

C# allows creating unsafe code that uses pointers

Yet it's sometimes necessary. For example, suppose you need to call existing non-CLR-based code, such as the underlying operating system, and the call includes a structure with embedded pointers. Or perhaps a particular section of an application is so performance critical that you can't rely on the garbage collector to manage memory for you. For situations like these, C# provides the ability to use pointers in what's known as *unsafe code*.

Unsafe code can use pointers, with all of the attendant benefits and pitfalls pointers entail. To make this "unsafe" activity as safe as possible, however, C# requires that all code that does this be explicitly marked with the keyword unsafe. Within an unsafe method, the *fixed* statement can be used to lock one or more values of a reference type in place on the managed heap. (This is sometimes called *pinning* a value.) Here's a simple example:

```
class Risky
{
    unsafe public void PrintChars()
    {
```

```
        char[] charList = new char[2];
        charList[0] = 'A';
        charList[1] = 'B';

        System.Console.WriteLine("{0} {1}",
            charList[0], charList[1]);
        fixed (char* f = charList)
        {
            charList[0] = *(f+1);
        }
        System.Console.WriteLine("{0} {1}",
            charList[0], charList[1]);
    }
}


class DisplayValues
{
    static void Main()
    {
        Risky r = new Risky();
        r.PrintChars();
    }
}
```

The PrintChars method in the class Risky is marked with the
keyword unsafe. This method declares the small character array
charList and then sets the two elements in this array to "A" and
"B," respectively. The first call to WriteLine produces

A B

just as you'd expect. The fixed statement then declares a character pointer f and initializes it to contain the address of the
charList array. Within the fixed statement's body, the first element of this array is assigned the value at address f+1. (The
asterisk in front of the expression means "return what's at this
address.") When WriteLine is called again, the output is

B B

The value that is one beyond the start of the array, the character
"B," has been assigned to the array's first position.

Unsafe code has limitations

This example does nothing useful, of course. Its intent is to make clear that C# does allow declaring pointers, performing pointer arithmetic, and more, as long as those statements are within areas clearly marked as unsafe. The language's creators really want you to be sure about doing this, so compiling any unsafe code requires specifying the /unsafe option to the C# compiler. Also, unsafe code can't be verified for type safety, which means that the CLR's built-in code access security features described in Chapter 3 can't be used. Unsafe code can be run in only a fully trusted environment, which makes it generally unsuitable for software that will be downloaded from the Internet. Still, there are cases when unsafe code is the right solution to a difficult problem.

Preprocessor Directives

Unlike C and C++, C# has no preprocessor. Instead, the compiler has built-in support for the most useful features of a preprocessor. For example, C#'s preprocessor directives include #define, a familiar term to C and C++ developers. This directive can't be used to define an arbitrary replacement string for a word, however—you can't define macros. Instead, #define is used to define only a symbol. That symbol can then be used together with the directive #if to provide conditional compilation. For example, in the code fragment

```
#define DEBUG
#if DEBUG
        // code compiled if DEBUG is defined
#else
        //code compiled if DEBUG is not defined
#endif
```

DEBUG is defined, so the C# compiler would process the code between the #if and #else directives. If DEBUG were undefined, something that's accomplished using the preprocessor directive #undef, the compiler would process the code between the #else and #endif directives.

Is C# Just a Copy of Java?

C# certainly does look a lot like Java. Given the additional similarities between the CLR and the Java virtual machine, it's hard to believe that Microsoft wasn't at least somewhat inspired by Java's success. By uniting C-style syntax with objects in a more approachable fashion than C++, Java's creators found the sweet spot for a large population of developers. I have seen projects that chose the Java environment rather than Microsoft technologies primarily because, unlike Java, neither Visual Basic 6 nor C++ was seen as a good language for large-scale enterprise development.

The arrival of C# and Visual Basic.NET will surely shore up Microsoft's technology against the Java camp. The quality of the programming language is no longer an issue. Yet this once again begs the question: Isn't C# like Java?

In many ways, the answer is yes. The core semantics of the CLR are very Java-esque. Being deeply object-oriented, providing direct support for interfaces, allowing multiple interface inheritance but only single implementation inheritance—these are all similar to Java. Yet C# also adds features that aren't available in Java. C#'s native support for properties, for instance, built on the support in the CLR, reflects the Visual Basic influence on C#'s creators. Attributes, also a CLR-based feature, provide a measure of flexibility beyond what Java offers, as does the ability to write unsafe code. Fundamentally, C# is an expression of the CLR's semantics in a C-derived syntax. Since those semantics are much like Java, C# is necessarily much like Java, too. But it's not the same language.

Is C# a better language than Java? There's no way to answer this question objectively, and it wouldn't matter if there were. Choosing a development platform based solely on the programming language is like buying a car because you like the radio. You can do it, but you'll be much happier if your decision takes into account the complete package.

If Sun had allowed Microsoft to modify Java a bit, my guess is that C# wouldn't exist today. For understandable reasons, however, Sun resisted Microsoft's attempts to customize Java for the Windows world. The result is two quite similar languages, each targeting a different development environment. Competition is good, and I'm confident that both languages will be in wide use five years from now.

C# is an attractive language. It combines a clean, concise design with a modern feature set. Although the world is littered with the carcasses of unsuccessful programming languages, C# isn't likely to join them. With Microsoft pushing it and its own quality pulling it, C# looks destined for a bright future.

Visual Basic.NET

Visual Basic is by a large margin the most popular programming language in the Windows world. Visual Basic.NET (VB.NET) brings enormous changes to this widely used tool. Like C#, VB.NET is built on the Common Language Runtime, and so large parts of the language are effectively defined by the CLR. In fact, except for their syntax, C# and VB.NET are largely the same language. Because both owe so much to the CLR and the .NET Framework class library, the functionality of the two is very similar.

Only Microsoft provides VB.NET compilers today

VB.NET can be compiled using Visual Studio.NET or vbc.exe, a command-line compiler supplied with the .NET Framework. Unlike C#, however, Microsoft has not submitted VB.NET to a standards body. Accordingly, while the open source world or some other third party could still create a clone, the Microsoft tools are likely to be the only viable choices for working in this language, at least for now.

A VB.NET Example

The quickest way to get a feeling for VB.NET is to see a simple example. The example that follows implements the same functionality as did the C# example shown earlier in this chapter. As you'll see, the differences from that example are largely cosmetic.

```
' A VB.NET example
Module DisplayValues
```

```
Interface IMath
    Function Factorial(ByVal F As Integer) _
        As Integer
    Function SquareRoot(ByVal S As Double) _
        As Double
End Interface

Class Compute
    Implements IMath

    Function Factorial(ByVal F As Integer) _
        As Integer Implements IMath.Factorial
        Dim I As Integer
        Dim Result As Integer = 1

        For I = 2 To F
            Result = Result * I
        Next
        Return Result
    End Function

    Function SquareRoot(ByVal S As Double) _
        As Double Implements IMath.SquareRoot
        Return System.Math.Sqrt(S)
    End Function

End Class

Sub Main()
    Dim C As Compute = New Compute()
    Dim V As Integer

    V = 5
    System.Console.WriteLine( _
        "{0} factorial: {1}", _
        V, C.Factorial(V))
    System.Console.WriteLine( _
        "Square root of {0}: {1:f4}", _
        V, C.SquareRoot(V))
End Sub

End Module
```

The example begins with a simple comment, indicated by the single quote that begins the line. Following the comment is an instance of the Module type that contains all of the code in this example. Module is a reference type, but it's not legal to create an instance of this type. Instead, its primary purpose is to provide a container for a group of VB.NET classes, interfaces, and

A Module provides a container for other VB.NET types

C# or VB.NET?

Before .NET, the language choice facing Microsoft-oriented developers was simple. If you were a hard-core developer, deeply proud of your technical knowledge, you embraced C++ in all its thorny glory. Alternatively, if you were more interested in getting the job done than in fancy technology and if that job wasn't too terribly complex or low level, you chose Visual Basic 6. Sure, the C++ guys abused you for your lack of linguistic savoir faire, but your code had a lot fewer obscure bugs.

This decade-old divide is over. C# and VB.NET are very nearly the same language. Except for relatively uncommon things such as writing unsafe code and operator overloading, they're equally powerful. Microsoft may change this in the future, making the feature sets of the two languages diverge. Until this happens, however (if it ever does), the main issue in making the choice is personal preference, which is really another way of saying "syntax."

Developers get very attached to how their language looks. C-oriented people love curly braces, while VB developers feel at home with Dim statements. Since many more developers use Visual Basic today than C++, I expect that VB.NET will be a more popular choice than C#. For the vast majority of VB developers who are fond of VB-style syntax, there's no reason to switch to C#. Even the .NET Framework documentation supplied by Microsoft is quite even-handed, usually providing examples in both languages. Given its much greater popularity today, I expect the dominant language for building Windows applications five years from now will still be Visual Basic.

In spite of this, however, I believe that any developer who knows C# can (and should) acquire at least a reading knowledge of VB.NET, and vice versa. The core semantics are identical, and after all, this is the really hard part of learning a language. In fact, to illustrate the near equality of these two languages, the examples in the following chapters of this book alternate more or less randomly between the two. In the world of .NET, you shouldn't think of yourself as a VB.NET developer or a C# developer. Whichever language you choose, you will in fact be a .NET Framework developer.

other types. In this case, the module contains an interface, a class, and a Sub Main procedure. It's also legal for a module to contain directly method definitions, variable declarations, and more that can be used throughout the module.

The module's interface is named IMath, and as in the earlier C# example, it defines the methods (or in the argot of Visual Basic, the functions) Factorial and SquareRoot. Each takes a single parameter, and each is defined to be passed by value, which means a copy of the parameter is made within the function. (The trailing underscore is the line continuation character, indicating that the following line should be treated as though no line break were present.) Passing by value is the default, so the example would work just the same without the ByVal indications. Passing by reference is the default in Visual Basic 6, which shows one example of how the language was changed to match the underlying semantics of the CLR.

By default, VB.NET passes parameters by value, unlike Visual Basic 6

The class Compute, which is the VB.NET expression of a CTS class, implements the IMath interface. Each of the functions in this class must explicitly identity the interface method it implements. Apart from this, the functions are just as in the earlier C# example except that a Visual Basic–style syntax is used. Note particularly that the call to System.Math.Sqrt is identical to its form in the C# example. C#, VB.NET, and any other language built on the CLR can access services in the .NET Framework class library in much the same way.

A VB.NET class is an expression of a CTS class

This simple example ends with a Sub Main procedure, which is analogous to C#'s Main method. The application begins executing here. In this example, Sub Main creates an instance of the Compute class using the VB.NET New operator (which will eventually be translated into the MSIL instruction newobj). It then declares an Integer variable and sets its value to 5.

Execution begins in the Sub Main procedure

As in the C# example, this simple program's results are written out using the WriteLine method of the Console class. Because this method is part of the .NET Framework class library rather than any particular language, it looks exactly the same here as it did in the C# example. Not too surprisingly, then, the output of this simple program is

```
5 factorial: 120
Square root of 5: 2.2361
```

just as before.

VB.NET's similarities to Visual Basic 6 both help and hurt in learning this new language

To someone who knows Visual Basic 6, VB.NET will look familiar. To someone who knows C#, VB.NET will act in a broadly familiar way since it's built on the same foundation. But VB.NET is not the same as either Visual Basic 6 or C#. The similarities can be very helpful in learning this new language, but they can also be misleading. Be careful.

VB.NET Types

Like C#, the types defined by VB.NET are built on the CTS types provided by the CLR. Table 4-2 shows most of these types and their VB.NET equivalents.

VB.NET doesn't support all of the CTS types

Notice that some types, such as unsigned integers, are missing from VB.NET. Unsigned integers are a familiar concept to C++ developers but not to typical Visual Basic 6 developers. The core CTS types defined in the System namespace are available in VB.NET just as in C#, however, so a VB.NET developer is free to declare an unsigned integer using

```
Dim J As System.UInt32
```

Unlike C#, VB.NET is not case sensitive. There are some fairly strong conventions, however, which are illustrated in the example shown earlier. For people coming to .NET from Visual Basic 6, this case insensitivity will seem entirely normal. It's one example of why both VB.NET and C# exist, since the more a new

Table 4-2   Some CTS Types and Their VB.NET Equivalents

CTS	VB.NET
Byte	Byte
Char	Char
Int16	Short
Int32	Integer
Int64	Long
Single	Single
Double	Double
Decimal	Decimal
Boolean	Boolean
Structure	Structure
String	String
Class	Class
Interface	Interface
Delegate	Delegate

environment has in common with the old one, the more likely people will adopt it.

Classes

VB.NET classes expose the behaviors of a CTS class using a VB-style syntax. Accordingly, VB.NET classes can implement one or more interfaces, but they can inherit from at most one other class. In VB.NET, a class Calculator that implements the interfaces IAlgebra and ITrig and inherits from the class MathBasics looks like this:

Like a CTS class, a VB.NET class can inherit directly from only one other class

```
Class Calculator
    Inherits MathBasics
    Implements IAlgebra
    Implements ITrig
. . .
End Class
```

Note that, as in C#, the base class must precede the interfaces. Note also that any class this one inherits from might be written in VB.NET or in C# or perhaps in some other CLR-based language. As long as the language follows the rules laid down in the CLR's Common Language Specification, cross-language inheritance is straightforward. Also, if the class inherits from another class, it can potentially override one or more of the type members, such as a method, in its parent. This is allowed only if the member being overridden is declared with the keyword Overridable, analogous to C#'s keyword virtual.

VB.NET doesn't support operator overloading

VB.NET classes can be labeled as NotInheritable or MustInherit, which means the same thing as sealed and abstract, respectively, the terms used by the CTS and C#. VB.NET classes can also be assigned various accessibilities, such as Public and Friend, which largely map to visibilities defined by the CTS. A VB.NET class can contain variables, methods, properties, events, and more, just as defined by the CTS. Each of these can have an access modifier specified, such as Public, Private, or Friend. A class can also contain one or more constructors that get called whenever an instance of this class is created. Unlike C#, however, VB.NET does not support operator overloading. A class can't redefine what various standard operators mean when used with an instance of this class.

Interfaces

Like a CTS interface, a VB.NET interface can inherit directly from one or more other interfaces

Interfaces as defined by the CTS are a fairly simple concept. VB.NET essentially just provides a VB-derived syntax for expressing what the CTS specifies. Along with the interface behavior shown earlier, CTS interfaces can inherit from one or more other interfaces. In VB.NET, for example, defining an interface ITrig that inherits from the three interfaces, ISine, ICosine, and ITangent, would look like this:

```
Interface ITrig
    Inherits ISine
    Inherits ICosine
    Inherits ITangent
...
End Interface
```

Is Inheritance Really Worthwhile?

Inheritance is an essential part of object technology. Until .NET, Visual Basic didn't really support inheritance, and so (quite correctly) it was not viewed as an object-oriented language. VB.NET has inheritance, since it's built on the CLR, and so it is unquestionably truly object-oriented.

But is this a good thing? Microsoft certainly could have added inheritance to Visual Basic long ago, yet the language's keepers chose not to. Whenever I asked Microsoft why this was so, the answers revolved around two main points. First, inheritance can be tricky to understand and to get right. In a class hierarchy many levels deep, with some methods overridden and others overloaded, figuring out exactly what's going on isn't always easy. Given that the primary target audience for Visual Basic was not developers with formal backgrounds in computer science, it made sense to keep it simple.

The second point often made about why Visual Basic didn't have inheritance was that in many contexts, inheritance was not a good thing. This argument was made most strongly with COM, a technology that has no direct support for implementation inheritance. Inheritance binds a child class to its parent very closely, which means that a change in the parent can be catastrophic for the child. This "fragile base class" issue is especially problematic when the parent and child classes are written and maintained by completely separate organizations or when the parent's source isn't available to the creator of the child. In the component-oriented world of COM, this is a more than plausible argument.

So why has Microsoft apparently changed its mind about inheritance? Inheritance still can be problematic if changes in a parent class aren't communicated effectively to all developers who depend on that class, and it can also be complicated. The arguments Microsoft made are not incorrect. Yet the triumph of object technology is complete: Objects are everywhere. To create new languages in a completely new environment—that is, to create the .NET Framework—without full support for inheritance would brand any organization as irretrievably retro. And the benefits of inheritance, especially those gained by providing a large set of reusable classes such as the .NET Framework class library, are huge. The pendulum has swung, and inheritance is now essential.

Besides, most of the people in Redmond who argued against inheritance in the 1990s have probably retired by now. Never underestimate the power of new blood in a development group.

Structures

VB.NET structures can contain fields, provide methods, and more

Because both are based on the structure type defined by the CTS, structures in VB.NET are very much like structures in C#. Like a class, a structure can contain fields, members, and properties, implement interfaces, and more. VB.NET structures are value types, of course, which means that they can neither inherit from nor be inherited by another type. A simple employee structure might be defined in VB.NET as follows:

```
Structure Employee
    Public Name As String
    Public Age As Integer
End Structure
```

To keep the example simple, this structure contains only data members. As described earlier, however, CTS structures—and thus VB.NET structures—are in fact nearly as powerful as classes.

Delegates

The idea of passing an explicit reference to a procedure or function and then calling that procedure or function is not something that the typical Visual Basic programmer is accustomed to. Yet the CLR provides support for delegates, which allows exactly this. Why not make this support visible in VB.NET?

VB.NET allows creating and using delegates

VB.NET's creators chose to do this, allowing VB.NET programmers to create callbacks and other event-oriented code easily. Here's an example, the same one shown earlier in C#, of creating and using a delegate in VB.NET:

```
Module Module1

    Delegate Sub SDelegate(ByVal S As String)

    Sub CallDelegate(ByVal Write As SDelegate)
        System.Console.WriteLine("In CallDelegate")
        Write("A delegated hello")
    End Sub

    Sub WriteString(ByVal S As String)
        System.Console.WriteLine( _
            "In WriteString: {0}", S)
    End Sub

    Sub Main()
        Dim Del As New SDelegate( _
            AddressOf WriteString)
        CallDelegate(Del)
    End Sub

End Module
```

Although it's written in VB.NET, this code functions exactly like the C# example shown earlier in this chapter. Like that example, this one begins by defining SDelegate as a delegate type. As before, SDelegate objects can contain references only to methods that take a single String parameter. In the example's Sub Main method, a variable Del of type SDelegate is declared and then initialized to contain a reference to the WriteString subroutine. (A VB.NET subroutine is a method that, unlike a function, returns no result.) Doing this requires using VB.NET's AddressOf keyword before the subroutine's name. Sub Main then invokes CallDelegate, passing in Del as a parameter.

CallDelegate has an SDelegate parameter named Write. When Write is called, the method in the delegate that was passed into CallDelegate is actually invoked. In this example, that method is WriteString, so the code inside the WriteString procedure executes next. The output of this simple example is exactly the same as for the C# version shown earlier in this chapter:

```
In CallDelegate
In WriteString: A delegated hello
```

Is VB.NET Too Hard?

Maybe. There have been lots of complaints about the changes, and certainly some Visual Basic 6 developers will get left behind. Microsoft has historically targeted quite separate developer markets with Visual Basic and C++, yet with the .NET Framework, this distinction is greatly blurred. VB.NET and C# are functionally almost identical.

The .NET Framework is certainly simpler in many ways than the Windows DNA environment. The complexity of COM for cross-language calls is no longer required, for example. But the Framework is also harder for a certain class of developers, especially those with no formal training in computer science. One reason for Microsoft's success in the developer market was the approachability of Visual Basic. The people who create software tools often forget that they're almost always much better software developers than the people who will use those tools. As a result, they tend to create tools that they themselves would like to use, tools that are too complex for many of their potential customers.

The creators of Visual Basic never made this mistake. Despite the opprobrium heaped on the language and its users by C++ developers, Microsoft kept a clear focus on the developer population and skill level they wished to target. This was a good decision, as Visual Basic is now perhaps the world's most widely used programming language.

And yet many Visual Basic developers wanted more. VB.NET certainly gives them more, but it also requires *all* Visual Basic developers to step up a level in their technical knowledge. The skills required to build the GUI-based client of a two-tier application, the original target for this language, are almost entirely unrelated to what's needed to build today's scalable, multitier, Web-accessible solutions. Given this, perhaps the original audience Microsoft targeted for Visual Basic, some of whom were just a step above power users, no longer has a role. With its complete object orientation and large set of more advanced features, VB.NET will certainly be too complex for many of them.

Yet building today's applications effectively was becoming more and more difficult with the old Visual Basic. Between a rock and a hard place, Microsoft chose to make this popular language both more powerful and more complex. Some developers will be very happy about this, but some won't. You can't please everybody, and the market will decide whether Microsoft has made the right decision.

Delegates are another example of the additional features Visual Basic has acquired from being rebuilt on the CLR. While this rethinking of the language certainly requires lots of learning from developers using it, the reward is a substantial set of features.

Arrays

Like arrays in C# and other CLR-based languages, arrays in VB.NET are reference types that inherit from the standard System.Array class. Accordingly, all of the methods and properties that class makes available are also usable with any VB.NET array. Arrays in VB.NET look much like arrays in earlier versions of Visual Basic. Perhaps the biggest difference is that the first member of a VB.NET array is referenced as element zero, while in previous versions of this language, the first member was element one. The number of elements in an array is thus one greater than the number that appears in its declaration. For example, the following statement declares an array of eleven integers:

Unlike Visual Basic 6, array indexes in VB.NET start at zero

```
Dim Ages(10) As Integer
```

Unlike C#, there's no need to create explicitly an instance of the array using New. It's also possible to declare an array with no explicit size and later use the ReDim statement to specify how big it will be. For example, this code

```
Dim Ages() As Integer
ReDim Ages(10)
```

results in an array of eleven integers just as in the previous example. Note that the index for both of these arrays goes from 0 to 10, not 1 to 10.

VB.NET also allows multidimensional arrays. For example, the statement

```
Dim Points(10,20) As Integer
```

creates a two-dimensional array of integers with 11 and 21 elements, respectively. Once again, both dimensions are zero-based, which means that the indexes go from 0 to 10 in the array's first dimension and 0 to 20 in the second dimension.

VB.NET Control Structures

VB.NET's control structures will look familiar to most developers

While the CLR says a lot about what a .NET Framework–based language's types should look like, it says essentially nothing about how that language's control structures should look. Accordingly, adapting Visual Basic to the CLR required making changes to VB's types, but the language's control structures are fairly standard. An If statement, for example, looks like this:

```
If (X > Y) Then
    P = True
Else
    P = False
End If
```

while a Select Case statement analogous to the C# switch shown earlier looks like this:

```
Select Case X
    Case 1
        Y = 100
    Case 2
        Y = 200
    Case Else
        Y = 300
End Select
```

As in the C# example, different values of x will cause y to be set to 100, 200, or 300. Although it's not shown here, the Case clauses can also specify a range rather than a single value.

VB.NET includes a While loop, a Do loop, a For...Next loop, and a For Each loop

The loop statements available in VB.NET include a While loop, which ends when a specified Boolean condition is no longer true; a Do loop, which allows looping until a condition is no longer true or until some condition becomes true; and a For...Next loop, which was shown in the example earlier in this section. And like C#, VB.NET includes a For Each statement, which allows iterating through all the elements in a value of a collection type.

VB.NET also includes a goto statement, which jumps to a labeled point in the program, and a few more choices. The innovation in the .NET Framework doesn't focus on language control structures (in fact, it's not easy to think of the last innovation in language control structures), and so VB.NET doesn't offer much that's new in this area.

Other VB.NET Features

The CLR provides many other features, as seen in the description of C# earlier in this chapter. With very few exceptions, the creators of VB.NET chose to provide these features to developers working in this newest incarnation of Visual Basic. This section looks at how VB.NET provides some more advanced features.

VB.NET exposes most of the CLR's features

Working with Namespaces

As mentioned in Chapter 3, namespaces aren't directly visible to the CLR. Just as in C#, however, they are an important part of writing applications in VB.NET. As shown earlier in the VB.NET example, access to classes in .NET Framework class library namespaces looks just the same in VB.NET as in C#. Because the Common Type System is used throughout, methods, parameters, return values, and more are all defined in a common way. Yet how a VB.NET program indicates which namespaces it will use is somewhat different from how it's done in C#. Commonly used namespaces can be identified for a module with the Imports statement. For example, preceding a module with

VB.NET's Imports statement makes it easier to reference the contents of a namespace

```
Imports System
```

would allow invoking the System.Console.WriteLine method with just

```
Console.WriteLine( . . .)
```

VB.NET's Imports statement is analogous to C#'s using statement. Both allow developers to do less typing. And as in C#,
VB.NET also allows defining and using custom namespaces.

Handling Exceptions

One of the greatest benefits of the CLR is that it provides a
common way to handle exceptions across all .NET Framework
languages. This common approach allows errors to be found in,
say, a C# routine and then is handled in code written in
VB.NET. The syntax for how these two languages work with
exceptions is different, but the underlying behavior, specified by
the CLR, is the same.

*As in C#, try/catch
blocks are used to
handle exceptions
in VB.NET*

Like C#, VB.NET uses Try and Catch to provide exception handling. Here's a VB.NET example of handling the exception
raised when a division by zero is attempted:

```
Try
    X = Y/Z
Catch
    System.Console.WriteLine("Exception caught")
End Try
```

Any code between the Try and Catch is monitored for exceptions. If no exception occurs, execution skips the Catch clause
and continues with whatever follows End Try. If an exception
occurs, the code in the Catch clause is executed, and execution
continues with what follows End Try.

*VB.NET offers
essentially the same
exception handling
options as C#*

As in C#, different Catch clauses can be created to handle different exceptions. A Catch clause can also contain a When
clause with a Boolean condition. In this case, the exception
will be caught only if that condition is true. Also like C#,
VB.NET allows defining your own exceptions and then raising
them with the Throw statement. VB.NET also has a Finally
statement. As in C#, the code in a Finally block is executed
whether or not an exception occurs.

Using Attributes

Code written in VB.NET is compiled into MSIL, so it must have
metadata. Because it has metadata, it also has attributes. The
designers of the language provided a VB-style syntax for specifying attributes, but the end result is the same as for any CLR-
based language: Extra information is placed in the metadata of
some assembly. To repeat once again an example from earlier
in this chapter, suppose the Factorial method shown in the
complete VB.NET example had been declared with the
WebMethod attribute applied to it. This attribute instructs the
.NET Framework to expose this method as a SOAP-callable
Web service, as described in more detail in Chapter 7.
Assuming the appropriate Imports statements were in place to
identify the correct namespace for this attribute, the declaration
would look like this in VB.NET:

A VB.NET program can contain attributes

```
<WebMethod()> Public Function Factorial(ByVal F _
As Integer) As Integer Implements IMath.Factorial
```

This attribute is used by ASP.NET to indicate that a method
contained in an .asmx page should be exposed as a SOAP-
callable Web service. Similarly, including the attribute

```
<assembly:AssemblyCompanyAttribute("QwickBank")>
```

in a VB.NET file will set the value of an attribute stored in this
assembly's manifest that identifies QwickBank as the company
that created this assembly. VB.NET developers can also create
their own attributes by defining classes that inherit from
System.Attribute and then have whatever information is defined
for those attributes automatically copied into metadata. As in
C# or another CLR-based language, custom attributes can be
read using the GetCustomAttributes method defined by the
System.Reflection namespace's Attribute class.

Attributes are just one more example of the tremendous se-
mantic similarity of VB.NET and C#. While they look quite

VB.NET and C# offer very similar features

different, the capabilities of the two languages are very similar. Which one a developer prefers will be largely an aesthetic decision.

Why Provide All of These Languages?

Microsoft says that more than twenty languages have been ported to the CLR. Along with the languages shipped by Microsoft itself, programmers will have plenty of options to choose from. Yet given the CLR's central role in defining these languages, they often have much in common. What's the real benefit of having multiple languages based on the CLR?

There are two key advantages. First, the existing pre-.NET population of Windows developers is split into two primary language camps: C++ and Visual Basic. Microsoft needs to move both groups of developers forward, and both certainly have some attachment to their language. Although the semantics of the CLR (and of languages built on it such as C# and Visual Basic.NET) are different from either C++ or Visual Basic 6, the fundamental look of these new languages will be familiar. If Microsoft chose to provide only, say, C#, it's a safe bet that developers who were wedded to Visual Basic 6 would probably be resistant to moving to .NET. Similarly, providing only a CLR-based language derived from Visual Basic wouldn't make C++ developers very happy. People who write code get attached to the oddest things (curly braces, for example), and so providing both C# and Visual Basic.NET is a good way to help the current Windows developer population move forward.

The second benefit in providing multiple languages is that it gives the .NET Framework something the competition doesn't have. One complaint about the Java world has been that it requires all developers always to use the same language. The .NET Framework's multilingual nature offers more choice, so it gives Microsoft something to tout over its competitors.

In fact, however, there are some real benefits to having just one language. Why add extra complexity, such as a different syntax for expressing the same behavior, when there's no clear benefit? Java's one-language-all-the-time approach has the virtue of simplicity. Even in the .NET world, organizations would do well to avoid multilanguage projects if possible. This isn't the problem it was with Windows DNA, since code written in different CLR-based languages can interoperate with no problems. Developers who know C# should also have no trouble understanding VB.NET, and vice versa. Still, having two or more separate development groups using distinct languages will complicate both the initial project and the maintenance effort that follows. It's worth avoiding if possible.

In the end, the diverse set of languages announced for the .NET Framework probably won't matter much. Because of Microsoft's strong support, expressed most powerfully in Visual Studio.NET, C# and Visual Basic.NET will be dominant for creating new CLR-based applications. The other languages might be interesting for universities, but for professional developers, good tools are essential. Most Windows developers today believe that Visual Studio is the best tool for building code on Windows. Just as in the pre-.NET world, I expect Visual Studio.NET and the languages it supports to be the dominant choices for Windows developers.

C++ with Managed Extensions

C++ is a very popular language, one that's been in wide use for more than a dozen years. Providing some way to use C++ with the .NET Framework is essential. Yet the semantics of C++ don't exactly match those of the CLR. They have much in common—both are object-oriented, for example—but there are also many differences. C++, for instance, supports multiple inheritance, the ability of a class to inherit simultaneously from two or more parent classes, while the CLR does not.

C++ was too popular for the .NET Framework's creators to ignore

Visual Basic 6 also differs substantially from the CLR, but Microsoft owns Visual Basic. The company was free to change it as they wished, so VB.NET was designed to match the CLR. Microsoft does not own C++, however. Unilaterally changing the language to match the CLR would have met with howls of protest. Yet providing no way to create .NET Framework–based applications in C++ would also have left many developers very unhappy. What's the solution?

Unlike Visual Basic, Microsoft isn't free to change C++ unilaterally to fit the CLR

Microsoft has defined a set of Managed Extensions for C++

The answer Microsoft chose was to create a set of extensions to the base C++ language. Officially known as *Managed Extensions for C++*, the resulting dialect is commonly referred to as just *Managed C++*. C++ is not simple to begin with, and Managed C++ adds new complexities. The goal of this chapter's final section is to provide an overview of the changes wrought by Managed C++.

Managed C++ defines several new keywords

Before looking at a Managed C++ example, it's useful to describe some of the extensions made to the language. In particular, several keywords have been added to allow access to CLR services, all of which begin with two underscores. (This follows

Managed C++ or C#?

C++ has legions of die-hard fans. And why shouldn't it? It's a powerful, flexible tool for building all kinds of applications. It's complicated, too, which means that learning to exploit all that power and flexibility takes a substantial amount of effort. Anyone who's put in the time to master C++ is bound to be less than thrilled about leaving it behind.

Yet for brand-new applications built from scratch on the .NET Framework, C++ probably should be left behind. For a C++ developer, learning C# isn't difficult. In fact, learning C# will probably be easier than using Managed C++ to write .NET Framework–based applications. As the short summary in this chapter suggests, Managed C++ adds even more complexity to an already complex language. For new applications, C# is probably a better choice.

For extending existing C++ applications with managed code, however, Managed C++ is a good choice. And if you plan to port an existing C++ application to run on the Framework, Managed C++ is also a good choice, since it saves you from rewriting large parts of your code. Although it's not as important in the .NET Framework world as either VB.NET or C#, Managed C++ is nevertheless a significant member of .NET's language arsenal.

the convention defined in the ANSI standard for C++ extensions.) Among the most important of these are the following:

- **__gc:** Indicates that a type is subject to garbage collection. In other words, this keyword means that the type being declared is a CTS reference type. Managed C++ allows this keyword to be applied to classes, arrays, and other types.

- **__value:** Indicates that a type is not subject to garbage collection; that is, that the type is a CTS value type.

- **__interface:** Used to define a CTS interface type.

- **__box:** An operation that converts a CTS value type to a reference type.

- **__unbox:** An operation that converts a boxed CTS value type back to its original form.

- **__delegate:** Used to define a CTS delegate type.

Given this brief introduction, we can now make some sense out of an example.

A Managed C++ Example

C# and VB.NET were both designed for the CLR, while C++ was not. As a result, code written in Managed C++ can look a bit odd. Here's the same example shown earlier in this chapter, this time in Managed C++:

```
// A Managed C++ example
#include "stdafx.h"
#using <mscorlib.dll>

__gc __interface IMath
{
        int Factorial(int f);
        double SquareRoot(double s);
};
```

```
__gc class Compute : public IMath
{
    public: int Factorial(int f)
    {
        int i;
        int result = 1;
        for (i=2; i<=f; i++)
                result = result * i;
        return result;
    };

    public: double SquareRoot(double s)
    {
        return System::Math::Sqrt(s);
    }
};

void main(void)
{
    Compute *c = new Compute;
    int v;
    v = 5;
    System::Console::WriteLine(
        "{0} factorial: {1}",
        box(v), __box(c->Factorial(v)));
    System::Console::WriteLine(
        "Square root of {0}: {1:f4}",
        box(v), __box(c->SquareRoot(v)));
}
```

*Managed C++
resembles C#*

The first thing to notice is how much this example resembles
the C# version. Most of the basic syntax and many of the operators are the same. Yet it's different, too, beginning with the
#include and #using statements necessary for creating managed
code in C++. Following these, the interface IMath is defined,
just as before. This time, however, it uses the __interface keyword and precedes it with the __gc keyword. The result is a
C++ incarnation of a CTS-defined interface.

Next comes the class Compute, which implements the IMath
interface. This class too is declared with the __gc keyword,
which means that it's a CTS class with a lifetime managed by
the CLR rather than the developer. The class varies a bit in syntax from the C# example, since C++ doesn't express things in
exactly the same way, but it's nonetheless very similar.

The example ends with a standard C++ main function. Just as before, it creates an instance of the Compute class and then calls its two methods, all using standard C++ syntax. The only substantive difference is in the calls to WriteLine. Because this method expects reference parameters, the __box operator must be used to pass the numeric parameters correctly. Boxing also occurred for this parameter in C# and VB.NET, but it was done automatically. Because C++ was not originally built for the CLR, however, the developer must explicitly request this operation. Finally, just as you'd expect, the output of this example is the same as before: the factorial and square root of five.

Managed C++ requires explicit boxing

Managed C++ Types

Managed C++ allows full access to the .NET Framework, including the types defined by the CLR and more. It's important to note that managed and unmanaged code, classes defined with and without __gc, can be defined in the same file, and they can exist in the same running process. Only the managed classes are subject to garbage collection, however; unmanaged classes must be explicitly freed as usual in C++. Table 4-3 shows some of the major CLR types and their equivalents in Managed C++.

Managed and unmanaged C++ code can coexist in a process

Other Managed C++ Features

Because it fully supports the CLR, there's much more in Managed C++. Delegates can be created using the __*delegate* keyword, while namespaces can be referenced with a *using namespace* statement, such as

Managed C++ allows full access to the CLR's features

```
using namespace System;
```

Exceptions can be handled using try/catch blocks, and custom CLR exceptions that inherit from System::Exception can be created. Attributes can also be embedded in code using the same syntax as in C#.

Table 4-3   Some CLR Types and Their Managed C++ Equivalents

CLR	Managed C++
Byte	unsigned char
Char	wchar_t
Int16	short
Int32	int, long
Int64	__int64
UInt16	unsigned short
UInt32	unsigned int, unsigned long
UInt64	unsigned __int64
Single	float
Double	double
Decimal	Decimal
Boolean	bool
Structure	struct
String	String*
Class	__gc class
Interface	__gc __interface
Delegate	__delegate

C++ is the only language in Visual Studio that can compile directly to native code

Managed C++ is a major extension to the C++ environment provided by Visual Studio.NET, but it's not the only new feature. This latest edition of Microsoft's flagship development tool also includes better support for building traditional applications, including COM-based applications. Except for C++, all languages in Visual Studio.NET compile only to MSIL, and they require the .NET Framework to run. Since all Managed C++ classes are compiled to MSIL, the language can obviously be used to generate Framework-based code, but C++ is unique in that it also allows compiling directly to a machine-specific

Is C++ a Dead Language?

C++ has been the workhorse of professional software developers for most of the last decade. It's been used to write Lotus Notes, a surfeit of business applications, and even parts of Windows. Yet in a world that offers C#, VB.NET, and Java, where does C++ fit? Has its usefulness come to an end?

Certainly not. C#, VB.NET, and Java are much better than C++ for many types of applications, even many for which C++ has commonly been used. But all three of these languages operate in a virtual machine environment. This has many benefits, but there's also a substantial price: performance and size. Some categories of applications, especially system-level software, can't afford this. Who's going to build an operating system in a garbage-collected language? Who wants to build embedded applications for memory-constrained devices in a language that requires a large supporting runtime library?

The day when C++ was the default choice for building a broad range of new applications is over. In the Microsoft world, C# and VB.NET will be the new defaults, while Java dominates elsewhere. Yet in cases where none of these is appropriate—and they do exist—C++ will still dominate. Its role will surely shrink, probably substantially, but C++ is not about to disappear.

binary. For building applications that don't require the CLR, C++ is the only way to go.

Conclusion

Programming languages are a fascinating topic. There appears to be wide agreement on what fundamental features a modern programming language should have and how it should behave. These features and behaviors are essentially what the CLR provides. There is little agreement on how a modern programming language should look, however, with everyone voting for his or her preferred syntax. By providing a common implementation

The .NET Framework brings a new approach to programming language design

of the core and then allowing diverse expressions of that core, the .NET Framework brings a new approach to language design. Even without Microsoft's backing, this would be an attractive model for creating a development environment. With the backing of the world's largest software company, it's bound to affect the lives of many, many developers.

5
___

The .NET Framework
Class Library

All software built on the .NET Framework uses the Common Language Runtime. Yet even the simplest CLR-based program requires using some part of the .NET Framework class library, and more capable software will use a much larger set of the services this library provides. Understanding the .NET Framework, perhaps the single most important part of Microsoft's .NET initiative, requires having a clear idea of what the .NET Framework class library offers to software developers. This long chapter provides a survey of this very large library.

The .NET Framework class library is essential for building .NET Framework applications

An Overview of the .NET Framework Class Library

The .NET Framework class library is organized into a hierarchy of namespaces. Each namespace can contain types, such as classes and interfaces, as well as other subordinate namespaces. The root namespace is System, and every .NET Framework application will use some of the types it contains. Yet the types in several other namespaces are also likely to be commonly used

The library is a hierarchy of namespaces

How Big Is Big?

If there's any one fact about the .NET Framework class library that you should internalize, it is that the library is big—very, very big. Microsoft claims that thousands of people have been working on .NET for several years, and from the looks of it, a large chunk of them were designing and building this class library. The steepest learning curve for most developers adopting the .NET Framework will be learning the .NET Framework class library.

Fortunately, you don't need to learn the whole thing. Unless you have a great deal of free time and remarkably catholic interests, you're unlikely ever to understand every type in the library. Instead, any developer working in the .NET world should first decide which parts of this mountain of software she absolutely needs to understand and then determine which parts she's really interested in. Every developer will need to understand some of its namespaces, but most will be able to ignore many others quite safely.

Providing a large set of generally useful code is clearly a good idea. While the .NET Framework class library probably isn't exactly on the mark in every way in this first release, it does appear to address the right set of problems in a reasonable way. And its straightforward design should make it as approachable as something this big can ever be.

by a broad swathe of developers. System is the foundation, but it's by no means the whole story.

The System Namespace

System is the root namespace of the .NET Framework class library

The System namespace is the ultimate parent of the .NET Framework class library. Along with its large set of subordinate namespaces, System contains many different types. Among the most interesting of these are the following:

- **The core types defined by the CLR's Common Type System,** including Int16, Int32, Char, Boolean, and all other standard value types, along with reference types such as Array and Delegate. The fundamental base type Object is also defined here.

- **Console,** the class whose WriteLine method was used in the previous chapter to output simple information. This class also provides a corresponding ReadLine method and several others.

- **Math,** the class whose Sqrt method was used in the previous chapter to compute the square root of a number. This class has more than two dozen members that provide standard ways to compute a number's sine, cosine, tangent, logarithm, and to perform other common mathematical functions.

- **Environment,** a class used to access information about the environment of the currently running application. An application can learn what its current directory is, find out what operating system it's running on, determine how much memory it's using, and more.

- **GC,** a class used to affect how and when garbage collection happens. By invoking this class's Collect method, an application can force garbage collection to happen immediately. (This isn't likely to be a good idea, however, since the CLR knows better than you when garbage collection should occur.)

- **Random,** a class whose members can be used to compute pseudorandom numbers.

Except for the base CLR types, the types in System sometimes seem to have been placed here because there was no obviously better namespace for them. Still, these types are useful in a broad range of applications.

The types in System are a diverse lot

A Survey of System's Subordinate Namespaces

Directly below System are some two dozen other namespaces, many of which have subnamespaces of their own. Providing even a short survey of these is a daunting task. Nonetheless, before moving on to examine the most important namespaces in some detail, it's important at least to attempt a broad view.

System directly contains more than two dozen namespaces

The Risks and Rewards of a Standard Class Library

The goal of creating a class library is to make life easier for developers. Rather than reinvent wheels from scratch, a developer can reuse existing wheels. Class libraries aren't a new idea, and several useful collections of code exist today. The most popular at the moment is surely the large set of packages defined for the Java environment, which collectively define a set of services that look much like the .NET Framework class library. (In fact, a Java package is very similar to a namespace in the .NET Framework.) The existence of this large set of prepackaged functionality is a major reason for Java's success.

There have been attempts to create broad class libraries that were doomed by their own ambition, however. One of the most visible (and probably most expensive) of these was a project undertaken by the joint Apple/IBM venture Taligent. I once gave a seminar for the technical staff at Taligent, and I don't think I've ever spoken to a more intelligent audience—those people were amazing. Yet in part because the class libraries they produced were so complex and had such a long learning curve, they ultimately weren't successful.

Does the .NET Framework class library suffer from this problem? I don't think so. It's certainly big, but a developer doesn't need to understand the whole thing to use just one part of it. Some degree of compartmentalization is critical to a successful class library, since the number of people willing to devote the necessary time to achieve complete mastery is much smaller than those who can benefit from exploiting some parts of it.

Whether what's in the library will meet developer needs remains to be seen. It's early days yet for the .NET Framework, and so we'll surely see some revisions made as this development platform matures. Also, some developers have complained about the lack of source code for the library. Without this, it's difficult to know exactly what's happening inside a class you're inheriting from. Yet the major Java products don't provide source code—big software companies are protective of their intellectual property—and they're still successful. While source code would be nice, I don't expect its absence to be a major impediment to adoption of the .NET Framework.

Overall, the .NET Framework class library strikes a good balance between power and complexity. While it will certainly require effort to understand, I don't think we're going to see a repeat of the Taligent experience here.

With this lofty goal in mind, this section takes a look at most of the namespaces directly below System, providing a brief description of what each one offers. To give you a visual guide, Table 5-1 shows the primary namespaces in the .NET Framework class library along with their most important children. Note that this chapter does not describe every namespace in this library, and so Table 5-1 is not a complete list.

System.Collections includes types for creating and working with hash tables, arrays, queues, stacks, lists, and other generally useful data structures. These types are defined quite generically. For example, the Stack and Queue classes are defined to contain Objects as their members, which means they can contain values of any CTS type. And like everything in the .NET Framework class library, these types can be used from any CLR-based language. This namespace also contains the subordinate namespace *System.Collections.Specialized*, which provides types for more narrowly applicable uses, such as a collection of Strings.

System.Collections defines generic types such as stacks and queues

System.ComponentModel contains types for creating various kinds of .NET Framework–based components. Among the types it includes is the Component class, which serves as the basis for components used by Windows Forms, described later in this chapter, and for many other classes in the .NET Framework class library. Components, which implement the IComponent interface defined in this namespace, exist inside instances of the Container class, also defined in this namespace. Each Container object implements two more interfaces defined in this namespace: one occurrence of the IContainer interface, along with one ISite interface for each component the container hosts. This namespace also contains types for licensing components. If you're familiar with the COM-based mechanisms for building ActiveX controls, the types defined in this namespace should suggest those commonly used models for building components. System.ComponentModel also contains the subordinate namespace *System.ComponentModel.Design,* which is full of types that can be used to allow design-time customization of .NET Framework–based components.

System.Component-Model provides a foundation for building software components

Table 5-1   The Hierarchy of Major Namespaces in the .NET Framework Class Library

System		
	Collections	
		Specialized
	ComponentModel	
		Design
	Configuration	
		Assemblies
		Install
	Data	
		OleDb
		SqlClient
	Diagnostics	
	DirectoryServices	
	Drawing	
		Drawing2D
		Imaging
		Printing
		Text
	EnterpriseServices	
	Globalization	
	IO	
	Management	
	Messaging	
	Net	
		Sockets
	Reflection	
		Emit

Resources		
Runtime		
	CompilerServices	
	InteropServices	
	Remoting	
	Serialization	
Security		
	Cryptography	
		X509Certificates
	Xml	
	Permissions	
	Policy	
	Principal	
ServiceProcess		
Text		
	RegularExpressions	
Threading		
Timers		
Web		
	Services	
	UI	
Windows		
	Forms	
Xml		
	Schema	
	Serialization	
	XPath	
	Xsl	

System.Configuration supports configuring assemblies and creating installers

System.Configuration provides types such as the ConfigurationsSettings class that allow accessing configuration information for a .NET Framework–based application. It also contains the subordinate namespaces *System.Configuration.Assemblies* for working with assembly-specific configuration information and *System.Configuration.Install* for building custom installers for CLR-based software.

System.Data contains the types that make up ADO.NET

System.Data is among the most important namespaces in the .NET Framework class library. The types in this namespace implement ADO.NET, the standard approach to accessing data for .NET Framework applications. Its subordinate namespaces include *System.Data.OleDb*, which allows access to data sources using OLE DB providers, and *System.Data.SqlClient*, which allows access to data stored in Microsoft's SQL Server. ADO.NET is described in more detail in Chapter 6.

System.Diagnostics supports tracing, assertions, and more

System.Diagnostics contains a large set of classes, interfaces, structures, and other types that help with debugging .NET Framework applications. For example, the Trace class allows adding to code assertions that verify key conditions, writing messages that trace the flow of execution, and performing other useful functions in released software. The Debug class, also defined in this namespace, provides similar services but is designed to be used during development rather than in a released product.

System.Directory-Services provides an API to Active Directory

System.DirectoryServices contains types for accessing Active Directory and other directory services. Prior to .NET, the standard way to expose Windows services was through COM-based interfaces. Active Directory, for instance, can be accessed via the Active Directory Services Interface (ADSI). The .NET Framework largely supersedes COM for new interface definitions, however, and so new ways to expose services must be created using managed code. The types in the System.DirectoryServices namespace are the .NET Framework's analog to ADSI.

System.Drawing provides a large set of types for using the services of the most recent version of Microsoft's Graphics Device Interface (GDI), known as GDI+. System.Drawing itself includes classes for working with pens, brushes, and other drawing tools, while several subordinate namespaces contain types for related uses. *System.Drawing.Drawing2D*, for example, contains types for vector graphics and other two-dimensional drawing functions; *System.Drawing.Imaging* contains types for working with metafiles and other more advanced GDI imaging; *System.Drawing.Printing* contains types for controlling printers; and *System.Drawing.Text* contains types for manipulating fonts.

System.Drawing supports creating text and several kinds of graphics

System.EnterpriseServices contains types for accessing the services provided by COM+, including support for distributed transactions, role-based authorization, and object pooling. Unlike most of the functions provided by the .NET Framework class library, the types contained here provide a wrapper around the existing COM+ software rather than reimplementing it as managed code. This important namespace is described in more detail later in this chapter.

System.Enterprise-Services allows access to COM+ services

System.Globalization contains types for creating national calendars, converting to national code pages, formatting dates and times, and other aspects of building software that supports multiple cultures. Globalized software is important, and so many of the .NET Framework's basic functions are automatically culture-aware. For example, conversion to a currency value can automatically examine the caller's culture setting to format the currency appropriately.

System.Globalization helps write software that works in diverse cultures

System.IO provides a large set of types for reading and writing files, directories, and in-memory streams. While access to database management systems is often the main route applications take to data, the ability to work with files is still important. This fundamental namespace is described in more detail later in this chapter.

System.IO supports access to files and directories

System.Management supports working with WMI data

System.Management provides types for accessing Windows Management Instrumentation (WMI) data from managed code. WMI is Microsoft's implementation of the Web-Based Enterprise Management (WBEM) initiative supported by many different vendors. A number of the types in this namespace provide support for the WMI Query Language (WQL), a dialect of SQL focused on accessing WMI-related information.

System.Messaging provides an API for MSMQ

System.Messaging contains types for accessing Microsoft Message Queuing (MSMQ). MSMQ has several other application programming interfaces (APIs), including a COM-based API and an API defined as a set of C function calls. System.Messaging's types define another API intended for use by managed code.

System.Net supports access to HTTP, TCP, and other protocols

System.Net provides types for accessing several common protocols, including HTTP and the Domain Name System (DNS). It also contains the abstract classes WebRequest and WebResponse, which allow building applications that are unaware of what protocol is being used to communicate. These applications can simply make requests to and get responses from specified URLs and let the underlying software worry about the details. System.Net also contains the subordinate namespace *System.Net.Sockets*. The types in this namespace provide a managed implementation of the traditional sockets interface to TCP and UDP—it's WinSock for the .NET generation. The sockets API, which first appeared in Berkeley UNIX some 20 years ago, refuses to die.

System.Reflection allows access to an assembly's metadata

System.Reflection contains a large set of types for examining an assembly's metadata. A subordinate namespace, *System.Reflection.Emit*, contains types that can be used to create other types dynamically. Reflection is described in more detail later in this chapter.

System.Resources allows manipulating resources

System.Resources provides types that allow managed code to work effectively with resources. Resources are parts of an application that can be separated from the source code, such as message strings, icons, and bitmaps. A primary use of this namespace's types is to allow an application to display different resources easily when used in different cultures. In other words, the contents of this namespace are especially relevant for internationalized software that must work in many different countries and languages.

System.Runtime is a parent namespace that contains several important subordinate namespaces. As its name suggests, System.Runtime.CompilerServices contains types useful for someone writing a compiler for a CLR-based language, and so it is of interest only to a very specialized developer audience. System.Runtime.InteropServices, however, is one of the .NET Framework class library's most important namespaces. It contains types that help in interoperating with non-CLR-based software, such as COM classes, and is described in more detail later in this chapter. System.Runtime.Remoting is another critically important namespace, as the types it contains allow accessing managed objects in other processes and other machines. This technology, known as .NET Remoting, is also described in more detail later in this chapter. Finally, System.Runtime.Serialization contains types for serializing a managed object's state. Serializing a managed object means copying its state (although not its code) into either memory or some more permanent medium such as a file. The ability to work with an object's state in this way is a fundamental feature of the .NET Framework—it's used by .NET Remoting, for example—so this namespace is also described in more detail later in this chapter.

System.Runtime provides interoperability, remoting, serialization, and other fundamental services

System.Security contains classes, interfaces, enumerations, and subordinate namespaces that provide various security-related functions. The namespace directly contains several fundamental classes, such as the SecurityManager class, which is the primary access point for working with the security system. The subordinate namespace System.Security.Cryptography contains types for using secret and public key cryptography services. Those

System.Security provides cryptography support and other security services

types can provide access to Windows Cryptographic Service Providers (CSPs) that actually implement algorithms such as DES, RC2, and RSA. System.Security.Cryptography itself also contains two subordinate namespaces. One of them, *System.Security.Cryptography.X509Certificates*, contains classes for creating and using X.509 version 3 public key certificates for use with Microsoft's Authenticode technology. The other, *System.Security.Cryptography.Xml*, contains a .NET Framework–specific mechanism for digitally signing data described using XML.

System.Security also contains three other subordinate namespaces. *System.Security.Permissions* defines types such as a class representing each of the possible permissions for code access security, while *System.Security.Policy* defines classes such as Site, URL, Publisher, Zone, and others used in defining security policy. How these concepts are used by the CLR was described in Chapter 3's section on code access security. The last of System.Security's three namespace children, *System.Security.Principal,* contains types for working with security principals. These classes are used by the CLR in implementing the role-based security described in Chapter 3.

System.ServiceProcess allows creating Windows services

System.ServiceProcess contains types for building .NET Framework applications that run as long-lived processes called *Windows services*. This kind of application was previously known as an *NT service* and is also sometimes referred to as a *demon* (often spelled *daemon*).

System.Text supports text conversion and working with regular expressions

System.Text contains just a small group of classes for working with text. For example, this namespace's UTF8Encoding class can convert Unicode characters from their default encoding into UTF-8 and vice versa. UTF stands for *Unicode Transformation Format,* and UTF-8 is compatible with the familiar ASCII character representation (although it also allows representing multibyte non-ASCII characters). System.Text also contains the namespace *System.Text.RegularExpressions.* The types in this namespace allow access to a generic regular expression engine that can be used from any CLR-based language.

System.Threading is another of the .NET Framework's more important namespaces. The types it contains provide a standard way for developers working in any .NET language to build multithreaded applications. Before .NET, Visual Basic, C++, and other languages all had their own unique approach to threading, with COM's apartments serving as a (complicated) cross-language solution. With the .NET Framework, all CLR-based languages can use the contents of System.Threading to work with threads in a consistent way. Perhaps the most important type in this namespace is the Thread class, which provides methods to start a thread, stop one, cause it to wait for another thread, and more. The namespace also contains classes for using fundamental synchronization constructs, such as mutexes and monitors, and for working with a thread pool.

System.Threading provides standard threading services used by all CLR-based languages

System.Timers contains types for specifying and handling recurring events. The most important class in this namespace is Timer, which allows a developer to specify an interval at which an Elapsed event, defined as part of the Timer class, will be raised in his application. The application can then catch this event and perform some function. For example, an application may wish to check for new mail once every ten minutes. Using this mechanism, the developer could cause the Elapsed event to take place every ten minutes, then put mail-checking code in the handler for this event.

System.Timers supports working with regularly occurring events

System.Web is, after System itself, perhaps the most important namespace in the .NET Framework class library. Comprising many types and many subordinate namespaces, the software it contains implements ASP.NET. The two most important children of System.Web are *System.Web.UI*, which contains types for building browser-accessible applications, and *System.Web.Services*, which contains types for creating

System.Web implements ASP.NET

applications that expose Web services. ASP.NET is described in some detail in Chapter 7.

System.Win-
dows.Forms sup-
ports building local
Windows GUIs

System.Windows.Forms contains types used to construct local Windows GUIs. Local GUIs are less important for application developers than they once were—a browser interface is now probably more common—but they're nonetheless an important topic. Accordingly, this namespace is described in more detail later in this chapter.

System.XML in-
cludes a wide
range of support for
working with XML-
defined data

System.XML contains types useful for working with XML documents. The .NET initiative is shot through with support for XML, and the contents of this namespace provide a great deal of support for developers working with XML-defined data. This namespace is also described in more detail later in this chapter.

Every .NET
Framework devel-
oper needs a basic
knowledge of the
class library

Code provided by a standard library isn't useful unless you know it's there. Accordingly, while memorizing the entire .NET Framework class library isn't necessary, any developer writing CLR-based code should have a broad grasp of what the library makes available. Some namespaces are more important than others, however, and so the remainder of this chapter takes a closer look at some of those that matter most.

Input and Output: System.IO

File access is an
essential service

Like most software, .NET Framework applications need some way to input and output data. These operations are most commonly done against a disk drive, but there are other possibilities too. The .NET Framework class library's System.IO namespace contains a substantial set of types that developers can use to read and write files, work with directories in a file system, and do other kinds of straightforward data access.

A Stream object
contains a sequence
of bytes and pro-
vides methods to
access those bytes

Among the most fundamental of these types is the Stream class. As defined by this class, a *stream* is a sequence of bytes together with methods to read the stream's contents, write those contents, perhaps seek to a specific location in the stream, and perform other operations. Specific stream classes inherit from a common abstract Stream class and so provide access to various kinds of information in a consistent way.

For example, information stored in files can be accessed using the File class. While an instance of File provides familiar methods for working with files such as Create, Delete, and Open, it doesn't provide methods for reading and writing a file's contents. Instead, a File object's Create and Open methods return an instance of a FileStream that can be used to get at the file's contents. Like all streams, a FileStream object provides Read and Write methods for synchronous access to a file's data, that is, for calls that block waiting for data to be read or written. Also like other streams, FileStream objects allow asynchronous access using the paired BeginRead/EndRead and BeginWrite/EndWrite methods. These methods allow a .NET Framework application to begin a read or write operation and then check later to get the result. Each FileStream also provides a Seek method to move to a designated point in the file, a Flush method to write data to the underlying device (such as a disk drive), a Close method to close the FileStream, and many more methods.

A FileStream object allows access to a file's contents as binary data

FileStreams work only with binary data, however, which isn't always what's needed. System.IO provides other standard classes to work with file data in other formats. For example, the FileInfo class can be used to create FileStreams, but it can also be used to create instances of the classes StreamReader and StreamWriter. Unlike File, whose methods are mostly static, an instance of a FileInfo class must be explicitly created before its methods can be used. Once a FileInfo object exists, its OpenText method can be used to create a new StreamReader object. This StreamReader can then be used to read characters from whatever file is associated with the FileInfo object.

A FileInfo object allows access to a file's contents as text

Here's a C# example that illustrates how these classes can be used:

```csharp
using System;
using System.IO;

class FileIOExample
{
    static void Main()
    {
        FileStream fs;
        FileInfo f;
        StreamReader sr;
        byte[] buf = new byte[10];
        string s;
        int i;

        for (i=0; i<10; i++)
            buf[i] = (byte) (65 + i);
        fs = File.Create("test.dat");
        fs.Write(buf, 0, 10);
        fs.Close();

        f = new FileInfo("test.dat");
        sr = f.OpenText();
        s = sr.ReadToEnd();

        Console.WriteLine("{0}", s);
    }
}
```

This admittedly unrealistic example begins with appropriate using statements and then defines the single class FileIOExample. This class contains only a Main method, which begins with several declarations. After this, the 10-byte buffer buf is populated with the characters "A" through "J." Because buf can accept only bytes, this is done by explicitly calculating each character's value and then forcing the result to be of type byte. (This forced type conversion is called *casting*.) File's Create method is then used to create a file, followed by a call to File's Write method. This method writes buf's ten characters into that file and is followed by a Close call that closes the file. Because the File class declares all of these methods to be static, they can be invoked without explicitly creating a File instance.

The example next opens the same file using an instance of the FileInfo class. Calling the FileInfo object's OpenText method returns a StreamReader object whose ReadToEnd method can be used to read the characters just written into a string. StreamReaders also provide methods to read single characters, blocks of characters, and lines of characters. Finally, the characters read from the file are written to the console, yielding the result

```
ABCDEFGHIJ
```

System.IO also defines several other useful types. The Directory class, for instance, provides methods such as CreateDirectory to create a new directory, Delete to destroy an existing directory and its contents, and several more. The MemoryStream class allows the typical operations defined for a stream, such as Read, Write, and Seek, to be carried out on an arbitrary set of bytes in memory. StringWriter and StringReader provide analogous functions to StreamWriter and StreamReader, except that instead of working with files, they work with in-memory strings. BinaryReader and BinaryWriter allow reading and writing values of types such as integers, decimals, and characters from a stream.

Many other classes are also defined for working with files, directories, and streams

While information stored in relational databases is more important for many applications, data stored in files still matters. The classes in System.IO provide a flexible set of options for working with that data.

Serialization: System.Runtime.Serialization

Objects commonly have state. An instance of a class, for example, can have one or more fields, each of which contains some value. It's often useful to extract this state from an object, either to store the state somewhere or to send it across a network. Performing this extraction is called *serializing* an object, while

Serialization extracts an object's state

the reverse process, recreating an object from serialized state, is known as *deserializing*.[1]

A formatter can be used to serialize an object

The .NET Framework class library provides support for serialization. The work of serialization is done by a particular *formatter;* each formatter provides a Serialize and Deserialize method. The NET Framework class library provides two varieties of formatter. The binary formatter, implemented by the BinaryFormatter class in the System.Runtime.Serialization.Formatters.Binary namespace, serializes an object into a straightforward binary form designed to be compact and quick to parse. The SOAP formatter, implemented by the SoapFormatter class in the System.Runtime.Serialization.Formatters.Soap namespace, serializes an object into a SOAP message like those shown in Chapter 2.

Both a binary formatter and a SOAP formatter are provided

Figure 5-1 illustrates the serialization process. As the figure shows, an instance of a class can be run through a formatter that extracts the state of this object in a particular form. As just stated, the binary formatter emits that state information in a simple and compact form, while the SOAP formatter generates the same information wrapped in XML and formatted as a SOAP message. While the outputs shown in the figure are simplified— the binary formatter actually stores integers in binary form, for instance—they illustrate the key difference between the two serialization options built into the .NET Framework class library.

An object's state is serialized into a stream

When a formatter serializes an object, the resulting state is placed into a stream. As described in the previous section, a stream is an abstraction of a sequence of bytes and so can hold any serialization format. Once it's in a stream, an object's state can be stored on disk (or in the jargon of objects, be made *persistent*), sent across a network to another machine, or used in some other way.

---

1. This is also sometimes referred to as *rehydrating* an object.

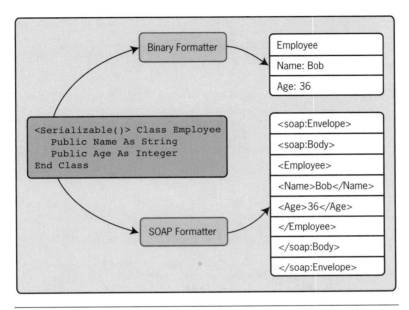

Figure 5-1   The System.Runtime.Serialization namespace provides two different formatters to serialize an object's state.

For a type to be serializable, its creator must mark it with the Serializable attribute, as Figure 5-1 illustrates. The Serializable attribute can be assigned to classes, structures, and other types or just to specific fields within a type to indicate that only they should be serialized. Also, a type marked with the Serializable attribute can indicate that certain fields should not be saved when an instance of this type is serialized by marking them with the NonSerialized attribute.

Not every type is serializable

Here's a simple VB.NET example that shows how serialization works:

```
Imports System
Imports System.IO
Imports System.Runtime.Serialization
Imports _
    System.Runtime.Serialization.Formatters.Binary

Module SerializationExample
```

```
<Serializable()> Class Employee
    Public Name As String
    Public Age As Integer
End Class

Sub Main()
    Dim E1 As Employee = New Employee()
    Dim E2 As Employee = New Employee()
    Dim FS As FileStream
    Dim BinForm As BinaryFormatter = _
        New BinaryFormatter()

    E1.Name = "Bob"
    E1.Age = 36

    FS = File.Create("test.dat")
    BinForm.Serialize(FS, E1)
    FS.Close()

    FS = File.Open("test.dat", FileMode.Open)
    E2 = BinForm.Deserialize(FS)
    Console.WriteLine("E2 Name: {0}", E2.Name)
    Console.WriteLine("E2 Age: {0}", E2.Age)
End Sub

End Module
```

This example begins with several Imports (using) statements. As always, these statements aren't required, but they make the code that follows more readable by removing the need to type fully qualified names. Following these, the module begins with the definition of a very simple Employee class. This class contains just two fields representing an employee's name and age and has no methods at all. (This is unrealistic, of course, but information about methods isn't stored anyway when a class is serialized.)

The example's Sub Main routine creates two instances of the Employee class, E1 and E2, and then declares a FileStream called FS. It next creates an instance of the BinaryFormatter class that will be used to serialize and deserialize the objects' state. Once that state has been created by initializing E1's fields to contain a name and an age, the file test.dat is created to hold the serialized state. The binary formatter's Serialize method is then called, which serializes the state in E1 into the stream FS. When the stream is closed, its contents are written to the file test.dat.

The example then reopens test.dat, associating it once again with the stream FS. This stream is passed into the binary formatter's Deserialize method, with the result assigned to E2. Although E2 has had just its default state so far, the deserialization process gives it the state that was extracted earlier from E1. Accordingly, the output of this simple program is

```
E2 Name: Bob
E2 Age: 36
```

Serialization can also be customized. For example, if a class implements the ISerializable interface, it can participate in its own serialization. This interface has only a single method that allows controlling the details of what gets serialized. Also, although it's not shown in this simple example, serializing an object will also serialize objects it refers to, causing them all to be serialized (or deserialized) at once. And for the brave of heart, it's possible to build your own formatter that does serialization in a completely customized way by inheriting from the abstract class System.Runtime.Serialization.Formatter. However it's done, serialization is useful, and in its basic form, at least, it's simple to use. As described later in this chapter, serialization plays a role in several parts of the .NET Framework class library.

Serialization has options

Working with XML: System.Xml

XML is certainly among the most important new technologies to emerge in the last few years. Recognizing this, Microsoft has chosen to use XML in many different ways throughout .NET. The company also apparently recognizes that its customers wish to use XML in a variety of ways. Accordingly, the .NET Framework class library includes a substantial amount of support for working with XML, most of it contained in the System.Xml namespace.

Microsoft has gotten XML religion

The XML Technology Family

XML is more than angle brackets

The basics of XML were described in Chapter 2. To get a feeling for what the System.Xml namespace provides, however, you need to understand a bit more about the family of XML technologies. From its beginning as a way to define documents, elements in those documents, and namespaces for those elements, XML has evolved into a significantly more powerful— and more complex—group of technologies.

XML Infosets

An Infoset provides an abstract view of the information in an XML document

The familiar angle bracket form of XML implies a logical hierarchy of related information. This abstract set of information and relationships is known as the XML document's *Information Set*, a term that's usually shortened to just *Infoset*. An Infoset consists of some number of *information items,* each of which represents some aspect of the XML document from which this Infoset was derived. For example, every Infoset has a *document* information item that acts as the root of the tree, with a single root *element* information item just beneath it. Most Infosets have some number of child element information items below this root element.

For example, consider this simple XML document:

```
<employees>
    <employee>
        <name>Bob</name>
        <age>36</age>
    </employee>
    <employee>
        <name>Casey</name>
    </employee>
</employees>
```

The Infoset for this document can be represented as shown in Figure 5-2. The root of the Infoset's tree is a document information item, while below it is a hierarchy of element information items, one for each element in the XML document. The leaves of the tree are the values of the elements in this simple document.

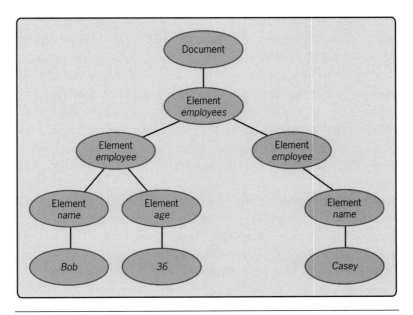

Figure 5-2   An XML document's Infoset is an abstract representation of the document's contents.

Other XML Technologies

XML documents and the Infosets they imply can provide the foundation for tools that manipulate a document's data. Among the most important of these is XPath, which provides a mechanism for identifying a subset of an Infoset. A simple and quite accurate way to think of XPath is as a query language for information in XML documents (that is, for XML Infosets). Just as SQL provides a standard language for querying information contained in a relational database, XPath provides a language for querying information represented as a hierarchy. Using an XPath expression, a user can identify specific nodes in a tree.

XPath allows querying an XML document

For example, imagine that this query is issued against the simple XML document just described:

```
/employees/employee/name
```

This simple XPath request first identifies each employee element below the root employees element and then identifies the values of each name element in each of those employee elements. Far more complex queries are also possible, including queries that use comparison operators, compute sums, include wildcards, and much more. With XPath, a developer need not write her own code to search through information. Instead, this abstract language can be used to find easily information represented as an in-memory XML document.

XSLT allows trans-forming XML documents

Another technology built on the abstract foundation provided by XML Infosets is the Extensible Stylesheet Language Transformations, universally referred to as XSLT. XSLT is a mechanism for specifying transformations of XML documents, transformations that can be described in an XSLT stylesheet. For instance, a set of XSLT rules that transforms an XML document from one schema to another can be defined. XSLT also relies on the abstract form of an XML document represented by its Infoset, and it relies on XPath for some of its functionality.

XML today is a unified family of technologies

Figure 5-3 summarizes the relationships among the fundamental XML technologies. An XML Schema definition describes the structure and contents of an XML document—it defines a group of types—while an XML document itself can be thought of as an instance of the document type defined by some schema.[2] This XML document, in turn, is the foundation for an Infoset, which provides an abstract view of the document's data. Technologies for working with that data, such as XPath and XSLT, are effectively defined to work against the Infoset, allowing them to remain independent of the specific representation used for the XML document itself. Note that because these technologies rely on the Infoset rather than the familiar angle bracket–based syntax of an XML document, they can actually

---

2. In effect, an XML document's metadata is provided by its associated XML Schema definition.

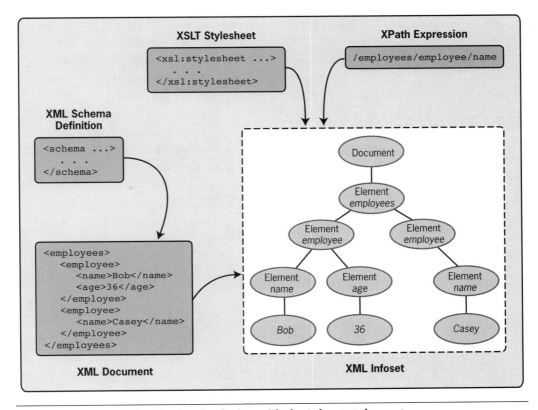

Figure 5-3   XML is a family of technologies, with the Infoset at the center.

be used with any data that can be represented in a strict hierarchy. That data need not necessarily come from a traditional XML document as long as it can be represented as an Infoset. For example, hierarchical data such as a file system or the Windows registry might be accessed in this way.

XML APIs

The XML standards don't mandate any particular approach to processing the information in an XML document. As it happens, two styles of APIs have come into common use. In one approach, the information in an XML document is read sequentially, traversing a document's tree in a depth-first search. An

SAX is a streaming API for accessing XML-defined information

API that supports this kind of access is referred to as a *streaming API*, and one common choice for this is the Simple API for XML (SAX). SAX was created by a group of volunteers independent of the W3C or other formal standards groups, but it is supported by many vendors today.

The DOM is a navigational API for accessing XML-defined information

In the second approach, the entire document is represented as an in-memory data structure (conceptually, at least), which allows an application to navigate through it, moving back and forth as needed. The most commonly used API for this option is an implementation of the Document Object Model (DOM) defined by the W3C. Because of the style of access it allows, the DOM is an example of a *navigational* API.

What System.Xml Provides

System.Xml includes support for XPath, XSLT, the DOM, and more

The System.Xml namespace has a great deal of built-in support for working with XML. Among the features available are support for both streaming and navigational APIs, the ability to use XPath queries, the ability to perform XSLT transformations, and more. While describing all of these features in any detail is well beyond the scope of this book, this section provides an overview of their most important aspects.

The XmlReader class allows streaming access to XML-defined information

The most fundamental types for handling XML-defined data are contained directly in System.Xml itself. One of these is the abstract class XmlNode. As its name suggests, this class represents a node in an XML document, such as a particular element. Another fundamental type in System.Xml is the abstract class XmlReader. XmlReader provides a streaming interface for accessing XML data. (Note that the .NET Framework does not directly support SAX; instead it bases all streaming access on XmlReader.) XmlReader is the parent for three concrete classes:

- **XmlTextReader:** Provides a streaming API that reads the information in an XML document sequentially, much like the SAX API. It's the fastest option for reading XML-defined data, but it's also somewhat limited in that no navigation is possible through the document. Also, this class makes no attempt to determine whether the document is valid, that is, whether it corresponds correctly with some XML Schema definition.

- **XmlValidatingReader:** Like XmlTextReader, this class reads the information in an XML document sequentially. It also makes sure that the document corresponds to a specified XML Schema definition, that is, that the document is valid.

- **XmlNodeReader:** Rather than reading from an XML document, this class provides forward-only access to a single XmlNode or a tree of XmlNodes. This is the same in-memory structure used to represent an XML document accessed via the DOM, but unlike the navigational DOM interface, XmlNodeReader allows only sequential access.

System.Xml also includes an abstract XmlWriter class, along with one implementation of a concrete class, called XmlTextWriter, that inherits from XmlWriter. The methods in this class allow writing XML information, angle brackets and all, to a stream. As described earlier in this chapter, a stream can be maintained in memory, written to a file, or used in some other way.

The XmlWriter class allows writing XML documents

System.Xml also includes the XmlDocument class. This class, which inherits from XmlNode, provides an implementation of the DOM API. While the various implementations of XmlReader just described are the fastest way to access information in an XML document, the XmlDocument class is more general because it allows navigation, moving backward and forward through the document at will. A developer is free to choose whichever approach best meets the needs of his application.

An XmlDocument object allows navigational access to XML-defined information

The methods and properties provided by XmlDocument give some idea of the kinds of operations the DOM allows. Those methods include the following:

- **Load:** Loads an XML document and parses it into its abstract tree form

- **Save:** Saves an in-memory document to a stream, file, or some other location

- **InsertBefore:** Inserts a new node, represented as an instance of the XmlNode class, in front of the currently referenced node in the tree

- **InsertAfter:** Inserts a new node, once again an XmlNode instance, in back of the currently referenced node in the tree

- **SelectNodes:** Allows selecting nodes using an XPath expression

XmlDocument also exposes a number of properties that allow navigation through the tree. They include the following:

- **HasChildNodes:** Indicates whether the current node has any nodes beneath it

- **FirstChild:** Returns the first child of the current node

- **LastChild:** Returns the last child of the current node

- **ParentNode:** Returns the parent, that is, the node immediately above the current node

Types for XPath, XSLT, and XML Schema support are provided in separate namespaces

Several other namespaces are defined beneath System.Xml:

- **System.Xml.Schema:** Contains classes for creating and working with XML Schema definitions. Because this language is quite complex, this namespace contains a large set of classes, including a class for each of the elements in the XML Schema language. Microsoft refers to these classes collectively as the Schema Object Model (SOM).

- **System.Xml.XPath:** Contains types that support using XPath expressions to query hierarchical data. Among them are the XPathNavigator class, which allows navigating through a document and issuing XPath queries, and the XPathExpression class, which can contain a compiled XPath query.

- **System.Xml.Xsl:** Contains types that support using XSLT. The most important of these is the XslTransform class, which allows transforming data using an XSLT stylesheet.

- **System.Xml.Serialization:** Contains types that allow serializing data into an XML format. This is another large namespace, but a key type within it is the XmlSerializer class. This class is similar to the SoapFormatter class described earlier, in that it provides Serialize and Deserialize methods that write and read an object's state in XML. This namespace also contains many other classes that allow customizing the serialization process, working with SOAP, and other aspects of converting between state information stored in a language object and the serialized XML form of that information.

XML has become an essential part of modern computing. By providing a standard way to describe information, it fills an important hole in the complex, multivendor world we live in. The .NET Framework's large set of namespaces and types devoted to XML are intended to make this increasingly important technology significantly easier to use.

The .NET Framework class library has a great deal of support for XML

Reflection: **System.Reflection**

Every assembly includes metadata. Always having metadata available is handy; it allows creating useful features such as Visual Studio's IntelliSense, which automatically displays the

An assembly's metadata is useless without some way to access it

Why Have Two Different XML Serializers?

At first glance, the XmlSerializer class in System.Xml.Serialization appears to do the same thing as the SoapFormatter class in the System.Runtime.Serialization.Formatters.Soap namespace. Both can serialize and deserialize the state of language objects to and from an XML representation. Why have both of them?

The answer lies in what each is intended to do. XmlSerializer attempts to produce standard XML, that is, XML that can be described using the XML Schema definition language, and it offers developers precise control over how that serialization happens. Because of this strong focus on standard XML, there are some aspects of the CLR type system that it cannot correctly serialize. For example, XML has no notion of private data, so when, say, a C# object with private members is serialized by the XmlSerializer, only the object's public members are included in the result. Accurately recreating the object given only the output of the XmlSerializer wouldn't be possible in this case—some information has been lost. If your goal is to produce completely XSD-compliant XML, however, this is the XML serialization option that you should choose. For example, ASP.NET's support for Web services uses the XmlSerializer to generate the XML it sends because those Web services are meant to be accessible from all kinds of systems.

The SoapFormatter, by contrast, is intended for use with .NET Remoting. Accordingly, this serialization engine wraps its output in a SOAP envelope, making it less useful for generalized XML work. More important, however, .NET Remoting typically assumes that the .NET Framework is on both sides of the communication, and so the interaction does not need to take into account anything but .NET. As a result, the SoapFormatter's primary goal is to reproduce the CLR types faithfully in XML. A CLR object serialized with the SoapFormatter can be exactly reconstructed by the receiving system's SoapFormatter—private members and everything else are transmitted correctly—but a non-Microsoft implementation would likely have trouble understanding some of the information it receives.

Mapping between different type systems is almost always challenging. Converting CLR types into XML types has its problems, as does the reverse translation, and different applications need to do it in different ways. Accordingly, the .NET Framework class library provides two choices for doing this translation.

methods available for a class and other useful information. But metadata is just information sitting in a file. It's useless without software that knows how to read and interpret that metadata. To support this software, it's useful to have a standard interface to an assembly's metadata, one that can be used by all kinds of applications.

For managed code, that interface is provided by the types contained in the System.Reflection namespace. Before taking a look at these types, recall what metadata consists of: information about the types in an assembly, such as what methods they implement, and information about the assembly itself, stored in the assembly's manifest. As mentioned in Chapter 3, the Ildasm tool can be used to examine an assembly's metadata. Figure 5-4 shows how Ildasm displays the metadata stored with the simple example application from Chapter 4. The manifest appears first, followed by entries for each of the three outermost types in the

The types in System.Reflection allow managed code to access metadata

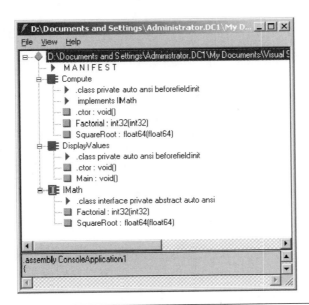

Figure 5-4   The metadata stored with Chapter 4's simple example application can be displayed using Ildasm.

program: the classes Compute and DisplayValues and the interface IMath. Each of these has associated information, the most interesting of which is the methods each type implements. Note that along with the familiar methods shown in Chapter 4's code, each class also has a constructor, labeled ".ctor" in the Ildasm display.

Each kind of metadata is represented by a specific class

To allow programmatic access to this information, the System.Reflection namespace includes a class for each type of information in an assembly's metadata. An application can create instances of these classes as needed and then populate them with the appropriate information from a particular assembly. As Figure 5-5 shows, instances of these classes are organized into a hierarchy. Once the appropriate instances have been created— Figure 5-5 shows a fairly complete picture for Chapter 4's sample application—the assembly's metadata can be accessed.[3]

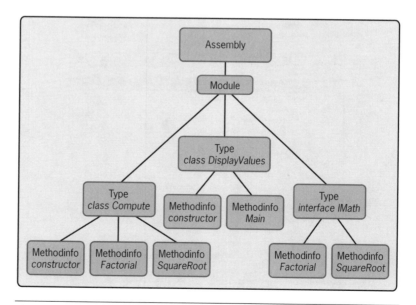

Figure 5-5   The classes in System.Reflection can be used to create a hierarchical in-memory structure that contains an assembly's metadata.

3. It's worth pointing out that full access to metadata requires appropriate code access security permissions.

Although it's not shown in the diagram, it's also possible to access any attributes this metadata contains.

For example, to list all methods contained in this assembly's Compute class, an application could create an instance of the Assembly class and then call this class's LoadFrom method with the name of the file containing the assembly. The Assembly class also provides a GetModule method that can be used to return an instance of the Module class that describes the module containing the Compute class. Once this Module instance exists, the application can call GetType with the name of the desired type in this module, which in this case is Compute. The result is an object of the class Type[4] that contains information about the Compute class. The Type class provides a large set of methods and properties for learning about its contents. For example, a call to Type.GetMethods can return a description of all methods that type implements, each contained in an instance of the class MethodInfo. In this case, three MethodInfo objects would be returned, each containing information about one of Compute's three methods. By examining the properties of each MethodInfo, the application can learn whatever it needs to know about these methods. Among the information available is the method's name, the types of its parameters, its return type, whether the method is final (sealed), and much more.

The Reflection namespace also contains the subordinate namespace Reflection.Emit. To understand what the types in this namespace do, it's first important to understand the two types of assemblies that can be used by the .NET Framework. As described in Chapter 3, the most common variety, *static*

The types in Reflection.Emit allow creating assemblies dynamically

---

4. This is the same Type that is returned by calls to GetType, one of the methods in the Object type that is the root of all others in the CLR type system. Because of this, Type is defined in the System namespace rather than in System.Reflection.

assemblies, are stored on and loaded from disk. All assemblies described so far have in fact been static assemblies. It's also possible to create *dynamic* assemblies, assemblies that are created directly in memory. With this approach, a running application creates MSIL code and metadata, building an assembly on the fly, and then executes it. The types in the Reflection.Emit namespace are used to do this.

Types in Reflection.Emit allow applications to generate explicitly and then execute MSIL code

Creating dynamic assemblies is not for the faint of heart. Reflection.Emit contains types that do very low-level things, including generating MSIL code one instruction at a time. Yet while most developers probably won't work directly with these types, it's useful to know that they exist. Class libraries are meant to make developers' lives easier, and you can't use code in a library if you don't know the code is there.

.NET Remoting: System.Runtime.Remoting

Distributed computing is a core technology today

Allowing communication between software running on different systems is the sine qua non of a modern computing environment. While providing a remote user interface in a browser is certainly important, providing a way for software running on different systems to communicate directly remains essential. Given that Web services provide a quite general mechanism for communication between software on different machines, a simple-minded view might suggest that Web services are all that's required. After all, this technology can be used on both intranets and the Internet, and it potentially allows the client and server to be written using software from different vendors.

Web services are necessary but not sufficient

Effective distributed computing requires more than just Web services, however. To see why, think about some of the limitations of standard Web services. For one thing, an explicit goal of Web services is to allow communication between different vendor implementations. Yet doing this isn't free. As described earlier in this chapter, mapping from the CLR's type system into the one defined by XML can be problematic, and depending on how it's done, this translation might lose some information. If both parties in the communication are built using the same technology, such as the .NET Framework, there's no reason to pay this price. Because using the .NET Framework at each end is a common scenario, some option that allows transmitting the complete set of CLR types must exist.

Another problem is that the XML-based serialization used in Web services is not very efficient. We may have to live with this for Internet-based communication, since XML and SOAP are becoming the world's common mechanisms for exchanging information. Yet for communication inside a firewall, such as on a corporate intranet, there's no need to use a relatively inefficient XML-based format for data. Instead, a faster binary representation can be used.

.NET Remoting addresses these concerns. While it is possible to expose SOAP-based Web services using .NET Remoting, it's more likely that this part of the class library will be used when both ends of the communication are using the .NET Framework. Whether they're communicating across an intranet or over the Internet through firewalls, the communicating systems will then have the same type system, a common set of available remoting protocols, and even the same implementation of those protocols.

.NET Remoting focuses on communication between CLR-based applications

As you might expect, .NET Remoting provides traditional remote procedure call (RPC) functionality, allowing a client to invoke a method in a remote object and have some result returned. It can also be used for asynchronous (nonblocking) calls, however, as well as one-way calls that have no result. The mission of .NET Remoting is to make all of these interactions as simple yet as flexible as possible.

.NET Remoting supports both synchronous and asynchronous communication

An Overview of the Remoting Process

.NET Remoting is used for communication between different app domains

Although the word *remoting* implies communication between different machines, it's used a bit more broadly in the .NET Framework. Here, remoting refers to any communication between objects in different application domains, whether those app domains are on the same machine or on machines connected by a network. Figure 5-6 shows a very high-level view of the major components of the remoting process.

Clients rely on proxy objects

When a client, such as an instance of some class, calls a method on an object in another app domain, that call is first handled by a *proxy* object running in the client's app domain. The proxy represents the remote object in the client's app domain, allowing the client to behave as if that object were running locally. The CLR automatically creates a proxy by using reflection to access the metadata of the remote object being accessed. (Note what this implies: The assembly containing the remote object's classes and/or interfaces must be available on the client's machine.)

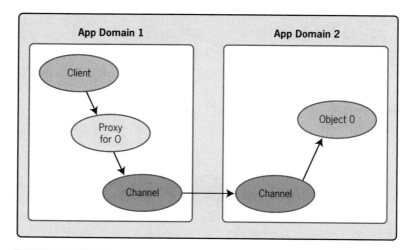

Figure 5-6   Calls to remote objects rely on a proxy object in the calling app domain and channel objects in both app domains.

A proxy eventually hands a call's information to a *channel* object. The channel object is responsible for using some appropriate mechanism, such as a TCP connection, to convey the client's request to the remote app domain. Once the request arrives in that app domain, a channel object running there locates the object for which this call is destined, perhaps creating it if the object isn't already running. The call is then passed to the object, which executes it and passes any results back through the same path.

Communication is handled by channel objects

At a high level, the process is simple. In fact, however, there's much more going on than this simple description shows. It's possible, for instance, to insert code that intercepts and customizes the in-progress call at several points in the path between caller and object. The details get quite involved—remote access is never simple to implement well—but most of the complexity can remain invisible to developers using .NET Remoting. The goal of this section is to present a broad overview of how this technology works.

.NET Remoting provides many opportunities for customization

Passing Information to Remote Objects

Calling a method in an object is straightforward when both the client and the object are in the same app domain. Parameters of value types such as integers are passed by value, which means that their contents are simply copied from client to object. Parameters of reference types, such as classes, are passed by reference, which means that a reference to the instance itself is passed—no separate copy is made. Calling a method in an object gets more complicated when the two are in different app domains, however, and so .NET Remoting must address these complications. Even accessing a remote object's properties or fields requires some way to transfer information across an app domain boundary. The process of packaging values for transfer to another app domain is called *marshaling,* and there are several options for how it gets done.

Values passed between app domains must be marshaled and unmarshaled

Marshal by value passes the value itself to another app domain

One option is *marshal by value (MBV)*. As the name suggests, transferring an instance of some type using this option copies its value to the remote app domain. For this to work, a user-defined type must be serializable, that is, its definition must be marked with the Serializable attribute. When an instance of that type is passed as a parameter in a remote call, the object's state is automatically serialized and passed to the remote app domain. Once it arrives, a new instance of that type is created and initialized using the serialized state of the original. (Note that the code for the type isn't passed, however, which means that for types such as classes, an assembly containing the MSIL for that type must exist on whatever machine the object's state is passed to.) An MBV object should usually be reasonably simple, or the cost of serializing and transferring the entire object to the remote app domain will be very high.

Marshal by reference passes only a reference to another app domain

It's also possible to pass an instance of a reference type across an app domain boundary by reference. This option, called *marshal by reference (MBR)*, is possible only if the reference type inherits from MarshalByRefObject, a class contained in the System namespace. When an MBR object is passed across an app domain boundary, only a reference to the object is passed. This reference, which is more complex than the one used to refer to the object in its own app domain, is used to construct a proxy back to the original object in its home app domain. When code in the remote app domain references this object, such as by calling one of its methods, those references are actually sent back to the original instance of this object. Passing MBR objects as parameters makes sense in cases where the overhead of accessing the object remotely is less than the cost of making a copy of the object.

Figure 5-7 illustrates the difference between MBV and MBR objects. When object X, an MBV object in app domain 1, is passed to app domain 2 as a parameter on a call to object O, a copy of X is created in the remote app domain. Passing object Y, however, does not result in a copy of Y being created in app

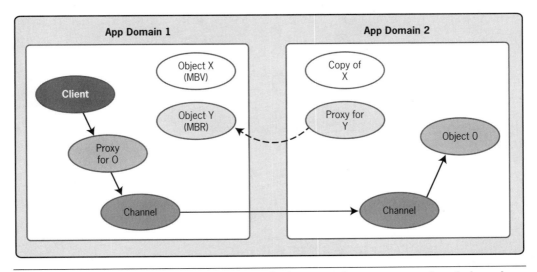

Figure 5-7   Marshal by value objects are copied when passed across an app domain boundary, while marshal by reference objects have a proxy created for them in the remote app domain.

domain 2 because Y is an MBR object. Instead, a proxy to Y is created, and all accesses to object Y are sent back to the instance of Y in app domain 1. (Although it's not shown in the picture, communication from Y's proxy back to Y itself relies on channels, just as described earlier.)

Finally, if a user-defined type isn't serializable and doesn't inherit from MarshalByRefObject, it is neither an MBV nor an MBR object. In this case, instances of that type can't be marshaled across an app domain boundary at all. In other words, any instance of this type can be used only within the app domain in which it is created.

Not all types can be marshaled

Choosing a Channel

Applications using .NET Remoting ultimately rely on channels to convey calls and responses between app domains. Two standard channels, called the *TCP channel* and the *HTTP channel*, are provided, and it's also possible to build custom channels.

.NET Remoting provides a TCP channel and an HTTP channel

While not especially simple to create, a custom channel might provide security services such as encryption, use a nonstandard protocol, or perform some other function in a unique way. It's safe to assume, however, that most applications will work happily with one of the two choices built into the .NET Framework.

The TCP channel sends binary information directly over TCP

The TCP channel is the simpler of the two. By default, it serializes and deserializes a call's parameters using the binary formatter described earlier in this chapter, although the SOAP formatter can also be used. Once the parameters have been serialized, they're transmitted directly in TCP packets. Somewhat surprisingly, the TCP channel provides no built-in support for authentication, data encryption, or any other security feature.

The HTTP channel sends SOAP envelopes over HTTP

The second option, the HTTP channel, uses the SOAP formatter by default to serialize and deserialize a call's parameters. Rather than sending those parameters directly over TCP, they're sent as SOAP requests and responses embedded in HTTP. It's also possible to use the binary formatter with the HTTP channel, which can be very useful. The binary formatter is more efficient than the SOAP formatter, so if the .NET Framework is on both sides of the communication, this option makes sense. For applications that need distributed security, the HTTP channel can use the security options provided by Internet Information Services (IIS). In this case, one possibility is to use the Secure Sockets Layer (SLL) protocol with HTTP, an option sometimes referred to as HTTPS.

Which channel is best depends on the situation

Deciding which channel to use depends on your goals. If the communication is entirely within an organization's intranet—if no firewalls will be traversed—use the fast and simple TCP channel. If the communication must go through firewalls, however, as do most packets sent on the Internet, use the HTTP channel. Although it's a bit less efficient, riding on HTTP means passing through port 80, the only port that virtually all firewalls leave open. Also, if the goal is to provide a standard Web service whose clients might not be based on the .NET Framework, the HTTP channel is the only .NET Remoting option you can use (although you might also choose to use the support for Web services provided by ASP.NET).

It's also possible to use different kinds of channels from the same app domain. This allows clients to communicate with remote objects using the mechanism that's most appropriate for each one. A single client, for instance, might use the more efficient TCP channel to talk to an object within the firewall while also invoking methods in an object across the Internet via the HTTP channel.

Creating and Destroying Remote Objects

One of the most challenging issues in designing a remoting technology is determining what options to support for creating remote objects, referred to as *activation*. .NET Remoting provides three options, each of which is illustrated in Figure 5-8.

.NET Remoting provides three styles of activation for remote objects

- **Single-call objects:** A new instance of the class is created for each call from each client and then is destroyed (that is, made available for garbage collection) when the call ends.

- **Singleton objects:** Only one instance of the class is created on a given machine, and that same instance handles all calls made by all clients to that class on this machine.

- **Client-activated objects:** A separate instance of the class is created for each client that wishes to use it and then is destroyed only when that client is finished with it.

Regardless of which option is chosen, the server will create each new object on its own thread. Also, any object that will be accessed from outside its app domain must be an MBR object, which means that the class must inherit from MarshalByRefObject. These similarities notwithstanding,

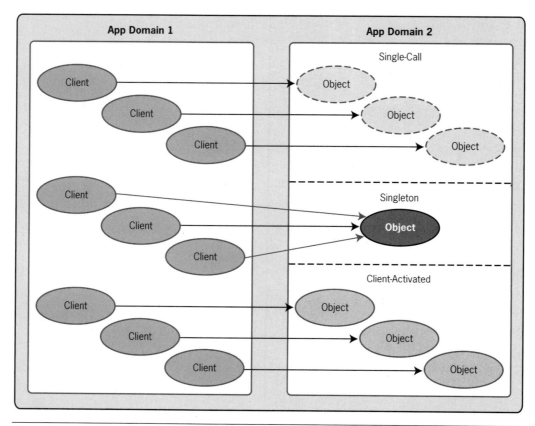

Figure 5-8   Objects accessed via .NET Remoting can be single-call, singleton, or client-activated.

however, each of these options varies in who creates the object, how the object is destroyed, as well as in other ways. Accordingly, each is worthy of its own short discussion.

Single-Call Objects

A new single-call object is created for each call and then is destroyed when the call ends

As the name suggests, single-call objects exist only for the life of one method call from one client. A new instance is created for each new call, and that instance is destroyed when the call ends. This model, typical of the way Web applications work, means that the object can't maintain any internal state between method calls since a new instance is created for each call. It works well with a load-balanced set of server machines, however, where each request might be handled by a different machine. Since the object stores no in-memory state, using different machines for a sequence of requests is not a problem.

To expose a single-call object to clients in other app domains, a server must register the object's type with the .NET Remoting infrastructure. There are two ways for servers to do this. One possibility is to perform the registration explicitly by calling methods provided by classes in System.Runtime.Remoting and its subordinate namespaces. For example, a server process can specify a channel that clients can use to access the single-call object by calling the RegisterChannel method of the ChannelServices class, found in the namespace System.Runtime.Remoting.Channels. Next, the server can call the RegisterWellKnownServiceType method of the RemotingConfiguration class, contained in System.Runtime.Remoting. The server specifies several things on this call, including the type being registered, the mode (which in this case is SingleCall), and the URL at which this object can be found.

Single-call objects must be registered with the .NET Remoting infrastructure

A second (and usually better) way for a server to register a single-call type is to specify the desired options in a configuration file and then tell the remoting infrastructure to read this file by passing the file's name as a parameter on a call to RemotingConfiguration's Configure method. This allows changing details of the exposed type, such as the URL at which it can be found, without recompiling the server code. However it's done, registering a type doesn't actually create an instance of that type. No running instance is created until it's absolutely necessary, as described later in this section.

Once a server is running and has registered an appropriate type for a single-call object, a client can invoke methods on that object. A client has two choices for how it does this. The first lets the client use the standard new operator provided by CLR-based

A client can use the new operator to access a single-call object

languages such as C# and VB.NET. With this option, the client application first tells the .NET Framework's remoting infrastructure various things, such as what channel to use, the type of the remote object, and a URL at which that object can be found. As with the server, this can be done either by using explicit calls or by referencing a configuration file. Note that to access a remote object, the client must know the URL at which it can be found (there's no built-in support for using a directory service such as Active Directory to learn this information). Alternatively, rather than explicitly passing the remoting infrastructure the information required to access the remote object, a client can specify this information in a configuration file, just like the server. Whichever approach a developer chooses, the client code can now create instances of the remote object using the new operator.

A client can also use Activator.GetObject to access a single-call object

If a developer is willing to forgo the relative convenience of using the standard new operator, she can use another approach for accessing a remote single-call object. Rather than setting up the configuration information and then calling new, a client can instead call the Activator class's GetObject method. The parameters to this call include the type of the object to be accessed and the URL at which the object can be found. Instead of specifying these separately, as in the previous case, they're passed directly on this call.

In either case, the server actually creates the single-call object

Whichever choice is used, however, neither one actually creates an instance of the remote object. Instead, single-call objects are server-activated, which means that the server creates an instance of the object only when a method call actually arrives. And because they're single-call objects, the object is destroyed after the call completes.

Singleton Objects

One singleton object handles all client requests for a particular class

Like single-call objects, singleton objects are activated by the server. Accordingly, the steps required for the server to register and the client to access a singleton object are similar to those just described for a single-call object. The only difference is that the server specifies a mode of Singleton instead of SingleCall on its call to RemotingConfiguration.RegisterWellKnownServiceType or in the configuration file. On the client, the code is exactly the same as with single-call objects.

The behavior of the object is not the same, however. Unlike a single-call object, which gets destroyed after each method call, a singleton object stays active until its (configurable) lifetime expires. Since a singleton object isn't destroyed between calls, it can maintain state internally. Yet because the same instance is accessed by all clients that use this singleton, that state is potentially accessible by any of these clients.

Singleton objects can maintain state between calls, unlike single-call objects

If another client makes a call on a singleton class after the running instance of that class has died, a new instance will be created. This new instance will handle all calls from all clients until its lifetime expires. Note, however, that for a singleton object accessible at a given URL, there is never more than one instance of the class active at any time.

Client-Activated Objects

Even though a client can use the new operator to "create" an instance of a single-call or singleton object, the server doesn't really create this instance until the first method call from the client arrives. This is why these two choices are called *server-activated:* The server is in charge of determining when activation occurs. *Client-activated* objects, by contrast, are explicitly created when the client requests it. The server still does the actual creation, of course, since that's where the object is running—the name is something of a misnomer. Still, the distinction between client-activated objects and the two types of server-activated objects is significant. The most important difference is that with client-activated objects, each client gets its own object instance, and each object can maintain internal state specific to its client between method calls—the object isn't destroyed after each call. Instead, as described later in this

Each client gets its own instance of a client-activated object

section, each client-activated object has a lease that determines when the object is destroyed.

A client can create a client-activated object using the new operator or Activator.CreateInstance

Just as with the first two types of remotely accessible objects, the server must register the type before the client can access it. As before, this can be done either through explicit calls or via a configuration file. To create the object, the client can also make explicit calls, much like the previous cases, or rely on a configuration file. In either case, the client can use either the new operator or make an explicit call to the CreateInstance method provided by the Activator class. (GetObject can't be used with client-activated objects.) Both of these directly contact the server, which then creates an instance of the specified client-activated type. All calls made by the client to this object will be handled by this instance, and each client that creates a client-activated object of this type will have its own instance.

One problem remains: When is a client-activated object destroyed? With single-call and singleton objects, the server decides when to destroy the object. With client-activated objects, however, the server can't destroy the object until it knows the client is finished using it. Theoretically, the client could tell the server when it's done with the object, but what happens if the client fails unexpectedly, or just forgets to do this? The server could wind up with objects that no longer have clients yet will never be destroyed.

A client-activated object is destroyed when its lease expires

To avoid this problem, each client-activated object has a lease assigned to it.[5] The lease controls how long an object can remain in existence. A client can set an object's lease time when that object is created, or an administrator can control default lease times. Optionally, each method call from a client can reset the lease timer to zero. If an object's lease time elapses,

---

5. In fact, leasing is used to control the lifetime of all remotely accessed MBR objects, including those passed as parameters.

the lease manager in the app domain that contains this object contacts any *sponsors* of the object. If any of these sponsors wishes to renew the lease, the object's lifetime is extended. If not, the object can be marked for garbage collection. Clients can also explicitly extend the lease of an object or even set it to infinity, ensuring that the server won't destroy it prematurely.

Remotely activating and accessing objects is inherently nontrivial. Is it better to provide many options, running the risk of making the technology too complex to use? Or should the design stay simple, supporting only the most common scenarios? .NET Remoting aims for a middle ground, offering built-in services for common situations while still allowing enough complexity to address more advanced applications. Pleasing everybody is hard, but this technology offers enough choice to please at least most of the people most of the time.

.NET Remoting provides a diverse group of options

.NET Remoting vs. DCOM

Until the arrival of .NET, Microsoft's primary protocol for intelligent communication between systems was DCOM. DCOM has certainly had some success, so why replace it? How is .NET Remoting better than DCOM?

First of all, DCOM assumes that both sides of the communication are implemented as COM objects. Because COM is no longer the fundamental technology on which applications are built in the .NET world, it's not surprising that DCOM has also been relegated to legacy status. Just as important, though, the world has changed since DCOM was designed. Intranets, DCOM's forte, are still important but so is access across the Internet, an area where DCOM has severe problems. Also, Microsoft's view of the world has at last expanded to include other vendors, something that DCOM's strong focus on Windows didn't allow.

At a more technical level, there are many differences between DCOM and .NET Remoting. For example, DCOM includes a way to launch a new server process automatically on the first request from a client, while .NET Remoting allows this only with IIS-based applications using the HTTP channel. DCOM relies on frequent pinging of clients to manage the lifetime of remote objects, an artifact of COM's reference counting mechanism. .NET Remoting uses a simpler and more efficient leasing scheme. Also, for people who delight in building their own infrastructure, the ability to add custom channels, custom formatters for serialization, and other low-level modifications to .NET Remoting is wonderful. DCOM is much more of a closed system, offering little in the way of extensibility. And too, developers must do special things to .NET objects to make them accessible remotely, such as inheriting from MarshalByRefObject. DCOM allows accessing vanilla COM objects—no modifications required—although getting the configuration details right is often a challenge.

Finally, one of the biggest differences in the two technologies is the approach each takes to distributed security. DCOM is a very secure technology. In fact, its strong emphasis on security is perhaps the most challenging thing about using it, since configuring DCOM correctly is not simple. If DCOM is at one end of the security scale, however, .NET Remoting is at the other. The HTTP channel allows access to IIS-based security, but the TCP channel has no built-in security services whatsoever. Given that this channel is designed for use on intranets, where the Kerberos-based services of a Windows domain are readily available, this omission is surprising. (In fact, I'd be surprised if Kerberos support isn't added in the next release of the .NET Framework or sooner.)

DCOM was a reasonably effective (although often complex to use) technology for the problem it addressed. But the problems we're interested in change, and so the technologies we use to address them must change too. DCOM had its day, but for the most part, that day is over.

Enterprise Services: System.EnterpriseServices

The types in System.Enterprise-Services allow access to COM+ services

Modern multitier applications often locate the bulk of their business logic in the middle tier. Much of the time, writing this logic with a technology such as ASP.NET is perfectly adequate. In some cases, however, especially for applications that need to

be very scalable and require features such as distributed transactions, more is required. Prior to .NET, the Microsoft technology that provided these services was known as COM+. With
the advent of the .NET Framework, those services are still available to CLR-based applications. In fact, the services themselves
haven't changed at all, but two things about them have: how
they're accessed and what they're called. Now commonly referred to as Enterprise Services, the traditional COM+ services
for building robust, scalable applications are also usable by
applications written on the .NET Framework.

Through the classes in the System.EnterpriseServices namespace, all COM+ services that are available to Windows DNA
applications on Windows 2000 are also available to .NET
Framework–based applications. Unlike most of the .NET
Framework, however, the code that provides COM+ services
was not rewritten as managed code. Microsoft tells us that this
rewrite will happen eventually, but in the Framework's first
release, the classes in System.EnterpriseServices provide a
wrapper around the existing implementation that allows managed objects access to these services in a natural way.

*All traditional
COM+ services are
available*

For a class to use COM+ services, that class must inherit from
EnterpriseServices.ServicedComponent. Because of this, a class
using these services is referred to as a *serviced component*.
Serviced components have access to the full range of services
COM+ provides, including the following:

*Classes that use
COM+ services are
known as serviced
components*

- Support for (possibly distributed) transactions

- Just-in-time activation (JITA), which optimizes server resources by allowing objects to exist only when they're
  needed

- Object pooling, which allows instances of a class to be
  pooled and reused rather than being destroyed and
  recreated

- Role-based authorization services that allow COM+ to verify a client's role and then grant services only to clients in specific roles

Serviced components can also use COM+ services that aren't directly related to building robust server applications, such as queued components, which is effectively an API to Microsoft Message Queuing (MSMQ); an event service; and others.[6] The key point is that .NET Enterprise Services allows managed code to use all COM+ services, but those services are unchanged—the .NET Framework doesn't add any new features in this area.

Traditional COM+ uses attributes to specify what services an application needs

One of the innovations brought by COM+ (or more correctly, by Microsoft Transaction Server, the original incarnation of this technology) was the ability to control what services a component received by setting attributes in a configuration file. To control how transactions are used, for example, a developer using COM+ can set a transaction attribute to Required, indicating that all methods in this component should be run within a transaction. When the component is executed, COM+ reads this attribute and provides the requested transaction support. In traditional COM+, these attributes are stored in something called the COM+ catalog, and they're typically set using the COM+ Explorer, a configuration tool designed for this purpose.

Serviced components use the CLR's built-in attributes to specify what services an application needs

In the .NET Framework, however, attributes are supported directly. As described in Chapter 3, every assembly can have extra metadata represented as attributes. Also, attribute values can be set in the source code of a CLR-based application—there's no need for a separate configuration tool—and those values can be read at runtime using reflection. Built-in support for attributes matches well with how COM+ provides its ser-

---

6. For a more detailed look at the services provided by COM+ in Windows 2000, see Chapter 8 of my earlier book *Understanding Windows 2000 Distributed Services* (Microsoft Press, 2000).

vices, and so .NET's Enterprise Services exploit this feature of the CLR. Developers are now able to specify how COM+ services should be used by including attributes directly in their code. And because it's sometimes useful to be able to change a component's attributes after the assembly that contains it has been installed, the COM+ Explorer can still be used to set or modify a component's attributes if desired.

Here's a simple VB.NET class that shows how attributes can be used to control the use of COM+ transactions:

```
<Transaction(TransactionOption.Required)> _
    Public Class BankAccount
        Inherits ServicedComponent

    <AutoComplete()> _
    Public Sub Deposit(Account As Integer, _
                          Amount As Decimal)
        ' Add Amount to Account
    End Sub

    <AutoComplete()> _
    Public Sub Withdrawal(Account As Integer, _
                            Amount As Decimal)
        ' Subtract Amount from Account
    End Sub
End Class
```

This class, called BankAccount, inherits from ServicedComponent, as is required for any CLR-based class that wishes to use COM+ services. The class definition is also preceded with an attribute indicating that this class uses the Required setting for transactions. This means that whenever a client calls one of the class's methods, COM+ will automatically wrap the work done by that method in the all-or-nothing embrace of a transaction.

The two methods in this simple class, Deposit and Withdrawal, each begins with the AutoComplete attribute (and since this is just an example, the code for these methods is omitted). This attribute indicates that if the method returns an exception, the serviced component will vote to abort the transaction of which it's a part. If the method completes normally, however, this

Attributes can be used to specify a class's transactional requirements

component will vote to commit the transaction to which it belongs. Note that different attributes are applied at different levels. The Transaction attribute, for example, can be applied only to a class—it can't be set per method—while AutoComplete can be applied only on a per-method basis. If the developer of this application wished to add a method to check the balance, she might well choose to put this method in some other class. Adding it to the BankAccount class would require the method to use a transaction, which isn't generally necessary for this kind of simple read operation so it would needlessly hurt performance.

Attributes can also be used to specify the use of other COM+ services

Many other attributes are available for controlling aspects of a serviced component's behavior. For example, the JustInTimeActivation attribute allows turning just-in-time activation on and off (although this feature is automatically turned on for classes that use transactions), while the ObjectPooling attribute controls whether pooling is used and, if it is, how large the pool will be. Other available attributes set application-wide options such as the name of the application as seen by COM+.

The methods in the traditional IObjectContext interface are still available

In standard COM+, an interface called IObjectContext contains fundamental methods that components can use. Perhaps the most important of these are SetComplete and SetAbort, the two methods that allow a component to cast its vote in a transaction if the autocomplete option isn't used. In .NET Enterprise Services, these same methods are available through a class called ContextUtil. If a transactional method wishes to control its commitment behavior explicitly, it can do so by directly calling these methods.

COM+ has not been completely rewritten as managed code

As mentioned earlier, the implementation of COM+ services is not managed code in the first release of the .NET Framework. In spite of this, serviced components are able to use those services without leaving the managed environment. As Figure 5-9 shows, key COM+ services such as transactions are provided using context information maintained by COM+ itself in un-

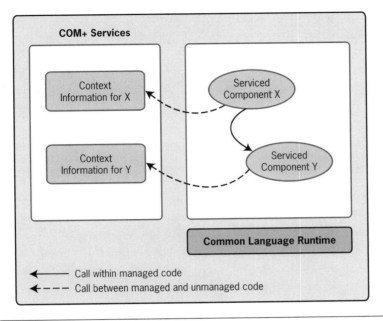

Figure 5-9   COM+ maintains context information for serviced components, allowing it to provide services across the managed/unmanaged boundary.

managed code. When this context is accessed, such as when a serviced component votes to commit or abort a transaction, that request flows across the boundary between managed and unmanaged code. Interactions among serviced components, however, remain completely within the managed environment provided by the CLR. Since crossing into unmanaged code incurs a slight performance penalty, this ability to remain almost entirely within the managed space is a good thing.

Enterprise Services also has a few more artifacts of its foundation in unmanaged code. For example, when a serviced component is accessed remotely, that access relies on DCOM rather than on .NET Remoting. Similarly, serviced components must have entries in the Windows registry, like traditional COM+ components but unlike other .NET classes. These entries can be created and

Remote access to serviced components is via DCOM

updated automatically by the Enterprise Services infrastructure—there's no need to create them manually—but requiring them at all betrays this technology's COM foundations. It's likely that all of these limitations will change in a future release of the .NET Framework when COM+ is completely rewritten in managed code.

Interoperability: System.Runtime.InteropServices

Software using pre-.NET technologies will not just disappear

Windows DNA is a successful group of technologies. Lots of applications that were built using COM, Active Server Pages, COM+, and the rest of the DNA family exist. Many of these applications play an important role in running businesses, so they're certain to remain in use for at least the next few years. No matter how successful the .NET Framework is, the Windows DNA technologies that preceded it are not going away anytime soon.

The types in System.Runtime.-InteropServices allow interoperability with existing software

Given the huge investment Microsoft's customers have made in these applications, the .NET Framework must provide some way for new applications to connect with them. Just as important, the Framework must provide an effective way for managed code to access existing DLLs that weren't built using COM and to invoke the raw services provided by the underlying operating system. Solutions to all of these problems are provided by the classes in the System.Runtime.InteropServices namespace.

Accessing COM Objects

A key aspect of interoperability is mapping from COM types to CLR types

The problem of interoperating with COM objects is in some ways similar to an issue we've seen earlier in this chapter: translating from one type system to another. Just as mapping between the CLR's type system and that defined by XML is problematic, so is mapping between the CLR type system and that defined by COM. You might expect mapping to COM to be a bit easier, since both the CLR and COM are Microsoft-owned

Rebuilding the World

By and large, the .NET Framework is a beautiful thing. It's well designed, consistent, and quite elegant. Microsoft has completely rethought what an application platform should look like and then redesigned the developer's world from the ground up. (What a once-in-a-lifetime treat for its designers: Build a new development environment, more or less from scratch, the way *you* think it should be.) The breadth of the company's ambition is breathtaking, and the degree to which it has succeeded is very, very impressive.

But it's not perfect. Nothing is perfect.

Rebuilding the world is a lot of work, and it's unreasonable to expect anybody to finish the job in the first release. Still, it is surprising that the implementation of COM+ services in the .NET Framework class library is just a wrapper around the existing code. COM+ is certainly a large piece of code, yet given the scale of the .NET effort, it's not really all that big. And there are some corollaries of this decision that are downright ugly, such as supporting remote access to serviced components only via DCOM.

Completely rewriting COM+ would have allowed Microsoft to rethink the way its services were provided rather than just exposing the existing programming model to managed code. While this rethinking may appear in the future, Microsoft has also committed itself to support this version indefinitely. The services provided by COM+ are important, and so leaving them in their initial form is unfortunate.

Yet while the Framework's current imperfections are sometimes annoying, they're hardly deadly, and they're likely to be fixed in a future release. Whatever its rough edges today, the .NET Framework is a remarkable piece of work. Its creators should be proud of what they've produced.

technologies. Yet the truth is that even though Microsoft owns it, COM is frozen in stone. The millions of lines of existing COM-based code in the world won't change to accommodate the new type system of the CLR, so the .NET Framework's solution for COM interoperability must adapt itself to the reality of the installed base.

Mapping between COM and managed objects can be simple, but it can also be complex

Doing this can be simple. In some cases, mapping from a COM interface to a CLR type is straightforward. It can also be quite difficult, however, especially when the COM interface involved uses complex types. While it's virtually always possible to map the two together in some way, it isn't always easy. To make even difficult mappings possible, the classes in System.Runtime.InteropServices provide very fine-grained control over how the mapping is done as well as many, many options. While most people won't use most of these options most of the time, it's still good to know that they're available.

Interoperability lets COM code and managed code each see the other as being like themselves

The fundamental model for interoperation between managed code and COM-based code is that each side sees the other in the form it expects: Managed code sees COM-based code as managed types, while COM-based code sees managed code as COM objects. How this looks is shown in Figure 5-10. To provide this illusion, the .NET Framework relies on two kinds of wrappers. One, known as a *runtime callable wrapper (RCW),* allows managed code to call a COM object. The other, a *COM callable wrapper (CCW),* allows COM code to access managed code.

Tools create wrappers for COM objects

But where does the information needed to create these wrappers come from? Managed code sees the world in terms of assemblies, so to access a COM object as managed code, an assembly that mimics the COM class must exist. Furthermore, this assembly must contain metadata that accurately reflects the COM class's interfaces. To create this interoperability assembly, the .NET Framework provides a tool called Tlbimp, also known as the Type Library Importer. The input to this tool is a COM type library, and the output is an assembly that contains metadata for the CLR analogs of the COM types in the type library.

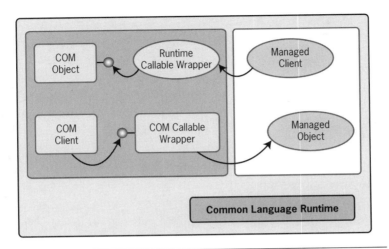

Figure 5-10   The .NET Framework's COM interoperability services can make a COM object look like managed code and managed code look like a COM object.

Once this assembly has been created, managed code can treat the library's COM classes just like any other managed code. When the managed code creates an instance of the class, the RCW actually creates the COM object. When the managed code invokes a method, the RCW makes a corresponding method invocation on the COM object. If an error occurs and the COM method returns an error HRESULT, as COM requires, the RCW automatically turns this into an exception that can be caught by the managed code. And when the managed code is finished using the object, it can behave just as it does when using any other managed object. The RCW will decrement the COM object's reference count before it is itself destroyed by the CLR's garbage collector.

The wrapper maps between COM's behavior and what managed code expects

When a COM client uses a managed class, the same kinds of things happen in the opposite direction. Rather than producing an assembly from a type library, the developer can now produce a type library from an assembly. The Type Library

Tools also create wrappers for managed objects

Exporter tool, known as Tlbexp, provides one way to do this. Also, because COM uses the registry to determine which code should be loaded for a particular class, assemblies that will be accessed by COM clients must have appropriate registry entries. The Assembly Registration Tool, Regasm, can be used to do this and optionally to register the assembly's generated type library as well. When a COM client creates and uses an instance of a managed class, translations between the two worlds are performed as before, but this time they're done by the CCW rather than the RCW.

A developer can customize the mapping between these two environments

All of this sounds simple and straightforward, and it often is. Yet what's not been addressed so far is the process of converting between the CLR type system and the COM type system. Much as with .NET Remoting, data must be marshaled between the two environments by the wrappers. Default mappings are defined, and if those defaults work, using code from the other world is simple. Marshaling an integer, for example, is straightforward, since a value of this type is the same in both environments. If the default mappings aren't appropriate, however, a developer's life gets more complex. What should a CLR string map to in the COM world, for example? COM has more than one string format, and it's not always obvious which one should be used. To control this and other marshaling choices, a developer can use the MarshalAs attribute to indicate the choice she prefers. Figuring out the right thing to do isn't always easy, but the fine-grained control the types in this namespace provide at least makes it possible.

Calls between managed and unmanaged code are expensive

One last point worth noting is that making calls across the boundary between managed and unmanaged code is noticeably more expensive than making calls solely within either environment. Marshaling data between the two takes time; writing managed code that interoperates with unmanaged code has performance implications. It's a good idea to do as much work as possible on each call across this boundary. If each one does only a small amount of work, an application that makes a large number of calls between the two worlds is unlikely to perform especially well.

Accessing Non-COM DLLs

While much of the existing code a .NET Framework application needs to use is accessible as COM classes, much of it isn't. Plenty of useful DLLs that don't use COM have been created. One important example of this is the Win32 API, exposed as a set of DLLs that allow direct access to Windows services. To allow managed code to call functions in these DLLs, the .NET Framework provides what are called *platform invoke* services, a phrase that's commonly shortened to just *PInvoke*.

PInvoke allows managed code to call existing DLLs

To use these services, a developer must specify the name of some DLL he wishes to use, the entry point to be called, the parameter list, and possibly other information. How this is done varies with the language in use. In VB.NET, for example, the Declare statement is used, while C# relies on an attribute called DllImport. Whichever choice is made, once a DLL function has been appropriately specified, it can be invoked as if it were a function in a managed object. The platform invoke services provide the necessary translations, including marshaling of parameter types, to carry out the call.

System.Runtime.InteropServices is a critically important part of the .NET Framework class library. Although the notion of legacy software is sometimes viewed pejoratively, it has one enormous thing going for it: We know it works. If new code written on the .NET Framework had no way to communicate with the installed base, this new platform would have been much less attractive. The Framework's strong support for interoperability with existing code recognizes this reality, doing its part to smooth the transition to the brave new .NET world.

Interoperability is an essential feature of the .NET Framework

How Many Customers Will Microsoft Lose in the Transition to the .NET Framework?

Suppose you're an organization that has made a substantial investment in Windows DNA. Just as Microsoft wanted you to, you've trained your entire staff in COM and other Windows DNA technologies, and you've built many mission-critical applications on this platform. Microsoft now tells you that you should build new applications in the completely different environment provided by the .NET Framework. Are you happy about this?

Developers may well be happy, because they often like learning the latest technologies. But the people who pay those developers' salaries are likely to be less thrilled. While the .NET Framework offers the potential of better productivity and new kinds of applications, it also incurs some immediate costs, such as retraining an entire development staff. Might the pain of this transition make some existing Microsoft customers bolt to a competing technology?

I doubt it. The only really viable alternative is the Java world, and I don't expect the advent of the .NET Framework to push many organizations into this other camp. For one thing, retraining a Windows DNA developer for the Java environment is likely to be even more expensive then retraining him for the .NET Framework, since few of his current language and operating system skills will apply. Furthermore, Java-based products don't have the built-in support for interoperability with Windows DNA code that is provided by the .NET Framework. By adding strong support for communicating with existing DLLs and COM objects, Microsoft has made migration to its new platform more attractive.

Customers who are unhappy with Microsoft for other reasons, such as poor support, may take this opportunity to switch sides. But because the difficulty and expense of moving from Windows DNA to the .NET Framework are significantly lower than the cost of moving to Java, I doubt we'll see many defections caused purely by this transition in technologies.

Windows GUIs: System.Windows.Forms

It can sometimes seem as if browser-based applications have taken over the world. While developers once devoted a great deal of time to getting the Windows GUI right, they now also sweat technical bullets over details of HTML and JavaScript. Browsers have become the new default interface for a whole generation of software.

Browser interfaces are very common today

But Windows GUIs still matter. The ascendancy of browsers notwithstanding, applications that directly access pixels on a screen are not going away. Recognizing this fact, the designers of the .NET Framework provided a new set of classes that allow CLR-based applications to build Windows GUIs. Contained in the System.Windows.Forms namespace, these classes are commonly referred to as Windows Forms.

Windows interfaces remain important

Building GUIs Using Windows Forms

Stripped to its essentials, an application that presents a GUI displays a form on the screen and then waits for input from the user. This input is typically processed by a message loop, which passes the input on to the appropriate place. For example, when the user clicks a button or hits a key or moves the mouse, events that are sent to the form the user is accessing are generated. The form and any code attached to it handle these events and then write output to the screen.

The typical model for a GUI is a form with code that responds to events

In Windows Forms, every form is an instance of the Form class, while the message loop that accepts and distributes events is provided by a class called Application. Using these and other classes in System.Windows.Forms, a developer can create a single-document interface (SDI) application, able to display only one document at a time, or a multiple-document interface (MDI) application, able to display more than one document simultaneously.

Windows Forms follows the traditional model

Forms have properties	Each instance of the Form class has a large set of properties that control how that form looks on the screen. Among them are Font, which indicates what font should be used for any text displayed on the form; Size, which controls the form's initial on-screen size; and nearly a hundred more properties. Developers can set these properties to customize a form's appearance and behavior.
Forms can contain Windows Forms controls	Forms commonly contain other classes called *Windows Forms controls*. Each of these controls typically displays some kind of output, accepts some input from the user, or both. The System.Windows.Forms namespace provides a large set of controls, many of which will be familiar to anyone who's built or even used a GUI. The control classes available in this namespace include Button, TextBox, CheckBox, RadioButton, ListBox, ComboBox, and many more. Also provided are more complex controls such as OpenFileDialog, which encapsulates the operations that let a user open a file; SaveFileDialog, which encapsulates the operations that let a user save a file; PrintDialog, which encapsulates the operations that let a user print a document; and several others.
Controls have properties	Like a form, each control has properties that can be set to customize its appearance and behavior. Many of these come from System.Windows.Forms.Control, a class from which every control inherits. (In fact, even the Form class inherits from System.Windows.Forms.Control.) The Button control, for example, has a Location property that determines where the button will appear relative to its container, a Size property that determines how big the on-screen button will be, and a Text property that controls what text will appear in the button.
Both forms and controls can respond to events	Forms and controls also support events. Some examples of common events include Click, indicating that a mouse click has occurred; GotFocus, indicating that the form or control has been selected by the user; and KeyPress, indicating that a key

has been pressed. In fact, all of these events and several more are defined in the base Control class from which all Windows Forms controls inherit. A control can also support unique events that have meaning only to it.

A developer can create code to handle events received by a form or control. Called an *event handler,* this code determines what happens when the event occurs. Handling events relies on delegates, the type provided by the CLR for passing references to methods in a type-safe way.

Code that responds to events is called an event handler

Here's a very simple C# example that illustrates the basic mechanics of forms, controls, and event handlers. While this example works, some things are simpler than they really should be, so you shouldn't necessarily view this as paradigmatic for your own code.

```
public class ExampleForm : System.Windows.Forms.Form
{
    private System.Windows.Forms.Button myButton;

    public ExampleForm()
    {
        Text = "An Example Form";
        myButton = new System.Windows.Forms.Button();
        myButton.Location = new
            System.Drawing.Point(50, 50);
        myButton.Size = new System.Drawing.Size(175,
            50);
        myButton.Text = "Click Here";
        myButton.Click += new
            System.EventHandler(myButton_Click);
        Controls.Add(myButton);

    }

    private void myButton_Click(object sender,
        System.EventArgs e)
    {
        System.Windows.Forms.MessageBox.Show(
            "Button clicked");
    }
}
```

```
class DisplayForm
{
    static void Main()
    {
        System.Windows.Forms.Application.Run(new
            ExampleForm());
    }
}
```

This example begins by declaring the class ExampleForm. Like all forms, this one inherits from System.Windows.Forms.Form. (This code contains no using statements, partly to make it shorter and partly to make clear where the various types can be found in the .NET Framework class library.) The ExampleForm class then declares a private instance of the System.Windows.Forms.Button class, one of the controls mentioned earlier, called myButton.

The next thing to appear is the constructor for the ExampleForm class. The constructor is automatically run whenever an instance of this class is created, and in this example, the constructor's job is to initialize appropriately the form and the control it contains. The first step in that initialization is to set the form's Text property. The constructor then creates an instance of the Button class and sets several of its properties. Those properties include Location, Size, and Text, all of which were described earlier. Once this is done, the constructor sets up an event handler for the Click event on myButton. This is done using EventHandler, a standard delegate provided in the System namespace. Finally, the myButton control is added to the control collection for this form, something that must be done to allow the control's output to be displayed.

Following the ExampleForm class's constructor is the method that will handle the Click event on myButton. By convention, the format of this method's name is the name of the control followed by an underscore and the name of the event: myButton_Click. This isn't required, however, and in fact any name can be used. The standard arguments to the event handler method allow learning more about the event, but they're not used in this simple example. Instead, the event handler just calls the Windows Forms MessageBox method to output a simple message.

The example ends with a class containing just one method—Main—which itself has only one statement, a call to the Run method of the System.Windows.Forms.Application class. This method provides a message loop that accepts and processes events. Passing it an instance of a form, as in this case, causes it to make that form visible when the application runs.

The output of this program is shown in Figure 5-11. As you would expect, it consists of a single form containing a button with the text "Click Here". The figure shows how things look after a user has clicked the button, causing the event handler for the Click event to run. The result is the message box that appears to the right of the form.

It's certainly possible to hand-code GUIs using the types in System.Windows.Forms, but only a masochist would do it.

Visual Studio.NET allows creating forms interactively

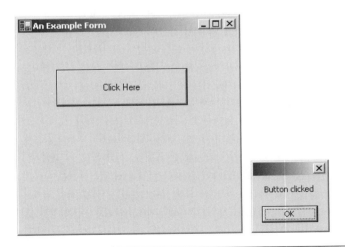

Figure 5-11   The simple application described in this section shows a form containing a button control; then it displays a message box when the button is clicked.

While it's useful to see a simple example to get a sense of how the mechanism works, the vast majority of Windows GUIs will be created using Visual Studio.NET or some other tool. Visual Studio.NET provides a full-featured designer that allows dragging controls onto a form, directly setting their properties, and adding code to handle events. The full implementation is then generated automatically by this tool. Creating a GUI in this way is faster, more accurate (since you can see what you're doing), and much less error-prone.

Windows Forms Controls

Developers can create custom Windows Forms controls

Windows Forms controls are a very useful way to package reusable chunks of functionality. Although the .NET Framework class library provides a large set of controls, the inventiveness of developers knows no bounds. Accordingly, the .NET Framework makes it straightforward to write custom Windows Forms controls. As already mentioned, every Windows Forms control must inherit either directly or indirectly from the class Control. It's also possible to inherit from one of the standard controls provided with the .NET Framework class library, basing a new control on existing functionality, or to combine two controls into one new one. Whatever choice the control's creator makes, a good chunk of the work is done for her. Because the new control can be built on what the .NET Framework already provides, building one is significantly easier than it was in the Windows DNA era.

Windows DNA applications can use COM-based components known as ActiveX controls. Despite being fairly complicated to create, huge numbers of these are available from third parties. Many containers capable of running ActiveX controls also exist, including Internet Explorer and the Windows shell. Given this large installed base of both ActiveX controls and containers for those controls, there must be some way for Windows Forms controls to interoperate with this world.

There is a way. To use an ActiveX control in a Windows Form environment, the ActiveX Control Importer, Aximp, can be used to create a wrapper for the control. As with other parts of the .NET Framework's support for COM interoperability, this tool reads the ActiveX control's type library and produces an assembly containing analogous metadata. To allow a Windows Forms control to be used in a container that expects only ActiveX controls, the Windows Forms control can inherit from the class UserControl. This class implements everything required to make the Windows Forms control look like an ActiveX control and thus be hostable in the many ActiveX control containers that exist today. Also, because ActiveX controls are COM-based, any Windows Forms control used in this way must have an entry in the Windows registry, just as in the COM interoperability scenarios described earlier in this chapter.

Windows Forms controls can emulate ActiveX controls

In Windows DNA, Visual Basic and C++ had completely different approaches to building GUIs. Because of this, ActiveX controls were based on COM, which allowed them to work with both languages. The predictable result was complexity. Windows Forms sweeps away the accumulation of GUI technologies that have built up on the Windows platform, replacing them with a single consistent approach. While you may lament the effort required to learn this new approach, there is certainly some appeal in finally having just one way to build Windows user interfaces.

Windows Forms provides a common mechanism for creating GUIs in any CLR-based language

Conclusion

This lengthy chapter has taken a tour of the .NET Framework class library, making the longest stops at the most important points in the journey. When you move to the .NET Framework, learning a new language will surely take some time. Yet neither C# nor VB.NET is all that different from other programming languages, so most developers won't have too much

Understanding the .NET Framework class library will take time

trouble learning these new tools. Learning to use the .NET Framework class library will probably take longer. There is just so much here, including some new features, such as reflection, and new versions of older Windows DNA technologies, such as ADO.NET. Probably no developer will need to master the entire library, but everybody will need to learn some parts.

Every Windows developer will need to learn the .NET Framework

The good news is that by providing a standard solution to many common problems, Microsoft has given us a large set of code that we'll never need to write again. While it will surely take some effort to master the relevant parts of this new technology, we should receive substantial benefits. And however you feel about it, the .NET Framework is the future for Windows-oriented software developers. Your choice isn't whether to learn it, but when.

6

Accessing Data: ADO.NET

Working with data—searching, updating, and processing it—is one of the fundamental tasks of software. Today, much of that data is commonly stored in some kind of database management system (DBMS), usually a relational DBMS. Developers need some mechanism that allows their applications to access this information. In Windows DNA, a group of COM classes called ActiveX Data Objects (ADO) solves this problem. In the .NET Framework, the solution is a radically updated version of ADO called ADO.NET.

ADO.NET provides access to stored data

Like everything else in the .NET Framework class library, ADO.NET is nothing more than a group of types, all of which reside in the System.Data namespace. These types are used by client applications that need to work with stored data, and they allow access to that data in various useful ways. As before, the most common need is to work with relational data, such as tables stored in Oracle or SQL Server, and so much of ADO.NET focuses here. Yet as described in Chapter 5, data defined using XML gets more important every day. Recognizing this, ADO.NET's creators also added support for working with

ADO.NET allows access to both relational and XML-defined data

Oh, No, Not Another Data Access Interface!

ODBC, OLE DB, ADO: The list goes on and on. If you've been working in the Microsoft world for a while, you've surely encountered some of these access technologies (and perhaps others—this is not a complete list). Each of them was at one time presented as the optimal way to access data, especially data in a relational database system. Yet today, each of them is a legacy technology, which means that while new applications shouldn't in general use them, somebody still has to support the old applications that do use them.

Why does Microsoft do this? Why can't the people in Redmond make up their minds in this terrifically important area? After all, the dominant database model hasn't changed in 20 years—a relation today is pretty much the same as it was then—so why should the way we access relational data be so volatile?

There are many answers. For one thing, the interface between object-oriented software and relational databases is inherently a messy place. With few exceptions, the database people never bought into objects as a core abstraction. There are good reasons for this—objects work much better for creating software than they do for storing data—but the result is a mismatch of models and a plethora of pain. In its attempts to make this difficult interface as useful as possible, Microsoft has taken a few wrong turns.

A more obvious reason for creating a new data access interface is that ADO, the currently dominant choice, is based on COM, while the .NET Framework is not. .NET Framework applications can use ADO through the Framework's COM interoperability features, but doing this is relatively slow. It makes more sense to offer a data access mechanism built solely with managed code, which is exactly what ADO.NET provides.

Another reason for the instability in data access interfaces is that the problem being addressed changes regularly. A primary goal of ODBC was to let applications written in C and C++ issue SQL queries against a database system. These applications were either running on just one system or were spread across two machines in a two-tier client/server configuration. Yet today the most common scenario is a browser talking to business logic on a middle-tier server. In this kind of application, it's this middle-tier logic that accesses data and then passes it across a network to the browser. ODBC didn't address this situation at all, since it provided no way to serialize its results for transmission across a network. ADO addressed it in a way that made some sense inside the firewall but didn't work well on the Internet, especially with browsers other than Internet Explorer. ADO.NET, however, was designed with exactly this style of application in mind. And because the older models are still the right approach for some applications, ADO.NET also allows writing code in a more traditional style.

Finally, new people join development teams at Microsoft all the time, and the existing people move on to other groups or other companies (or they retire at 30, although this looks like less of an issue in these post-bubble years). New people bring new ideas, and as ownership of a technology changes, that technology will also change. I don't believe Microsoft is intentionally making developer's lives difficult, but that has sometimes been the result of the technology churn in data access interfaces. Still, ADO.NET is a clean, attractive, and relatively simple technology for today's applications. All historical confusion aside, it's a good fit for the world of the .NET Framework.

XML documents. This chapter takes a look at what ADO.NET provides for applications built on the .NET Framework.

.NET Data Providers

An application that uses ADO.NET to access data commonly relies on some *.NET data provider,* software able to access a particular source of data such as SQL Server. Figure 6-1 shows how clients, .NET data providers, and DBMSs fit together. The client, written as managed code running on the CLR, can use various .NET data providers to access stored data. Each .NET data provider is also written as managed code, but a data provider might also rely on software that doesn't use the .NET Framework to accomplish its task.

A .NET data provider allows access to stored data, such as data in SQL Server or Oracle

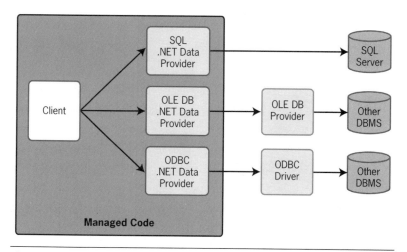

Figure 6-1   Applications using ADO.NET can rely on .NET data providers to access information.

The .NET Framework provides various .NET data providers

The .NET Framework class library includes two .NET data providers:

- **SQL provider:** Written completely as managed code, this .NET data provider can be used to access Microsoft's SQL Server DBMS 7.0 or later. Access to earlier versions of SQL Server requires using another provider option.

- **OLE DB provider:** Traditional ADO applications rely on OLE DB providers for access to data, so several of these providers exist. The OLE DB .NET data provider implements a wrapper around an OLE DB provider, such as those for Oracle or older versions of SQL Server, that lets it be used by .NET Framework applications.

A third option, called the ODBC provider, will also be made available, although it's not officially part of the first .NET Framework class library release. The Open Database Connectivity (ODBC) API is another of the many data access interfaces Microsoft has provided for Windows developers, and applications that use it rely on ODBC drivers to get at stored data. ODBC is even older than ADO, so many, many ODBC drivers exist. The ODBC .NET data provider provides a wrapper around an ODBC driver, allowing managed code to use it for accessing data.

It's conceivable that other .NET data providers, such as a native provider for Oracle, will appear in the future. Doing this would improve performance for clients accessing databases other than SQL Server, because crossing the boundary between managed and unmanaged code burns more cycles than staying completely within the managed environment. Also, it's worth pointing out that .NET Framework applications can still use the traditional ADO interface via the COM interoperability support described in Chapter 5.

.NET data providers built from managed code have the best performance

Each .NET data provider is implemented as a group of types. The primary types that implement the SQL provider are located in the System.Data.SqlClient namespace, while those that implement the OLE DB provider are in System.Data.OleDb. Regardless of which provider you choose, each one offers an analogous set of classes. Figure 6-2 shows the fundamental kinds of objects supported by any .NET data provider. They are as follows:

Each .NET data provider exposes the same core set of classes

- **Connection:** Allows establishing and releasing connections and can also be used to begin transactions.

- **Command:** Allows storing and executing a command, such as a SQL query or stored procedure, and specifying parameters for that command.

- **DataReader:** Provides direct, sequential, read-only access to data in a database.

- **DataAdapter:** Built on a DataReader, this class creates and populates instances of the class DataSet. As described later in this chapter, DataSets allow more flexible access to data than is possible using just a DataReader.

With the exception of DataSet, these names are generic rather than actual class names defined in the .NET Framework class library. There is no DataReader class, for example. Instead, each .NET data provider implements its own version of these classes. The DataReader for the SQL .NET data provider, for example, is implemented by the SqlDataReader class, while that for the OLE DB .NET data provider is implemented by the OleDbDataReader class.

Clients can access data through a DataReader or by using a DataSet

Using these four kinds of objects, a .NET data provider gives clients two options for accessing data. Both use Connections and Commands to interact with a DBMS, but they differ primarily in how a client can work with the result of a query. As Figure 6-2 shows, a client that needs only straightforward one-row-at-a-time access to a query's results can use a DataReader object to read those results. Clients with more complex requirements, such as accessing a query's result in an arbitrary order, filtering that result, combining the results of multiple queries, or

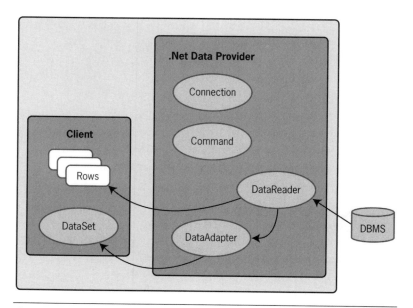

Figure 6-2   A .NET data provider allows clients to access data either directly as rows or through a DataSet.

sending those results across a network, can use a DataAdapter object to retrieve data wrapped in a DataSet. Each of these choices is described next.

Does the .NET Framework Require SQL Server?

Obviously, the answer to this question is no. After all, the OLE DB .NET data provider explicitly supports Microsoft's OLE DB provider for Oracle, which means that .NET Framework applications aren't limited to SQL Server. Still, it's too much to expect Microsoft not to favor its own product. By initially providing a native .NET data provider only for SQL Server, Microsoft is effectively guaranteeing that using its product will give the best performance with .NET Framework applications. And the next release of SQL Server will allow running the CLR natively in the DBMS, much like products such as Oracle that host the Java virtual machine. I'd be surprised to see Oracle or IBM's DB2 add this kind of native CLR support, so going forward it's reasonable to expect that SQL Server will have even more of an edge for .NET Framework applications. As usual, Microsoft technologies work best with other Microsoft technologies. This is generally true for all vendors, but no one does it as consistently or as assertively as Microsoft.

Here's a related issue: Is it possible to write an ADO.NET application that's portable across different DBMSs? After all, one of the reasons for using a common interface such as ADO.NET is to access different vendors' DBMSs in a common way. Yet each .NET data provider implements some parts of this technology differently. For example, the SQL provider's DataReader class is called SqlDataReader, while the OLE DB provider's DataReader class is called OleDbDataReader. A client that explicitly creates and uses an instance of either of these classes will be wedded to just one .NET data provider.

Although it's easy to create a client that works with only one particular provider, there are enough similarities that it's still possible to write code that works across different providers. Both SqlDataReader and OleDbDataReader implement the IDataReader interface, for instance, so code that instantiates and accesses either of these classes purely through this interface will work with either. As usual, writing portable code takes some work, and some DBMS-specific features may be lost, but it can be done.

Direct Access to Data

A client uses a Connection object's Open method to open a connection to a DBMS

Regardless of what approach is used to access data, an ADO.NET client application relies on a connection to the DBMS. The application can explicitly open a connection by calling the Open method of a Connection object. To open a connection to SQL Server, for example, the client invokes this method on an instance of the SqlConnection class. To open a connection to some other database using the OLE DB .NET data provider, the client invokes the Open method on an instance of the OleDbConnection class. In either case, the client must first set the class's ConnectionString property, indicating which database it's interested in and other information.

A client relies on Command objects to issues queries and other DBMS operations

Once a connection exists, a client can issue queries and other commands on it using a Command object. An application can create a Command object by invoking a Connection object's CreateCommand method. Once again, different data providers use different Command object classes: The SQL provider uses SqlCommand, while the OLE DB provider uses OleDbCommand. Whichever is used, both allow specifying a SQL query for a Command object by setting the object's CommandText property.

A Command object provides several options for executing the operation it contains

Once a Command object exists, a client can choose one of several methods this object provides to execute the command it contains. Those methods are as follows:

- **ExecuteReader:** Returns a DataReader that can be used to read the results of the query. A DataReader can access the result of a SQL query one row at a time.

- **ExecuteScalar:** Returns a single value, such as the result from a SQL SUM function. If the result of the query contains more than one value, this method will return the value in the first column of the first row—everything else will be ignored. The value it returns is of the type

System.Object, which means that it can contain a result of any type.

- **ExecuteNonQuery:** Returns no data, but instead sends back the number of rows affected by the query. This method is used with commands that don't return results, such as SQL UPDATEs, INSERTs, and DELETEs.

The SqlCommand class also has another choice, one not provided by OleDbCommand: ExecuteXmlReader. This method returns an XmlReader object that can be used to access XML-formatted data returned by SQL Server.[1] Command objects can also be used to execute stored procedures and can have parameters whose values can be set before the command is executed.

Connections must be explicitly closed

When finished, an ADO.NET client must invoke either the Close or the Dispose method on an in-use Connection object. You can't just forget about the object and rely on garbage collection to shut down the open connection—it won't work. Each connection must be explicitly closed.

Clients can start and end DBMS transactions

Connection objects are also used to start a transaction in the DBMS. Calling the BeginTransaction method on a SqlConnection object instructs the DBMS to start a new transaction. This method allows the client to specify the transaction's isolation level, offering the usual choices: Serializable, RepeatableRead, ReadCommitted, and a few more. Interestingly, however, although the Connection object is used to start a transaction, it is not used to end one. Instead, a call to SqlConnection.BeginTransaction returns an instance of the SqlTransaction class, and a client ends the transaction by calling a method in this object rather than in SqlConnection. To

---

1. This option works with SQL Server 2000, which supports the "FOR XML" clause in a SQL statement, but it doesn't work with earlier versions.

commit the work done in the transaction, the client calls
SqlTransaction.Commit, while calling SqlTransaction.Rollback
instructs the DBMS to abort the transaction, rolling back all
changes made to data since the call to
SqlConnection.BeginTransaction.

A DataReader ob-
ject provides fast
access to data

Direct access to data relies on DataReader objects.
DataReaders are fast, and they don't use much memory, because only one row of data at a time is made accessible (although more may be cached). An application using a
DataReader can read a query's results only one row at a time,
and can move forward only through those results—no random
access is allowed. This is very simple, but it's the right solution
for a significant set of applications. Like everything else, data
access should be as simple as possible. There's enough inherent
complexity in software development without unnecessarily
adding more.

A client reads data
from a DataReader
one row at a time

To read a row, the application calls a DataReader's Read
method, which makes the next row from the result of the executed query accessible. (This method returns FALSE when there
are no more rows to be read from the result.) Once this has
been done, the contents of that row can be accessed in various
ways. If you know the types of the columns in the result (which
is the usual case since you probably wrote the query), the values from the current row can be read by calling the appropriately typed Get methods (officially called *typed accessor*
methods) provided by the DataReader. For example, if a SQL
query asks for a list of all employee names and ages, each row
in that query's result will contain a string and an integer. To
read these, a client application could use the DataReader's
GetString and GetInt32 methods, respectively. The
SqlDataReader and OleDbDataReader classes provide many
more Get methods, each capable of reading a particular type of
data in a row. It's also possible to access each column of the
current row by the column name or position, but using the Get
methods is more efficient.

Here's a C# class that illustrates opening a connection, creating a command, and reading the results using a DataReader:

```csharp
using System.Data.SqlClient;
class DataReaderExample
{
    public static void Main()
    {
        SqlConnection Cn = new SqlConnection(
            "Data Source=localhost;" +
            "Integrated Security=SSPI;" +
            "Initial Catalog=example");
        SqlCommand Cmd = Cn.CreateCommand();
        Cmd.CommandText =
            "SELECT Name, Age FROM Employees";
        Cn.Open();
        SqlDataReader Rdr = Cmd.ExecuteReader();
        while (Rdr.Read())
        {
            System.Console.WriteLine(
                "Name: {0}, Age: {1}",
                Rdr.GetString(0),
                Rdr.GetInt32(1));
        }
        Rdr.Close();
        Cn.Close();
    }
}
```

This example uses the SQL .NET data provider, so it begins with the appropriate using statement for this set of classes. Following this is a single class, DataReaderExample, containing the single method Main. This method begins by creating a new Connection object, passing in a very simple connection string. (The connection string format used by the OLE DB .NET data provider is essentially the same as that used by ADO, but the format used by the SQL .NET data provider is just a little different.) The example then creates a Command object and sets its CommandText property to contain a simple SQL query. Next, the Connection object's Open method is used to open a connection to the database, the command is executed by a call to ExecuteReader, and a DataReader object is returned. The result of the query is read using a simple while loop. Each iteration reads an employee name and age from the current row in the result using the appropriate Get method. When there are no more results, first the DataReader and then the Connection object are closed. And although it's not shown in this simple example, using a try/catch block to handle any exceptions that occur is a common thing to do.

DataReaders are useful, but they're not always the best approach

Accessing relational data in a DBMS using a DataReader object is simple and fast. For applications that need nothing more than sequential access to data or straightforward updates, this approach is perfect. Not all applications can get by with this simple mechanism, however. For those that need more, ADO.NET provides the much more flexible (and much more complicated) alternative of a DataSet, described next.

Accessing Data with DataSets

A DataSet is an in-memory cache that can store data from various sources

An instance of the class DataSet, contained in the System.Data namespace, is an in-memory cache for data. Most commonly, that data is the set of rows resulting from one or more SQL queries, but it can also include information derived from an XML document or from some other source. Unlike Connection, Command, and DataReader, each of which has a unique class for each .NET data provider, there is only one DataSet class used by all .NET data providers.

DataSets allow much more flexible access to data than is possible with a DataReader

DataSets are very general things, so they're useful in many different situations. For instance, if a client application wishes to examine data in an arbitrary way, such as scrolling back and forth through the rows resulting from a SQL query, a DataReader won't suffice—but a DataSet will. DataSets are also useful for combining data from different data sources, such as two separate queries, or different types of data, such as the result of a query on a relational DBMS and the contents of an XML document. DataSets are also useful if data needs to be sent across a network, because DataSets are serializable. In fact, once it's been created, a DataSet can be passed around and used independently—it's just a managed object with state and methods like any other—but it cannot itself maintain an open connection to any underlying database.

Figure 6-3 shows a simplified picture of a DataSet object. Each DataSet can contain zero or more DataTable objects, which are instances of a class defined in System.Data. Each DataTable can contain the result of some query or perhaps something else. A DataSet can also maintain relationships among DataTables using DataRelation objects. For example, a column in one table might contain a foreign key for another table, a relationship that could be modeled by a DataRelation. These relationships can also be used to navigate through the contents of a DataSet. A simple DataSet, one that contains the result of just a single SQL query, might have only one DataTable and no DataRelations. DataSets can be quite complex, however, so an application that needed to maintain the results of several queries in memory could stuff them all into one DataSet, each in its own DataTable.

A DataSet contains DataTables

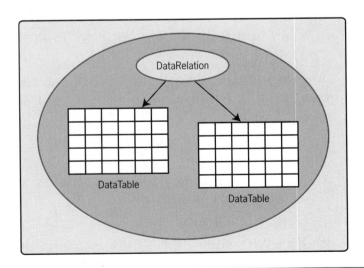

Figure 6-3   A DataSet contains DataTables, and it can also have DataRelation objects that describe relationships among those tables.

A DataSet has a schema

Each DataSet has a schema. Since DataSets hold tables, this schema describes those tables, including the columns each one contains and the types of those columns. Each DataSet and DataTable also has an ExtendedProperties property that can be used in various ways. For example, the ExtendedProperties value for each DataTable might contain the SQL query that generated the information stored in that table.

Creating and Using DataSets

A DataAdapter object can be used to create a DataSet

As mentioned earlier, DataSet objects can be created using a .NET data provider's DataAdapter object. The SQL .NET data provider uses the class SqlDataAdapter, while the OLE DB .NET data provider uses OleDbDataAdapter. Both classes provide a similar set of properties and methods for creating and working with DataSets. Among the most important properties of a DataAdapter are the following:

- **SelectCommand:** Contains a Command object that can be used to populate a DataTable within some DataSet with the results of a query on some database. The Command typically references a SQL SELECT statement.

- **InsertCommand:** Contains a Command object used to insert rows added to a DataTable into an underlying database. The Command typically references a SQL IN-SERT statement.

- **UpdateCommand:** Contains a Command object used to update a database based on changes made to a DataTable. The Command typically references a SQL UPDATE statement.

- **DeleteCommand:** Contains a Command object used to delete rows in a database based on deletions made to a DataTable. The Command typically references a SQL DELETE statement.

The contents of these properties, which can be explicit SQL statements or stored procedures, are accessed by various methods provided by the DataAdapter. The most important of these methods is Fill. As shown in Figure 6-4, this method executes the command in the DataAdapter's SelectCommand property and then places the results in a DataTable object inside whatever DataSet is passed as a parameter on the Fill call. The connection to the database can be closed once the desired results are returned, since a DataSet object is completely independent of any connection to any data source.

A DataAdapter's Fill method can be used to execute a query and store the result in a DataSet

Here's a simple C# example that shows how a DataAdapter can be used to add a DataTable containing the results of a query to a DataSet:

```
using System.Data;
using System.Data.SqlClient;

class DataSetExample
```

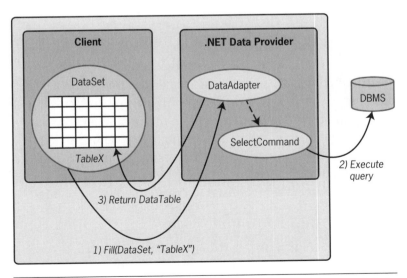

Figure 6-4   **Calling a DataAdapter's Fill method causes the associated SelectCommand to be executed and the results placed in a DataSet as a DataTable.**

```
{
    public static void Main()
    {
        SqlConnection Cn = new SqlConnection(
            "Data Source=localhost;" +
            "Integrated Security=SSPI;" +
            "Initial Catalog=example");
        SqlCommand Cmd = Cn.CreateCommand();
        Cmd.CommandText =
            "SELECT Name, Age FROM Employees";
        SqlDataAdapter Da = new SqlDataAdapter();
        Da.SelectCommand = Cmd;
        DataSet Ds = new DataSet();
        Cn.Open();
        Da.Fill(Ds, "NamesAndAges");
        Cn.Close();
    }
}
```

This example begins with using statements for the System.Data namespace, home of the DataSet class, and for System.Data.SqlClient, because this example will once again use the SQL .NET data provider. Like the previous example, this class's single method creates Connection and Command objects and then sets the Command object's CommandText property to contain a simple SQL query. The example next creates an instance of the SqlDataAdapter class and sets its SelectCommand property to contain the Command object created earlier. The method then creates a DataSet and opens a connection to the database. Once this connection is open, the method calls the DataAdapter's Fill method, passing in the DataSet in which a new DataTable object should be created and the name that DataTable object should have. Closing the connection, the last step, doesn't affect the DataSet in any way—it never had any idea what connection was used to create the data it contains anyway.

A DataSet can contain results from different queries on different DBMSs

The DataSet created by this (completely useless) example contains just one DataTable. To add other DataTables with different contents to this same DataSet, the Fill method could be called again once the SelectCommand property of the DataAdapter had been changed to contain a different query. Alternatively, as shown in Figure 6-5, another DataAdapter could be used on a different data source. In the figure, one DataSet is being populated with DataTables from two different .NET data providers accessing two different databases. In each case, the same DataSet is passed into a call to the appropriate DataAdapter's Fill method. The result of each call is a DataTable within this DataSet whose contents are the result of running whatever query is represented by the SelectCommand object associated with the DataAdapter.

It's also possible to modify information in a DBMS using a DataSet. Once one or more DataTables have been created in the DataSet, the information in those tables can be changed by the client in various ways, as described later in this section. As shown in Figure 6-6, calling a DataAdapter's Update method

DataSets can also be used to modify data in a DBMS

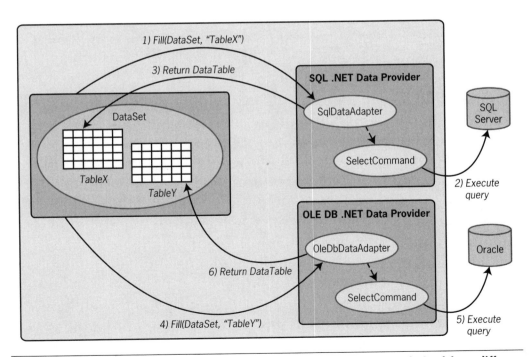

Figure 6-5   A single DataSet can contain DataTables whose contents are derived from different databases.

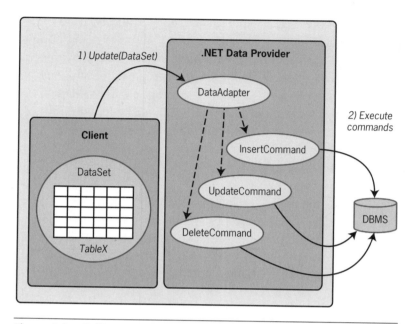

Figure 6-6   Calling a DataAdapter's Update method updates the DBMS to reflect any changes made to a DataSet.

will cause the DataAdapter to examine the changes in any DataSet or DataTable passed into this call and then modify the underlying database to reflect those changes. These modifications are made using the commands stored in the DataAdapter's InsertCommand, UpdateCommand, and DeleteCommand properties described earlier. Because these commands can be stored procedures as well as dynamically executed statements, these update operations can be reasonably efficient.

A DataSet can't itself maintain a lock on data

Note, however, that there is no way for the DataSet itself to maintain a lock on the underlying data from which its contents were derived. As a result, it's possible that the data in the database has changed since some of its information was copied into the DataSet. Whether updates succeed if the underlying data has changed depends on what commands are placed into the

InsertCommand, UpdateCommand, and DeleteCommand properties of the DataAdapter. For example, it's possible to generate those commands automatically using a CommandBuilder object supplied by the .NET Framework class library. If this is done, the automatically generated update commands are designed to fail if any of the affected data has changed since it was originally read. This need not be the case for commands created manually, however—it's up to the developer to decide what's best.

Every DataSet has a few collections that logically group some of the DataSet's objects. For example, all of the DataTables in a DataSet belong to the Tables collection. An application can create a free-standing DataTable object, one that's not part of any DataSet, and then explicitly add it to some DataSet object.[2] To do this, the application can pass this DataTable object as a parameter on the Add method of the DataSet's Tables collection. Similarly, each DataSet has a Relations collection that contains all of the DataRelation objects in this DataSet, each of which represents a relationship of some kind between two tables. Calling the Add method of a DataSet's Relations collection allows creating a new DataRelation object. The parameters on this call can be used to specify exactly which fields in the two tables are related.

The contents of a DataSet are grouped into collections

Accessing and Modifying a DataSet's Contents

DataSets exist primarily to let applications read and change the data they contain. That data is grouped into one or more DataTables, as just described, and so access to a DataSet's information is accomplished by accessing these contained objects. Because applications need to work with data in diverse ways, DataTables provide several options for accessing and modifying the data they contain. Whatever option is used, two

Applications access a DataSet's contents by examining the DataTables it contains

---

2. DataTable objects can also be used on their own without belonging to some DataSet, although with some limitations. A DataTable can't be marshaled, for example, while a DataSet containing a DataTable can be.

classes are commonly used to work with information in a
DataTable:

- **DataRow:** Represents a row in a DataTable. Each
  DataTable has a Rows property that allows access to a
  collection containing all of that table's DataRows. The
  data in a DataTable can be accessed by examining its
  DataRows. In fact, perhaps the most common way to
  access a DataTable's information is by directly accessing
  the Rows property as a two-dimensional array.

- **DataColumn:** Represents a column in a DataTable. Each
  DataTable has a Collections property that allows access
  to a collection containing all of that table's
  DataColumns. Rather than defining the table's data, however, this collection defines what columns the table has
  and what type each column is. In other words, this collection defines the table's schema.

A DataTable's
Select method can
be used to choose
a subset of its data

For more complex examinations of data, each DataTable provides a Select method. This method allows an application to
describe the data it's interested in and then have that data returned in an array of DataRow objects. Select takes up to three
parameters: a filter, a sort order, and a row state. The filter allows
specifying a variety of criteria that selected rows must meet,
such as "Name='Smith'" or "Age > 45." The sort order allows
specifying which column the results should be sorted by and
whether those results should be sorted in ascending or descend-
ing order. Finally, the row state parameter allows returning only
records in a specific state, such as those that have been added
or those that have not been changed. Whatever criteria are used
on the call to Select, the result is an array of DataRows. The
application can then access individual elements of this array as
needed to work with the data each one contains.

New rows can be
added to a
DataTable

To add data to a DataTable, an application can create a new
DataRow object, populate it, and insert it into the table. To

ADO.NET vs. ADO

Microsoft sometimes changes a technology's name but doesn't change the technology itself. Renaming "OLE" as "ActiveX" some years ago was one visible example of this. In other cases, however, the company leaves the name more or less the same while radically revamping the technology it identifies. ADO.NET is an instance of this second phenomenon. While the name sounds familiar, it is in fact very different from ADO.

The differences aren't arbitrary, however. Instead, they stem from the nature of the problem to be solved. ADO.NET is very different from ADO in large part because the problem it must solve is also very different. While ADO was designed for an inside-the-firewall world of Windows clients communicating through DCOM, ADO.NET was designed to work well in both intranet and Internet scenarios, as well as to fit with browser clients.

The most obvious expression of these different goals is the difference between an ADO Recordset and a DataSet. Recordsets contain the result of a single query, and by default, they maintain an open connection to the database against which that query was performed. A disconnected Recordset breaks that connection, but still maintains some memory of where its data came from. Also, while disconnected Recordsets can be passed to DCOM clients quite easily, there's no simple way to pass the data in a Recordset to a browser other than Internet Explorer, especially across the Internet.

DataSets, by contrast, are free and easy, unconcerned with the DBMS from which their contents came. (This is similar to a disconnected Recordset, although a DataSet might contain the results of more than one query.) Also, as described later in this chapter, DataSets can be easily serialized into an XML format. This makes them a good match for the Web world, since any browser can handle a stream of XML-defined data. Also, passing the data in a DataSet using XML makes it easy to send over HTTP, which allows slipping through firewalls.

ADO and ADO.NET are more different than they are similar. Both allow accessing data, and both have names that start with "ADO". Beyond these superficial similarities, they're very different beasts.

create the new DataRow, the application can call a DataTable's NewRow method. Once this DataRow exists, the application can assign values to the fields in the row, then add the row to the table by calling the Add method provided by the DataTable's Rows collection. It's also possible to modify the contents of a DataTable directly by assigning new values to the contents of its DataRows and to delete rows using the Remove method of the Rows collection.

Each row in a DataTable keeps track of its state

The state of a DataRow changes as that DataRow is modified. The current state is kept in a property of the DataRow called RowState, and several possibilities are defined. Changes made to a DataRow can be made permanent by calling the DataRow.AcceptChanges method for that row, which sets the DataRow's RowState property to Unchanged. To accept all changes made to all DataRows in a DataTable at once, an application can call DataTable.AcceptChanges, while to accept all changes made to all DataRows in all DataTables in a DataSet at once, an application can call DataSet.AcceptChanges. It's also possible to call the RejectChanges method at each of these levels to roll back any modifications that have been made.

Using DataSets with XML-Defined Data

DataSets can also be used with XML-defined data

Information stored in relational DBMSs probably comprises the majority of business data today. Increasingly, though, data defined using XML is also important, and XML's hierarchical approach to describing information will probably matter even more in the future. Recognizing this, the designers of ADO.NET chose to integrate DataSets and XML-defined data in several different ways. This section describes the available choices.

Translating Between DataSets and XML Documents

An XML document can be read directly into a DataSet

So far, the contents of a DataTable inside a DataSet have always been generated by a SQL query. It's also possible, however, to create DataTables in a DataSet the contents of which come from an XML document. To do this, an application can call a

The Revenge of Hierarchical Data

The relational model has been the dominant approach for storing and working with data for more than 20 years. Older systems that organized data hierarchically, such as IBM's IMS, were shoved aside by the more flexible notion of putting everything into tables. Today, relations rule.

Yet the idea of hierarchical data refuses to die. The object database crowd attempted to revive this notion, reasoning that since objects in software were commonly organized into a tree, organizing data the same way could give better performance and a better match between code and data. This insight was correct, but since the information in most databases is shared by multiple applications, no single hierarchy worked well for all of them. The more general relational approach was still better in most cases.

XML is the latest technology to exploit the utility of hierarchical data. Unlike the object database people, XML proponents aren't trying to displace the entrenched relational world. Instead, they'd like to work with it. This strategy looks far more likely to succeed than anything we've seen up to now. The truth is that some kinds of information really are better modeled as a tree than as a table. And given XML's tremendous value as a common interchange format among applications, software to work with XML documents is required anyway. Since XML is going to be around, merging the hierarchical structure it uses with relational data access is a very good idea.

Microsoft got XML religion some years ago. One way the company expressed its new-found faith was by combining the groups in Redmond responsible for relational data access and those responsible for XML data access. ADO.NET was one major result of this religious conversion, as were the XML features described in the previous chapter. Each has a streaming API—DataReader and XmlReader, respectively—along with a navigational API—DataSet (which has at least some navigational characteristics) and XmlDocument. More important, the .NET Framework's integration of these two models, described later in this chapter, allows the same data to be accessed as either a relational table or an XML hierarchy.

Relational dominance notwithstanding, there's still a place for trees. XML, the modern expression of hierarchical data, is the latest technology to remind us of this fact.

DataSet's ReadXml method, passing as a parameter an indication of where the XML data can be found. The possible sources for this data include a filename, a stream, and an XmlReader object. Wherever it comes from, the XML-defined information is read into a DataTable in the DataSet.

There's an obvious problem here. Both XML and the relational model have the notion of schemas for describing data. Yet the two technologies view this notion in very different ways. An XML schema defines a hierarchy using the XML Schema definition (XSD) language. The relational model defines a schema as a set of tables, each having a particular group of columns in a particular order. DataSets and the DataTables they contain are firmly in the relational camp. When an XML document is loaded into a DataSet, what should the schema of the resulting table look like?

A schema for a DataSet can be automatically created from an XML document

Like most questions, the answer to this one is, it depends. The DataSet.ReadXml method allows passing an XmlReadMode parameter to control how the XML document's schema is mapped into the schema for the DataTable in which that document's information will be stored. One option is to tell the DataSet to read an XSD schema that appears in the XML document being read, while another instructs the DataSet to infer a relational schema from the XML schema.

Mapping between a hierarchical XML document and a relational DataSet can get complicated

Mapping the hierarchical form of an XML document into the tables contained in a DataSet can be a nontrivial undertaking. In particular, the rules for inferring a relational schema are not especially simple. Some parts are easy, though. For instance, all columns have the type String, since in the absence of an XSD schema, a DataSet has no way to identify any other types. Mapping the document's hierarchy into tables is more interesting. When inferring a relational schema, a DataSet assumes that an element with attributes should become a table, with the attributes and the element value represented as columns in that table. Similarly, an element with child elements will also become a table containing some number of values.

Figure 6-7 shows how the simple XML document we saw in Chapter 5 might be mapped into a DataSet if it were read with DataSet.ReadXml. The <employee> elements are placed into a single DataTable named *employee*, with the information in each of the child elements mapped into a row in that table. Notice that because there's no age present for Casey, that value is of the type null (or more exactly, the type DBNull defined in the System namespace).

While this simple example worked fine, inferring a relational schema from an XML document is in general likely to produce a less attractive result than creating one directly from an XSD schema. When possible, then, it's better to tell the DataSet to read an XML document's schema. Also, if an XML document is being read into a DataSet that contains data and already has a schema, the ReadXml method can be instructed just to use the DataSet's existing schema. Note too that it is possible to read explicitly an XML schema from a stream, a file, or somewhere else into a DataSet by calling the DataSet's ReadXmlSchema method.

A DataSet can also explicitly read an XSD schema

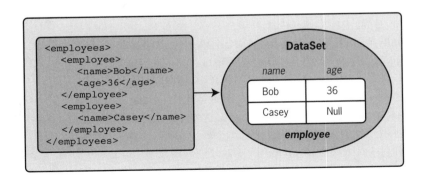

Figure 6-7   A DataSet can infer a relational schema from an XML document read with DataSet.ReadXml.

Any DataSet's contents can be serialized as an XML document

Once an XML document has been loaded into a DataSet, the data it contains can be treated just like any other data in any other DataSet—there's nothing special about it. And just as an application can populate a DataSet from an XML document, so too it's possible to write out a DataSet's contents as an XML document. In other words, the contents of any DataSet can be serialized as XML, whether or not its data originally came from an XML document. A primary choice for doing this is the DataSet's WriteXml method. This method writes the DataSet's contents as an XML document to a stream, an XmlWriter, or some other destination. A parameter on this method can be used to control whether an XSD schema is written with the data. If desired, a developer can specify how columns are mapped to XML and control other options in the transformation from a relational format to a hierarchy.

One common reason for serializing a DataSet as an XML document is to allow the information it contains to be sent to a browser. Similarly, an XML document received from a browser can be read into a DataSet and then used to update a DBMS or in some other way. It's also worth noting that because DataSets are serializable, they can be passed as parameters by applications that use .NET Remoting. Data wrapped in XML can be applied in many contexts, and so being able to easily serialize a DataSet into this format is quite useful.

Synchronizing a DataSet and an XML Document

A DataSet can be synchronized with an XmlDataDocument object

Reading an XML document into a DataSet converts the information it contains into a set of tables. Similarly, writing the contents of a DataSet as an XML document converts the information in that DataSet into a hierarchical form. Being able to translate data between tables and trees is certainly a useful thing. Yet sometimes you'd like the ability to treat the same data as either relational tables or an XML tree at the same time. Rather than converting between the two formats, something that can result in losing information, you'd like to maintain the flexibility to view the same data in either form depending on your requirements. ADO.NET allows this by synchronizing a DataSet with an instance of a class called XmlDataDocument.

Figure 6-8 shows how this looks. By having the data available in a DataSet, it can be accessed using standard operations such as DataTable.Select. Yet having the same data available in an XmlDataDocument allows running XPath queries on the data, performing XSLT transforms, and doing other kinds of hierarchically oriented access. XmlDataDocument inherits from XmlDocument, a class described in the preceding chapter that implements the standard navigational API for XML, the DOM. Since it derives from XmlDocument, XmlDataDocument also allows its contents to be accessed using this navigational interface. Along with this, however, XmlDataDocument also allows its user to work simultaneously with the data it contains as a DataSet.

Relational data can now be accessed with tools such as XPath

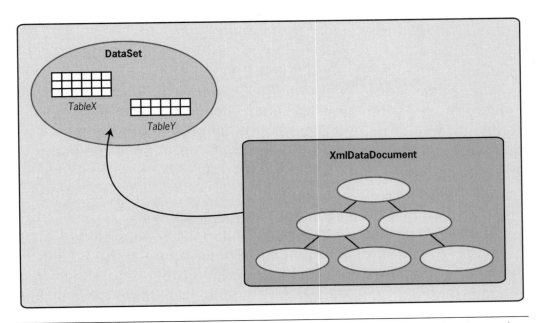

Figure 6-8   Synchronizing a DataSet with an XmlDataDocument allows an application to view the same data either relationally or hierarchically.

There are several ways to create a synchronized DataSet/XmlData-Document pair

To view an existing XmlDataDocument's information as a DataSet, an application can simply access the XmlDataDocument's DataSet property. The result is a DataSet object containing the XmlDataDocument's information in a relational form. There are also other ways to create a synchronized DataSet/XmlDataDocument pair. One choice is to create an instance of an XmlDataDocument and pass in a DataSet on the new operation. This will create an XmlDataDocument that provides a hierarchical view of whatever data is in that DataSet. Another option is to create a DataSet containing only relational schema information rather than data, then pass this DataSet on the new operation that creates an XmlDataDocument. An XML document can now be loaded into the XmlDataDocument using its Load method, and the data in that document will be both loaded as an XML hierarchy and mapped to tables using the DataSet's existing schema. However it's done, the ability to use the same data either hierarchically or relationally is an interesting idea, one that's likely to be quite useful for some kinds of applications.

Conclusion

ADO.NET is an important part of the .NET Framework class library

In some ways, ADO.NET is just another group of types in the .NET Framework class library. It's an important part of this library, however, one that will be used by a large percentage of .NET developers. All of ADO.NET's types are built on the CLR and the foundation types it defines, all can be accessed from any CLR-based language, and all are contained within the library's consistent namespace hierarchy. Yet despite their visibility, the types that comprise ADO.NET are really just more soldiers in the army of support provided by the .NET Framework class library.

7

Building Web Applications: ASP.NET

Accessing software over the Web has become the norm. Most new enterprise applications offer at least the option of a browser interface, and many offer nothing else. Given this, an application platform that doesn't provide first-class support for building Web-based software is doomed to failure. And yet how we use software via the Web is changing. While communicating with a user through a browser is certainly important, Web services are also on the scene. The Web is expanding from a world driven solely by eyeballs to one that's also driven by applications.

Web-based applications are important

ASP.NET is the .NET Framework's primary foundation for building Web applications. Part of the .NET Framework class library, it supports creating both browser applications and Web services applications, and it relies on a common infrastructure for both. Given the popularity of Active Server Pages (ASP), ASP.NET's predecessor, this technology is certain to be among the most widely used parts of the .NET Framework.

ASP.NET allows creating browser applications and Web services applications

263

ASP.NET's types are contained in the System.Web namespace

Like everything else in the class library, ASP.NET is defined as a group of types contained in several namespaces. (As described later in this chapter, however, ASP.NET also provides an executable process for hosting its applications.) The root namespace for ASP.NET is System.Web, and immediately below it are several more namespaces. The most important of these are System.Web.UI, which contains the types used to build browser Web applications, and System.Web.Services, which contains the types used to build Web services applications. This division is central, so this chapter first describes how ASP.NET supports browser applications and then examines how the technology can be used to build Web services.

Browser Applications: System.Web.UI

Active Server Pages has been a successful technology

The idea of Web scripting—embedding executable code within a Web page's HTML—has been very successful. The original Active Server Pages technology was certainly one reason for this. Easy to learn and use, ASP was also widely available because it was included with the server versions of Windows NT and Windows 2000. Many thousands of ASP applications are in use today, so what this technology offers is clearly attractive. When Microsoft created ASP.NET, its successor, they faced an interesting problem: How could this new version exploit the simplicity and the installed base of ASP while still taking advantage of the consistency and power provided by the .NET Framework?

ASP.NET applications are .NET Framework applications

The solution chosen by the designers of ASP.NET was to create an environment that can look very much like traditional ASP pages. To build browser applications, a developer can create Web pages that mix HTML and executable code just like traditional ASP pages. A relatively naïve ASP developer, one who just wrote simple scripts, could likely begin doing the same thing in ASP.NET with at most a few hours of retraining. Yet thinking about ASP.NET in this simple-minded way isn't the best approach for understanding this new technology. Instead, more advanced developers must understand that every ASP.NET application, no matter how it's constructed, is really a CLR-based application running on the .NET Framework.

Unlike traditional ASP technology, in which a scripting engine executes code contained in ASP pages and possibly accesses compiled COM objects, ASP.NET applications are just ordinary .NET Framework applications. Every line in a pure ASP.NET application is ultimately managed code. Yet to make them look familiar to ASP developers and to make them easy to create, Microsoft chose to allow ASP.NET browser applications to be built using pages, just like before.

As Figure 7-1 shows, an ASP.NET page that is accessed directly from a browser is stored in a text file with an extension of .aspx. When this page is accessed, it is transformed into one or more managed objects. As the figure shows, those objects can use Web controls (described later in this chapter), rely on ADO.NET to access data, and perhaps can use other services.

Browser applications rely on .aspx pages

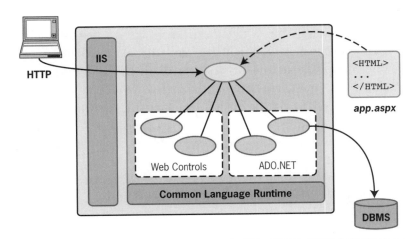

Figure 7-1   Each .aspx page becomes one or more managed objects when it is accessed.

Managed objects always belong to some assembly, however, so each .aspx page is compiled into its own assembly. To understand how ASP.NET supports browser applications, it's useful to know a little bit about how this translation occurs.

How Browser Applications Work

An .aspx page can mix text, HTML, and code

An .aspx page can contain text, HTML, and executable code. Any code in the file must either be in a *script block*, bracketed by the tags <script> and </script>, or be wrapped in the symbols "<%" and "%>". Here's a very simple example of an .aspx page that contains text, HTML, and a few lines of VB.NET code:

```
<html>
<script runat="server" language="vb">
Sub ShowNumbers()
    Dim I As Integer
    For I = 0 To 5
        Response.Write(I)
    Next
End Sub
</script>

The date and time: <% =Now() %>
<hr>
Some numbers: <% ShowNumbers() %>
</html>
```

VB.NET is the default language for .aspx pages

After the opening <html> tag, this page contains some very simple code inside a script block. The attributes in the opening <script> tag indicate that this code should be run at the server rather than at the client and that the code is written in Visual Basic.NET. (VB.NET is the default language for .aspx pages, so this second attribute isn't strictly required.) The code in the script block defines a method called ShowNumbers containing a simple loop that writes out the numbers 0 through 5. To accomplish this, that code calls the Write method of the Response object, a built-in ASP.NET mechanism described later in this chapter.

After the script appear some text and, wrapped as code, a reference to Now, which returns the current date and time. The horizontal rule tag, <hr>, appears next, followed by more text and a call to the ShowNumbers method. Accessing this page from a browser produces the following:

```
The date and time: 9/5/2002 5:21:05 PM
```

```
Some numbers: 012345
```

If you're familiar with traditional Active Server Pages, this is old hat. The script above could execute almost unchanged if it were accessed with traditional ASP technology. The only required modifications would be changing the language to "vbscript" and deleting the Dim statement in the ShowNumbers method. (Despite the similarities between the two technologies, most existing ASP pages will require at least small changes such as these to work with ASP.NET.)

.aspx pages look much like .asp pages

In fact, however, what's happening when this page is executed by ASP.NET is very different from what happens when a page is executed by traditional ASP. If this were an ASP page, the code it contains would be interpreted by the server, with the output it generated inserted in the stream of data sent to the browser. The text and HTML in the page would be passed through directly to the browser unchanged. If the page used COM objects, they would be written and compiled in some other language and then created and used via the standard COM mechanisms.

Traditional ASP interprets each ASP page when a request arrives

Accessing this page through ASP.NET results in a completely different execution process. ASP.NET applications are .NET Framework applications, just like those seen throughout this book. An .aspx page does look quite different from an ordinary VB.NET program, but that's only because the designers of ASP.NET wanted to maintain the familiar, easy-to-use model of Web scripting. The truth is that every .aspx page is automatically turned into a class and then compiled into an assembly the first time it's accessed by a client.

ASP.NET converts each .aspx page into a class that gets compiled into an assembly

An .aspx page is really just another way to define a class

Figure 7-2 gives an abstracted view of how this simple example page gets converted into a class. (What's shown here isn't literally correct—the complete truth is somewhat more complicated.) The generated class's name is derived from the name of the file containing this page, and this new class must inherit from the Page class defined in System.Web.UI. As the diagram shows, any code contained in a script block is inserted into the class itself. In this case, the page's simple ShowNumbers method becomes a method in the generated class. The rest of this page, including any text, HTML tags, and code wrapped in "<% . . . %>", gets dropped into a single Render method for this class.[1]

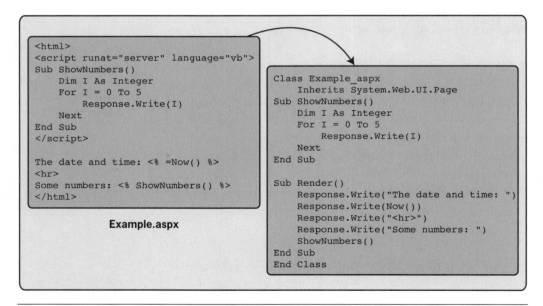

```
<html>
<script runat="server" language="vb">
Sub ShowNumbers()
    Dim I As Integer
    For I = 0 To 5
        Response.Write(I)
    Next
End Sub
</script>

The date and time: <% =Now() %>
<hr>
Some numbers: <% ShowNumbers() %>
</html>
```

Example.aspx

```
Class Example_aspx
    Inherits System.Web.UI.Page
Sub ShowNumbers()
    Dim I As Integer
    For I = 0 To 5
        Response.Write(I)
    Next
End Sub

Sub Render()
    Response.Write("The date and time: ")
    Response.Write(Now())
    Response.Write("<hr>")
    Response.Write("Some numbers: ")
    ShowNumbers()
End Sub
End Class
```

Figure 7-2   Each .aspx page is converted into a class, with the page's contents inserted in various places.

---

1. This is why code wrapped in "<% ... %>" can't define a method in ASP.NET. Doing this is allowed in traditional ASP, but any method defined here would become part of the body of the page class's Render method. The CLR doesn't allow one method definition to be nested inside another one, so methods in .aspx pages can be defined only inside a script block.

The class is then compiled into MSIL and packaged into an assembly. What is produced is not a static assembly, however, but rather a dynamic assembly built directly in memory using types provided by the .NET Framework class library. Once this dynamic assembly has been created, it's written to disk and then used to handle all future requests for this page. If the page is changed, the process happens again, and a new assembly is generated. In the absence of any changes, the original assembly is all that's needed, so only one compilation is required for each .aspx page.

The compiled assembly handles requests until the underlying .aspx page is changed

Understanding how a traditional ASP page generated its output was easy: The page was processed sequentially. As we've already seen, though, this isn't the case in ASP.NET. Given that each page is turned into a class before it's executed, how does that execution happen? The answer is that in place of the simple sequential processing of traditional ASP, ASP.NET uses an event-driven model. When a page is accessed, the assembly generated from that page is executed, and an instance of that assembly's page class is created. This page object receives a series of events. The object can provide a method to handle each event, and each of those methods can produce output that gets sent to the client's browser. Once all events have been handled, the page object is destroyed.

.aspx pages are executed using events

The first event every page object receives is Page_Load, sent immediately after the page object has been created. Every page object also receives a Page_Unload event just before it is destroyed. In between these two bookend events, the page object can receive and process various other events. For example, sometime prior to receiving Page_Unload, every page object will receive a Render event. This event causes the object's Render method to execute and thus displays the page's output.

Every .aspx page receives several standard events

Event-based programming will be new to many ASP developers, and understanding it will require some work. Yet a primary goal of Web scripting technologies such as ASP.NET is to create effective user interfaces. User interfaces by their nature are event driven, so it makes sense to apply this model here.

Web Controls

GUIs tend to have many of the same elements

Event-driven user interfaces have always been the norm for Windows applications. As described in Chapter 5, for example, Windows Forms applications depend on events to get input from users. But along with events, there's another idea that's long been popular in building Windows GUIs: packaging discrete chunks of reusable functionality into controls. Each control commonly provides some part of a user interface, such as a button or text box, so they can be combined as needed to build more easily an effective GUI. Since ASP.NET has adopted the notion of event-based programming, why not introduce reusable interface components to the Web as well?

Web controls provide packaged functionality for creating a browser GUI

This is exactly what ASP.NET's Web controls do. They're conceptually close to the Windows Forms controls described in Chapter 5, in that each one provides its own user interface and carries out its own function. Unlike Windows Forms controls, however, Web controls run on the server—they're classes that become part of a page class—and they produce their user interfaces by generating appropriate HTML for a browser. It's even possible for a Web control to learn what kind of browser it's communicating with and then to send the appropriate output— HTML, Dynamic HTML, or something else—for that browser.[2]

ASP.NET includes many Web controls

ASP.NET provides a large set of standard Web controls. All of them inherit from the base class WebControl in the namespace System.Web.UI.WebControls. The available choices include the

---

2. Applications that target mobile devices such as cell phones and PDAs typically can't use standard ASP.NET Web controls effectively—the screens are too small. Accordingly, Microsoft provides the Mobile Internet Toolkit for building applications that target this environment. The Toolkit includes a separate parent class for .aspx pages and a specialized set of Web controls, both specifically designed to work with small devices.

common atoms of GUI design, such as Button, TextBox, CheckBox, RadioButton, and ListBox. Several more complex controls are also provided. There's a Calendar control, for instance, that displays months and allows users to select dates and an AdRotator control capable of automatically cycling through a series of Web-based advertisements. And of course, it's possible to create custom Web controls, just as there are custom Windows Forms controls. Sometimes called *user controls,* third parties have created a reasonably large selection of these quite quickly.

Here's a simple example, once again using VB.NET, that illustrates using Web controls:

```
<html>
<form runat="server">
<asp:Button runat="server" height="81px"
      width="288px" text="Click Here"
      onClick="Button_Click"/>
<asp:Label id="Label1" runat="server"/>
</form>

<script runat="server">
Sub Button_Click(Sender As System.Object, _
                 e As System.EventArgs)
    Label1.Text = "Button clicked"
End Sub
</script>
</html>
```

This .aspx page begins by defining a form containing two Web controls: a Button and a Label. The tag identifying both controls begins with "asp:", which indicates that these controls are defined by ASP.NET. Both of these controls, along with many more, are contained in the namespace System.Web.UI.WebControls. The Button element contains a number of attributes, specifying where the control should run (on the server), its height and width in pixels, and the text the Button should display. The element ends with the onClick attribute, specifying that a method called Button_Click should be run when this Button

Web controls can handle events

receives a Click event. The Label element also contains a few attributes. One of them, id, gives this Label a name so it can be referred to later in the page. This simple Label initially displays no text but is instead used to provide a way to send output to the browser, as described next.

Web controls allow building browser GUIs in a familiar style

Following the form is a short script containing just the single method Button_Click. When the button is clicked, this method will be executed. The only thing this method does is assign a value to the Label's Text property, causing it to be displayed on the screen. Figure 7-3 shows the result of loading this page and clicking the button it displays. If you recall the Windows Forms example from Chapter 5, this should look familiar. Once again, a Button control is created, its size is determined, and an event handler is associated with the Button's Click event. By using Web controls, developers can build browser-based applications in a familiar style.

Web controls are similar to, but not the same as, Windows Forms controls

ASP.NET's event-driven approach certainly is very similar to the event-driven model used in Windows Forms applications, and

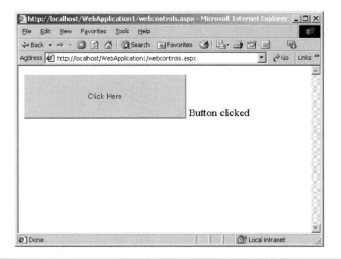

Figure 7-3   The simple .aspx page described in this section shows a button and then displays a message when the button is clicked.

many Web controls even have the same names as their
Windows Forms analogs. Still, there are significant differences
between the controls used in Windows Forms applications and
those used with ASP.NET applications. The most important of
these grows out of the fact that while Windows applications
handle events that were generated on the same machine,
ASP.NET events are typically generated on the client machine
and then are handled by the server system. This greatly
increases the cost of raising an event, since each one results in
a round trip from the browser to the ASP.NET application and
back. Accordingly, there are some kinds of events that just don't
make sense for Web controls.

For example, both Windows Forms and ASP.NET include a
Button control. Yet the number of events supported by the Web
control Button is much smaller than that supported by its
Windows Forms cousin. Both Buttons support an event called
Click, for instance, so an application using either one can write
an event handler that runs when the control is clicked, as
shown earlier. The Windows Forms control, however, also has
an event called MouseMove that occurs when the mouse
pointer is moved over the on-screen button, along with many
other mouse-related events. None of these is available in the
Web control Button. Raising each of these events on a single
machine is cheap, but to send an indication to the Web server
every time the mouse moves over a new control in the browser
would result in an unacceptably large amount of network traffic. Accordingly, Web controls are substantially more limited in
the events they can accept and process than their Windows
Forms brethren.

*Web controls sup-
port fewer events
than Windows
Forms controls*

Another difference between Windows Forms controls and those
used with ASP.NET is how they maintain their state. Each control
has properties, such as the text it displays or its on-screen size.
Windows Forms controls maintain this state in the control's
memory, which is simple and efficient. Sadly, because HTTP is a
stateless protocol, this isn't possible with Web controls. Like all

*Web controls main-
tain state automati-
cally between
requests*

Web-based applications, ASP.NET applications are stateless. Every object created to handle a request is destroyed when that request is completed, so an application does not by default maintain any in-memory state about a client between requests. This makes Web-based applications easy to load balance, since different requests from the same client can be sent to different machines with no problems; however, it also creates problems. One of those problems is finding a way for Web controls to maintain their state between client requests. The solution adopted by ASP.NET is to insert each control's state into the Web page sent back to the browser. When the user submits another request, the page is sent back, and this state information is copied back into each Web control. The process is arguably inelegant, but given the limitations imposed on Web-based applications, it's a good solution.

Visual Studio.NET provides a graphical tool for building browser GUIs

One more important point remains to be made about using Web controls. Despite the simple example shown earlier, building browser GUIs by hand makes no more sense than building Windows GUIs by hand. Using a tool that allows creating a browser GUI graphically is a much better approach. Visual Studio.NET, for example, allows a developer to drag and drop Web controls on a form, set their properties, and attach code to the events they generate, just as with Windows Forms. (In fact, ASP.NET applications are sometimes referred to as *Web Forms*.) While it's useful to know what's going on under the covers, real applications should be built using real tools whenever possible.

Separating the User Interface from the Code

Code and HTML can be separated using the code-behind option

One problem with creating browser-based applications is the inescapable need to combine HTML and code written in a language such as VB.NET or C#. Simple pages like those shown earlier in this chapter don't create much of a problem, but real applications can get very hard to read when HTML and code are mingled on the same page. While ASP.NET allows doing this, as the examples so far have shown, it also provides a mechanism for cleanly separating the GUI-oriented HTML from the code behind that GUI. Appropriately, this mechanism is called *code-behind*.

Code-behind is a straightforward idea. Rather than mixing HTML and code in a single file, using the code-behind option allows putting all of a page's HTML in its .aspx file and then inserting a reference in that file to another file that contains the code. The result is significantly easier to work with, since the two very different worlds of HTML and a CLR-based programming language can remain distinct from one another.

Code-behind can make applications more maintainable

Here's how the simple application just shown might look if this option were used. The file containing just the code is as follows:

```
Imports System
Imports System.Web.UI.WebControls

Public Class Example
    Inherits System.Web.UI.Page
    Protected Label1 As Label
    Protected myButton As Button
    Sub Button_Click(sender As Object, _
                    e As EventArgs)
        Label1.Text = "Button clicked"
    End Sub
End Class
```

This is effectively the same code that appeared in the script block in the previous example. It begins with a couple of Imports statements to make what follows more readable; then it declares a class named Example. This class inherits from the base Page class that underlies all .aspx pages. The two controls, both of which are contained in the System.Web.UI.WebControls namespace, are declared next. Both are marked as Protected, which means they can be accessed only from within this class or a child of this class. The class ends with the definition of Button_Click, the same simple method shown in the previous example.

With the code cabined off in a separate file, the .aspx file now looks like this:

```
<%@Page Inherits="Example" Src="Code.vb" %>

<html>
<form runat="server">
<asp:Button runat="server" height="81px"
        width="288px" text="Click Here"
        onClick="Button_Click"/>
<asp:Label id="Label1" runat="server"/>
</form>
</html>
```

The file begins with a Page directive. This line tells the ASP.NET infrastructure that the code for this page is in a class named Example in the file Code.vb. In other words, this directive connects this purely HTML file with the VB.NET code that it uses. The rest of the file is just the HTML from the example shown earlier. With the code removed, the user interface aspects of this very simple application are much clearer, as the entire page can now contain purely HTML.

Using code-behind is a good idea. Visual Studio.NET, for example, automatically creates new Web applications in this format. For anything beyond the simplest ASP.NET browser applications, it's the way to go.

Other Topics

Processing .aspx pages, using Web controls, and understanding the idea of code-behind are arguably the most important aspects of ASP.NET. There are plenty more, however, and really understanding this technology requires a grasp of ASP.NET applications, state management, and other issues. This section takes a brief look at these topics.

ASP.NET Applications

An ASP.NET application can contain .aspx pages, assemblies, and more

ASP.NET allows grouping .aspx pages, assemblies, and other files into an ASP.NET application. To do this, the files that com-

Is ASP.NET Too Hard?

Microsoft's original Active Server Pages technology was a huge hit. A primary reason for this was that it was incredibly easy to use, and so everybody and his dog Rover wrote ASP applications. True, this initial ease of use tended to devolve into unmaintainable code for applications of any size, but the barriers to entry for this technology were very low.

ASP.NET provides much more than the original ASP. Accordingly, it's more complex. In fact, using ASP.NET effectively requires understanding the CLR, since all code must be written in a CLR-based language such as VB.NET or C#. Classes, events, inheritance, and a host of other more advanced concepts will descend on unsuspecting ASP developers like fog on a San Francisco evening. While writing real ASP applications required some technical knowledge—using COM components well isn't simple—ASP.NET asks even more of at least some of its developers.

Suppose Microsoft had shipped ASP.NET originally and that the original ASP technology had never existed. Would ASP have become so widely used? I'm inclined to doubt it. ASP.NET's barriers to entry are noticeably higher for beginners. Still, this new technology does make some accommodation for newcomers, while still providing plenty of functionality for serious developers. Like many other things in the .NET Framework (VB.NET comes immediately to mind), ASP.NET expects more from developers than did Windows DNA. Upping the technical ante will please most customers, but some are likely to be left behind.

prise the application must be installed beneath a common directory. Each ASP.NET application can also have application-wide logic stored in a global.asax file. This file, analogous to the global.asa files used with traditional ASP, can contain code that runs when the application is first executed, when it ends, when a new client begins a session with the application, and at various other times. Each ASP.NET application also has its own web.config file that controls many aspects of the application's behavior.

Figure 7-4 shows the files comprising two different ASP.NET applications. The simple retirement calculator application has two .aspx files and a web.config file. The slightly more complex account management application has two .aspx files, a global.asax file and a web.config file. It also has two assemblies, each of which consists of only a single DLL. As the figure shows, assemblies that are part of an ASP.NET application are stored in a bin directory below the application's root directory.

ASP.NET applications can be installed by just copying their files

Because ASP.NET applications are .NET Framework applications, installing an ASP.NET application requires just copying the application's files to the target machine. No registry entries are required (unless COM interoperability is used), and there's no need to restart IIS to begin using the new application. Deleting the application is equally simple—all that's required is deleting the application's files. It's even possible to install new versions of pages or assemblies while an ASP.NET application is running. Requests in progress will complete using the old code, while new requests will automatically use the new version.

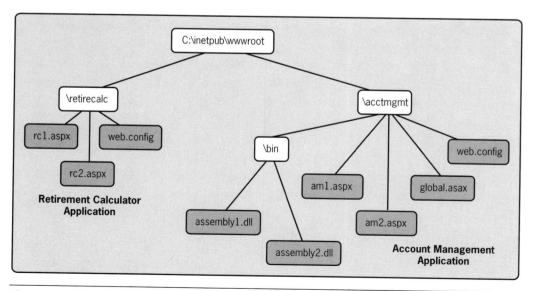

Figure 7-4   Each ASP.NET application can include pages, assemblies, a configuration file, and more.

Although it may seem odd at first, all code from all ASP.NET applications is loaded into the same Windows process. Sometimes called the ASP.NET *worker process,* it's implemented in aspnet_wp.exe. Requests from clients are handled first by IIS and then passed on to the appropriate ASP.NET application within this worker process. Loading a group of unrelated applications into a single process sounds dangerous. What happens if code from one application accesses the memory space of another one? This is a potential problem in the traditional ASP world, but it's not something developers need to worry about with ASP.NET. As Figure 7-5 shows, each ASP.NET application is loaded into its own application domain, so each application is completely isolated from any other. This is just another example of the myriad ways in which the traditional ASP model has been adapted to the .NET Framework.

The ASP.NET worker process hosts all ASP.NET applications, each in its own app domain

Built-in Objects

When a request from a client is processed, that request passes through a series of objects sometimes referred to collectively as the *HTTP pipeline.* These objects all need access to information about the request, so an instance of the HttpContext class,

.aspx pages can use several different built-in objects

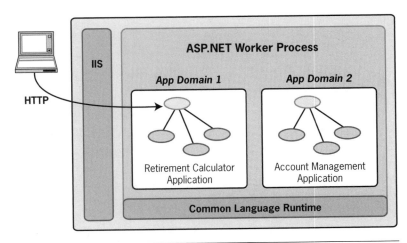

Figure 7-5   Each ASP.NET application runs in its own application domain.

contained in the System.Web namespace, is created for each incoming request. This object is available throughout the HTTP pipeline, allowing the objects in the pipeline to share information about a particular request. To allow this sharing of information, the HttpContext object contains a large number of properties, including the following:

- **Request:** Allows access to the HttpRequest object for this request. This object's properties contain information about the request, such as the HTTP query string that accompanied it, the client's IP address, any cookies that accompanied it, and much more.

- **Response:** Allows access to the HttpResponse object for this request. This object provides a large group of methods and properties focused on sending information back to the requesting client. Perhaps the most commonly used of these is the Write method illustrated in the example pages shown earlier, which directly sends output back to the client.

- **Application:** Allows access to the HttpApplicationState object for this request. This object stores information relevant for the entire ASP.NET application. Its methods include Add, which allows adding an arbitrary object to a collection maintained by this object; Get, which allows accessing an object in this collection; and Set, which allows modifying an object in this collection.

- **Cache:** Allows storing information for an ASP.NET application. The Cache object is similar to the Application object, but it provides several extra features. For example, information stored in this object can be set to expire in a specific period of time or to exist only as long as a specific file exists.

- **Session:** Allows access to the HttpSessionState object for this request. This object stores information solely about the client that made this request. Like

HttpApplicationState, it allows adding, reading, and modifying arbitrary objects in a collection. This object is especially important, so it's described in more detail later in this chapter.

- **Error:** Allows access to an Exception object for an error that occurred during processing of this request.

- **User:** Contains the identity of the client that initiated this request.

- **Handler:** Allows access to the instance of an HttpHandler class associated with this request. HTTP handlers allow access to the low-level functions of processing a request. Rather than writing code using the Internet Server API (ISAPI), such as an ISAPI extension, you can create a custom HTTP handler instead. As was true for ISAPI extensions, most people won't need to write their own handlers, but ASP.NET provides this relatively low-level option for hard-core .NET developers.

If you're familiar with traditional ASP, many of these objects will look familiar. In the ASP world, Request, Response, Session, Application, and Error are all COM objects available to applications. With ASP.NET, the same information (and more) is available via the HttpContext object. In fact, the most important properties of this object are also accessible directly through the Page class. The properties that Page provides include Request, Response, Session, Application, Error, and Cache, each of which is actually a way to access the corresponding property of the HttpRequest object for this request. Since Page is the parent class for every .aspx page, this information is readily accessible to every application.

Many of these objects are also available in traditional ASP

Among the most interesting of these objects are those used to manage an application's state. State management is a key issue for most ASP.NET applications, and as described next, there are several choices for how it's done.

Managing State

Objects in an .aspx page can't maintain their state internally between requests

Every request a client makes to an ASP.NET application causes the objects on the loaded page to be created, used, and then destroyed. This helps in building scalable applications, since no resources are taken up on the server for clients that aren't currently running requests. It can also make writing those applications more difficult, however. If all of an application's objects forget everything they've been told after every request, the application won't be very intelligent. To make it easier to create smarter software, ASP.NET provides several different ways for an application to maintain state information between client requests.

Information used by a page can be saved in a state bag

As already described, the properties in Web controls are automatically saved by inserting their values into the Web pages sent to the user and then reading those values out again when the page is sent back. Using a *state bag,* an application developer can rely on this same approach to store any other information maintained by a particular page. This inelegantly named mechanism allows an application to store any values it wishes and have them restored when the user resubmits the page. Like Web controls, the information in the state bag is saved as fields in the page sent to the user.

Information used throughout an application can be saved in the Application object

Yet the state bag saves information only for a particular page in an ASP.NET application. What if you want to save information used by several pages in the application? To do this, an application can use the Application object mentioned earlier. Rather than being sent to the client with each page, information placed in the Application object is maintained on the server and made accessible to all pages in an application. A reference to the Application object from any page in an ASP.NET application will always access the same instance. For example, if an application wishes to record the time at which some event takes place and then let that time be accessed by another page in the same application, it might contain the following line:

```
<% Application("Timestamp") = Now() %>
```

A page that wished to access the value of this variable can reference it directly, as in

```
<% response.write (Application("Timestamp")) %>
```

This book hasn't said much about threading in the .NET Framework, but it's important to note that ASP.NET applications are multithreaded. Since there's only one Application object for an entire ASP.NET application, if two different pages running on two different threads write to it simultaneously, problems can occur. Depending on the threading choices an application uses, explicit concurrency controls might be needed to avoid conflicts.

Alternatively, the Cache object can be used instead of the Application object. As mentioned earlier, the objects are broadly similar in function. The biggest difference is that the Cache object allows much more control over how long information is held and what causes it to be removed. An application can also ask that it be informed when a particular item is deleted from the Cache object, providing an event handler that runs when the information is deleted.

Information used throughout an application can also be stored in the Cache object

Storing state in either of these objects has a problem, however: Both are physically stored on a single machine. If an ASP.NET application is deployed on several Web servers, with client requests load balanced across those servers, storing state in the Application or Cache objects will be problematic. Each copy of the application will have its own instance of these objects, so the information these instances contain will likely be different. Applications that will be load balanced should be careful about how, or even if, they use these objects.

Load balancing complicates state management

The options just described can be useful ways for an application to store state. Yet none of them addresses the most common state management problem in building ASP.NET applications: maintaining per-client state. Think, for example, of

Information used throughout a single client session can be stored in the Session object

a Web application that allows its user to add items to a shopping cart. Given that the objects created by the application are destroyed after every request, how can that information be retained? Every page accessed by that client (and only that client) within an ASP.NET application should have easy access to this per-client state, but nothing described so far provides this. Yet building reasonable applications requires some way to store client-specific information across the life of a client session. In ASP.NET, the Session object provides a way to do this.

Accessing a Session object looks much like accessing the Application object. To store a value, an .aspx page can contain a line such as

```
Session("ItemSelected")= 13
```

To access that value, the page can simply refer to it as in

```
response.write(Session("ItemSelected"))
```

One Session object can exist for each active client

Even though Session and Application objects are accessed in a similar way, don't be confused. There's only one Application object shared by all pages in an ASP.NET application, while every client has its own Session object. When an application accesses the Session object, it will always get the instance associated with the client that made this request. To figure out which client each request comes from, ASP.NET assigns each client a unique 120-bit session identifier that gets stored in a cookie. The client then presents this cookie with each request it makes, allowing ASP.NET to identify all requests that come from the same client. Users can turn off cookies if they wish, however, so ASP.NET is also capable of embedding this identifier in the URL string returned to a user. However it's done, the creator of an ASP.NET application doesn't need to worry about determining which request comes from which user—it's done for him.

In traditional ASP, the Session object worked much as described here. Yet while that older version of the Session object is easy to use, it's also deadly. The ASP Session object is bound to a single machine, much like the Application object today. If an ASP application is load balanced across several different machines, only one of those machines will store this object. Requests from this client that get sent to other machines due to load balancing won't be able to access the object's contents, so they won't execute correctly. As a result, using ASP's Session object greatly limits an application's scalability.

Traditional ASP's Session object doesn't work well with load balancing

This limitation doesn't exist in ASP.NET. The Session object for a particular client can still be stored on just one machine, as in traditional ASP, but it can also be stored in a separate Session State Store. If this is done, the contents of the Session object are available to all copies of the application running on all machines in a load-balanced configuration. And because the state is in another process (and perhaps another machine), it can remain available even if the ASP.NET application itself is restarted.

ASP.NET's Session object does work well with load balancing

The standard Session State Store server provided with the .NET Framework provides four options:

The Session object can store its state in several different ways

- **InProc:** The Session object is stored in the same process as the application. This is much like the Session object in traditional ASP, and it's the default setting.

- **StateServer:** The Session object's state is stored in another process that can run locally or on another machine.

- **SQLServer:** The Session object's state is stored on disk using SQL Server.

- **Off:** The Session object is disabled.

Any state in the Session object is automatically destroyed when a client hasn't accessed the application for a configurable length of time. It's also possible to write your own session state server and plug it in to the ASP.NET infrastructure (or more correctly, insert it into the HTTP pipeline) in place of a standard solution. Note too that how the Session object's state is stored depends entirely on the contents of an application's web.config file. No code in the application needs to be modified to change which option is used.

Output caching allows saving recently accessed results in memory

Finally, although it's not state management in quite the same way as the choices just described, ASP.NET's output caching option is also worth describing here. (Don't confuse this with the Cache object described earlier, which is a separate idea.) Caching repetitively accessed data is an effective way to speed up applications. Rather than doing the work required to recreate that data each time it's requested, the information can be read quickly from an in-memory cache and returned. To use ASP.NET's caching mechanism, an .aspx page can contain a directive such as

```
<%@ OutputCache Duration="60" VaryByParam="none" %>
```

The duration specifies how long (in seconds) the results of that page can be cached before the information must be recreated. Requests that arrive for the same information within this period will have their responses returned immediately from the cache.

Output caching has several options

The required VaryByParam attribute is set to none in this example, but if desired, it can be used to control exactly which results are cached. The parameter this attribute refers to can be any named value contained in a query string, which is the text following a "?" on a client request. For example, suppose an .aspx page contained the directive

```
<%@ OutputCache Duration="60" VaryByParam="name" %>
```

Suppose further that this page received two requests with these query strings:

```
http://www.qwickbank.com/page1.aspx?name=Bob
http://www.qwickbank.com/page1.aspx?name=Casey
```

Because output caching was instructed to vary by a parameter called "name," the results of each request would be cached. Requests to this page with names of either Bob or Casey that are received within the 60-second window specified on the Duration attribute will return cached results. Other things, such as the type of browser from which a request originated, can also be used to control exactly which pages are cached. The result is a more responsive application, especially if the same data is accessed over and over.

ASP.NET Security

Securing Web applications is incredibly important. Internet viruses have made even nonprofessionals aware of the dangers of too little security. Unfortunately, really understanding Web security is a large topic, one that's outside the scope of this chapter's short description. Nevertheless, it's worth making a few points about what ASP.NET provides in this area.

Browser applications must be secure

The System.Web.Security namespace contains a large set of types that can be used to provide security services for ASP.NET applications. The primary focus is on authentication, that is, on proving you are who you say you are. Although a developer is free to create her own authentication mechanism, ASP.NET applications have several authentication options provided for them. The choices include the following:

ASP.NET provides several options for authenticating users

- **Windows authentication:** Based on what's built into IIS, there are three options. Basic authentication, simplest of the three, requires a client to send an unencrypted password across the network, which by itself is no one's idea of good security. Digest authentication, the second choice, requires a client to send a hashed version of a password and other information, which provides somewhat better security. The third option, called Integrated Windows Authentication, allows using the authentication protocol available in a Windows domain, such as Kerberos. This choice is quite secure, but it's generally available only on intranets and only when the client browser is Internet Explorer.

- **Forms authentication:** A mechanism new with ASP.NET, this option allows an application to display a custom form to acquire user credentials, such as a login name and password and then to decide whether the user is who she claims to be. It relies on the Secure Sockets Layer (SSL) protocol to ensure that those credentials are encrypted when initially sent across the network.

- **Passport authentication:** Allows using Microsoft's Internet-based Passport service. System.Web.Security contains several classes that allow applications to access Passport and then use the authenticated client identity it provides.

ASP.NET applications can make an authorization decision in different ways

Once a client has been authenticated, the next step is to make an authorization decision for that client, that is, to determine what the client is allowed to do. If one of the Windows authentication options is used, a client's attempt to access a particular file such as an .aspx file will be subject to the usual access controls. This means that Windows will automatically check the access control list (ACL) on the file to ensure that the user's request is allowed. With Windows authentication or any of the other authentication options, an approach called URL authorization is also available. This option allows fine-grained control over who is allowed to perform what operations against a particular ASP.NET application.

With .aspx pages, ASP.NET lets developers create what has become the norm today: applications that are accessed through a browser. While the name and some parts of the technology are derived from the original ASP technology, ASP.NET is a complete rewrite—and a rethink—of how to build browser-accessible applications on the .NET Framework. Implemented almost entirely as types in the .NET Framework class library, the services it provides will be used by many, many developers. Yet browser-accessible applications aren't the only way to use the Web today. Web services also matter, and ASP.NET allows creating this new kind of application as well. How this can be done is described next.

ASP.NET redesigns ASP from the ground up

Web Services Applications: System.Web.Services

The fundamental concepts of Web services—SOAP, WSDL, and the rest—were described in Chapter 2. The chapters since then have described the suite of technologies provided by the .NET Framework. ASP.NET's support for Web services combines these two things, providing a way to build .NET Framework applications that expose and use SOAP-callable methods.

Web Services Servers

Like the browser applications described so far, the server side of an ASP.NET Web services application relies on pages. As shown in Figure 7-6, the files containing those pages have an .asmx extension rather than .aspx, and they don't contain any HTML. Apart from an occasional directive, they're just code. No HTML is required because a Web service is accessed by software, not by people, so it doesn't display a user interface. Ultimately, of course, there is often some human being whose request triggered the Web service, but the interface that person uses to accomplish this is outside the scope of the Web service itself. Web services don't define GUIs; .asmx pages don't contain

Web services applications rely on .asmx pages

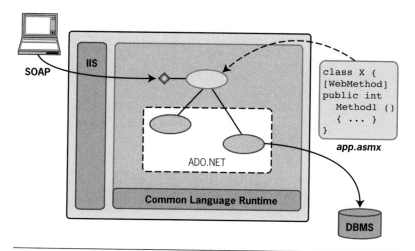

Figure 7-6   A Web services application is built using .asmx pages, which produce managed objects when they're accessed.

HTML. As the figure also indicates, Web services applications are nothing more than managed objects, so they can use ADO.NET for data access and other available services.

The WebMethod attribute is used to expose a method as a Web service

To expose a method contained in an .asmx file as a Web service, all that's required is to insert the attribute WebMethod in front of the method declaration. That's it. When the file is compiled, this attribute will be stored in the metadata of the resulting assembly, like all attributes. Its presence signals to the ASP.NET infrastructure that this method should be made accessible as a Web service. To give you a sense of how simple this is to do, think back to the Compute class used in Chapter 4's language examples. An .asmx file that exposed the C# version of that class's two methods as Web services might look like this:

```
<%@ WebService Language="c#" Class="Compute" %>
using System.Web.Services;
public class Compute
{
    [WebMethod]
    public int Factorial(int f)
    {
```

```
        int i;
        int result = 1;
        for (i=2; i<=f; i++)
            result = result * i;
        return result;
    }
    [WebMethod]
    public double SquareRoot(double s)
    {
        return System.Math.Sqrt(s);
    }
}
```

The file's contents begin with a WebService directive. Similar in form to the Page directive shown earlier, this line indicates that the Web service specified in this .asmx page is written in C# and defines a class named Compute. Next appears a using statement for the namespace System.Web.Services, followed by the definition of the Compute class. This class is virtually identical to what was shown in Chapter 4. For simplicity, this version doesn't use an interface, although that's not an important distinction here. What is important is the presence of the WebMethod attribute before each of the class's methods. This attribute is defined in System.Web.Services, hence the using statement that precedes this class, and it's the only addition required to expose these methods as Web services. Note, however, that only public methods can be marked with the WebMethod attribute.

Web services applications are ASP.NET applications, too

Web services applications are deployed as ASP.NET applications, just like applications built using .aspx pages. As with .aspx pages, an .asmx page is compiled when it is first accessed by a client. The resulting assembly is stored on disk and then reused until the .asmx page that produced it is modified. Changing this page results in an automatic recompile the next time the page is accessed.

ASP.NET allows accessing an .asmx page from a browser

When an .asmx page is accessed through a browser, ASP.NET uses reflection to learn what Web services it exposes. ASP.NET uses this knowledge to create a Web page that allows learning about these services. The Web page provides a way to invoke the services, examples of what calls to these services look like on the wire, and even a full WSDL definition of the Web services defined in this .asmx page. In reality, of course, the clients for Web services will usually be software other than a browser, but it's still nice to have this Web page generated for you as it provides an easy way to verify that your methods are available.

Web services appli-
cations can use the
code-behind option

Like browser-focused ASP.NET applications, ASP.NET applications that provide Web services can also use a code-behind option. In this case, the .asmx file contains just the WebService directive with a reference to the assembly that contains the class. The actual code for that class is in a separate file, just as with browser-accessible ASP.NET applications.

Web Services Clients

Web services
clients depend on
proxies

Servers are useless without clients. To create a client capable of invoking the Web services in some server, a developer must first create a proxy class that exposes the same methods. This proxy can be created in Visual Studio.NET just by adding a Web reference to a project or by specifying an .asmx file, a WSDL file, or something else. Given this information, Visual Studio.NET will extract the information it needs to build a proxy for the desired Web service. It's also possible to create a proxy manually using wsdl.exe, a command-line tool that reads in a WSDL file and produces a proxy in the desired programming language. Once this proxy exists, the client can create an instance of that class and call its methods just like any other class. The proxy will forward each call to the destination Web service, that method will execute, and any results will be returned though the proxy.

This is much like .NET Remoting, where a proxy object communicates through channel objects to interact with an object in another app domain. With Web services, however, the remote object might well be written in Java and running on Linux. ASP.NET's SOAP implementation is distinct from the one provided by .NET Remoting, even though the concepts and terminology are similar.

It's also possible to invoke a Web service asynchronously. Rather than make the call and then block waiting for a response, a client can call the Web service and go about its business. When it gets the chance, the client can check to see what results, if any, the call has returned. To do this, the client uses two methods provided by the proxy along with the normal synchronous method for each Web service it supports. The first of these begins the call, passing in any parameters, and then returns control to the client. The second ends the call, returning any results that have come back. Other options are also possible, allowing the client to avoid repeatedly checking for the call to be completed.

Web services can be called asynchronously

Options for Web Services Applications

Building straightforward Web services such as those just shown could hardly be simpler. Adding one attribute isn't much work, and building a client proxy is also dead easy. But then, the methods in this example's Compute class don't do much either. Web services methods that do real work commonly require a bit more complexity than what's been shown so far. This section describes some of the options ASP.NET provides for creating more powerful and more useful Web services.

For example, what if a Web services application needs to maintain state about its client between requests? Just as with the .aspx pages of a browser application, object instances defined via an .asmx page are created, used, and then destroyed for each request. Without some outside help, a Web services application can't store any in-memory information between requests. Fortunately, this outside help is available in the form of the standard objects provided by ASP.NET for this purpose. If a class that includes Web services methods inherits from System.Web.Services.WebService, code in that class can access the Session

Web services applications can use built-in objects to manage their state

Why Are There Two Separate SOAP Implementations in the .NET Framework?

As described in Chapter 5, .NET Remoting includes an implementation of SOAP. ASP.NET includes another implementation of SOAP. On the face of it, this makes no sense. Why include two completely separate implementations of the same technology in the .NET Framework class library?

The short answer is: different groups, different goals. Recall that the goal of .NET Remoting is to communicate effectively across a network when both client and server are running the .NET Framework. SOAP is used primarily because, when mapped to HTTP, it allows this communication to pass through firewalls. In ASP.NET, on the other hand, the goal is to interoperate with any other implementation of SOAP, not just with the .NET Framework. SOAP is used both because it can pass through firewalls and because it's supported by many vendors.

A primary result of these different goals was described in Chapter 5: how serialized CLR types are mapped into XML. .NET Remoting uses the SOAP formatter, which allows everything that can be expressed by a CLR-based application to be passed across the network, including private data members and more. ASP.NET's SOAP implementation is not so committed to full-fidelity transfer of CLR types. Instead, it strives to produce a purely standard XML representation in everything it transmits, so it uses the XmlSerializer class to serialize and deserialize information. Sending a serialized type across ASP.NET's SOAP implementation won't send any private data members, for example, since XML has no notion of private members. The XmlSerializer emphasizes faithfulness to XML's XSD type system, while the SOAP formatter used in .NET Remoting emphasizes faithfulness to the CLR types.

Where .NET Remoting targets the homogeneous case, ASP.NET's Web services are optimized for heterogeneity. In a perfect world, the imperfections that drive this division wouldn't exist. Given the complexities engendered by different type systems, different vendors, and the still-emerging technology of Web services, we shouldn't be surprised to find that they do exist, at least for today.

object, the Application object, and others. Through these, a Web services application can maintain state about its clients, access the User object to learn who the client is, and use the other services provided by these objects.

To use the Session object, although not the others, a method within this class must also specify the EnableSession parameter in its WebMethod attribute. For example, if the Factorial method in the Compute class shown earlier were to do this, its declaration would look like this:

Using the Session object requires specifying the EnableSession parameter

```
[WebMethod(EnableSession=true)]
    public int Factorial(int f)
    { ...}
```

Here's another concern: What if a method exposed as a Web service needs to group the work it does into a transaction? If the method uses ADO.NET to access a DBMS, it can certainly use the services of the Connection and Transaction objects to demarcate transaction boundaries, just like any other ADO.NET client. But suppose the method needs to create a transaction that spans multiple DBMSs or includes work done by other components? In the .NET Framework, these services are provided by the classes in System.EnterpriseServices, as described in Chapter 5, and ultimately by COM+. To access these services, a method exposed as a Web service can use another parameter of the WebMethod attribute called TransactionOption. If a method to transfer money between two bank accounts were exposed as a Web service, for example, that method might be declared like this:

Web services applications can also use transactions

```
[WebMethod(TransactionOption=
    TransactionOption.Required)]
public bool MoveMoney(int fromAccount,
    int toAccount, decimal amount)
{ ... }
```

When the method executes, it will automatically run within a transaction managed by code in System.EnterpriseServices. It's

Transactions don't span SOAP calls

important to note that this transaction includes only the work done by the MoveMoney method, which might, say, add to one account and subtract from another. It does not involve the client, whose only role is to call MoveMoney. The value of transactions that span SOAP calls is an open topic today, one on which reasonable people can disagree. While a way to do this might one day exist, currently the TransactionOption property controls only conventional COM+-based transactions.

ASP.NET supports processing SOAP headers

Another issue that might confront the creator of a Web services method is how to deal with SOAP headers. As Chapter 2 described, a SOAP packet can include various headers, and each of those headers can have a mustUnderstand attribute. Given that SOAP headers are allowed to contain virtually anything, ASP.NET provides quite generic support for working with them. The foundation of that support is the SoapHeader class, contained in the namespace System.Web.Services.Protocols. This class defines common properties found in a SOAP header, including a MustUnderstand property to contain the value of a header's mustUnderstand attribute. By inheriting from this class, a developer can more easily create a class that reflects the specifics of a particular SOAP header. To populate an instance of a SoapHeader class, a SoapHeader attribute can be added to a Web method's definition, identifying a variable of the appropriate header class. When a SOAP packet that contains this header is received, the header's information will be copied into the SoapHeader class, allowing the method to examine it.

A Web services application can define its own namespace

One more concern stems from every Web service's dependence on XML, the representation for all information sent and received via SOAP. This information, including method names and more, will belong to a default XML namespace unless an explicit alternative is provided. It's a good idea to provide this alternative since XML namespaces are used to differentiate between information carried by different services. The WebService attribute, defined in System.Web.Services, can be applied to the class, with the attribute's Namespace parameter used to specify the XML namespace. For example, if the Compute class shown earlier were provided by the fictitious QwickBank, its declaration might look like this:

```
[WebService(Namespace=
    "http://www.qwickbank.com/mathinfo")]
public class Compute
{ . . . }
```

Recall that even though it looks like a URL, an XML namespace identifier is actually a URI. Typing this identifier into a browser isn't guaranteed to lead anywhere at all—it's just a convenient way to specify a unique name.

Microsoft-Specific Support for Web Services Applications

The basic standards for Web services are largely complete today, and ASP.NET supports them quite well. SOAP and WSDL are an intrinsic part of ASP.NET, as already described. Visual Studio.NET also has built-in support for accessing a UDDI registry on the Internet to find and add references for publicly available Web services. But given the nascent state of Web services, most vendors who implement them add some extras, and Microsoft is no exception.

One option ASP.NET provides is the ability to access Web services using pure HTTP rather than sending SOAP messages over HTTP. If HTTP's GET method is used, a call's parameters are passed in a simple form—not XML—as part of the URL string handed to the server. If HTTP's POST method is used, a call's parameters are passed in the body of the HTTP message, with each parameter identified by name. For clients that are unable to bear the weight of SOAP, these simpler protocol choices might be useful.

ASP.NET allows invoking Web services using just HTTP

Another addition is the simpler alternative to UDDI called Disco, mentioned in Chapter 2. Intended for discovering available Web services on a single machine or in a local

Disco provides a straightforward way to learn about available Web services

environment, Disco uses a simple XML-defined format to describe available Web services and access their WSDL descriptions. Visual Studio.NET automatically produces Disco files and just as with UDDI, allows searching for and adding references to Web services with Disco descriptions. Without a Web service's WSDL definition, it's tough to build a client for that service. Given both the early state of UDDI and its relative complexity, Microsoft has chosen also to provide this simple, concrete mechanism for discovering Web services in a more localized environment.

Conclusion

To understand ASP.NET, first understand the .NET Framework as a whole

For traditional ASP developers, ASP.NET is a new world. Some parts will look familiar, and much of the knowledge picked up in the old world will be useful in this one. Much of it won't, however, and some might be downright misleading. Because of this, the best way to understand ASP.NET isn't to think in terms of the technology it replaces. The best approach is first to understand the .NET Framework in general and then to grasp how ASP.NET builds on this foundation. ASP.NET applications are created in special ways using .aspx and .asmx pages, but in the end, they're just .NET Framework applications. As always, everything boils down to assemblies executing on the CLR.

8

.NET My Services

How many different ways are there to apply Web services? No one knows. Some of the possibilities—B2B integration over the Internet, application integration inside the firewall, and others—were described in Chapter 2. Yet Web services are a powerful idea that can be used in all sorts of ways. New technologies create new applications, and Web services are no exception.

Web services are a broadly useful technology

For instance, the advent of Web services makes possible new approaches to storing and accessing information. Rather than keeping your personal address book on your desktop computer, why not store it on the Internet and access it as a Web service? This would allow information about the people you commonly contact to be accessed from your desktop machine, your personal digital assistant (PDA), your mobile phone, and other devices. Similarly, why not store your calendar or other generally useful information in a similar way? And why not use Web services to notify you when, say, a book that you're interested in arrives at your favorite Web bookstore?

Web services can be used to access personal information on the Internet

.NET My Services provides Internet access to personal information via the Internet

.NET My Services, originally code-named HailStorm, is a set of Internet-accessible Web services that provide services such as these. By defining documented interfaces for accessing the information it stores, .NET My Services makes it possible to access that information from a variety of applications and devices. And since storing personal information on the Internet raises significant privacy and security concerns, .NET My Services provides substantial security services for the data it stores. By offering a standard set of Internet-accessible services that can be exploited by software running on any connected device, .NET My Services makes possible a new class of Web-based applications.[1]

Defining .NET My Services

.NET My Services consists of a network authentication service together with a group of SOAP-callable Web services. These services are provided by a distributed group of server machines, run by Microsoft (and potentially other organizations as well), that can be accessed over the Internet. Each service stores a particular kind of data or supports a specific function.

Passport authenticates clients that access .NET My Services

For example, allowing a client to prove its identity is essential for a wide range of applications. Accordingly, as in most distributed environments, .NET My Services provides a core authentication service that is used by all other .NET My Services. This service is provided by Microsoft's Passport technology, which in its .NET My Services version is extended to support Kerberos. All clients that access .NET My Services rely on Passport, and thus on Kerberos, for authentication.

---

1. This chapter describes the original version of the .NET My Services technology. More recently, Microsoft has announced that .NET My Services will be made available as software for use on both the Internet and internal networks.

Once a client has been authenticated, that client can access other services. Some examples of these services include the following:

.NET My Services stores a variety of information about people

- **.NET Profile:** Stores various personal information about a user, such as the user's name, telephone number, e-mail address, mailing address, and so on.

- **.NET Calendar:** Maintains a user's personal calendar. Applications might use this information for things such as determining when a user is able to receive a delivery; recording a flight that's been scheduled; checking when a user is free to attend a meeting; or synchronizing a user's schedule between his office computer, his home machine, and his PDA.

- **.NET Alerts:** Manages a stream of notification messages directed to a particular user. From a developer's point of view, this service provides a standard way to send events asynchronously to a user wherever she might be. The services in .NET My Services themselves can use this—you might be notified of an upcoming event on your calendar, for example—as can applications that make use of .NET My Services. An auction Web site could use this service to notify you when a higher bid has been received for an item you're interested in, or an application selling tickets might notify you that a friend has purchased two seats for a show and invited you to join her.

- **.NET Contacts:** Provides a list of names, addresses, and other contact information for a user, that is, an address book. Stored along with this is information needed by .NET My Services that, among other things, allows mapping from a name to what's required to send an alert to that person.

- **.NET Inbox:** Allows access to a user's e-mail. Because it provides programmatic access to mail from any

Internet-connected device, this service could potentially allow new kinds of mail applications.

- **.NET Lists:** Stores lists of various kinds. Some potential examples include a user's to-do list, a shopping list, and a list of desired gifts posted by a bride-to-be.

- **.NET Documents:** Provides Internet-accessible storage for a user's documents, allowing the same information to be accessed (and possibly shared) from multiple devices and multiple users at multiple locations.

- **.NET Presence:** Maintains a list of electronic endpoints where a user can be contacted. For example, a user might have an active Instant Messenger client that can receive notifications and other immediate communications. Applications that send alerts can rely on this service to route those messages to a device near the user, such as a desktop computer or PDA.

- **.NET Devices:** Maintains a list of devices and device characteristics for a user. For example, an entry for a PDA might indicate its screen and bandwidth limitations. An application could use this information to determine that a particular device isn't appropriate for, say, video-conferencing.

- **.NET Wallet:** Contains payment information such as a user's credit card number. A Web site might access this and allow a user to select one of the credit cards contained in the wallet along with ship-to and bill-to addresses. This information could then be transferred to the appropriate fields on a form on the Web site, saving the user from having to enter the information manually.

- **.NET Application Settings:** Maintains information about a user's application settings. For example, Office might store settings such as a user's toolbar and dictionary preferences here. This would allow the user to see the same

Office environment from any .NET My Services–aware system she logs into.

- **.NET Services:** Maintains a list of services a user has subscribed to (or in the jargon of .NET My Services, has been *provisioned* for). This is actually a simple directory used by .NET My Services–based applications to locate other services provided by .NET My Services.

One important fact to grasp about these services is that with the exception of Passport, the information stored in each one is defined using XML and accessed via SOAP. Don't be confused by the similarity between what's provided by .NET My Services and the Internet mail and calendar services provided today by Microsoft, AOL, Netscape, and others. These existing services are all designed to be accessed directly by people through browsers. The .NET My Services offerings, by contrast, are exposed programmatically—they're Web services. Rather than being accessed through a browser, each of these services is meant to be accessed by client software making SOAP calls.

Most services provide access to XML-defined data through SOAP

Reflecting the heterogeneity of the Internet, Microsoft's goal is that .NET My Services will be usable from all kinds of systems. This includes Windows, of course, and so the .NET Framework will provide good support for building applications that access .NET My Services. Target clients also include Macintosh desktops, Linux machines, PDAs running Windows CE or PalmOS, mobile phones, and any other intelligent device. Because .NET My Services is accessed using the industry-standard SOAP and Kerberos protocols, this is at least theoretically possible, and Microsoft has demonstrated access to .NET My Services from diverse clients. Also, Microsoft has indicated that it plans to submit to standards bodies the extensions it makes to SOAP and Kerberos for .NET My Services. Given the challenges that exist in Web services interoperability, however, the goal of universal access to .NET My Services is not simple to accomplish. Yet with the increasing popularity of small devices, a majority of

.NET My Services is potentially accessible from all kinds of clients

which don't run Windows, it's easy to see why Microsoft wishes to make .NET My Services broadly accessible.

Each user has her own logical instance of what .NET My Services provides

Figure 8-1 illustrates how .NET My Services can be accessed. As the figure shows, both clients and servers can use the services. In fact, if a user contacts .NET My Services from any of her client devices, the same instance of each service will be accessed. Whether a user accesses her .NET Inbox from her PDA, from her desktop computer, or from her mobile phone, for example, she will be recognized as the same user and have access to the same information. No matter what client her access comes from, she is always authenticated using Passport.

Applying .NET My Services

Applications can exploit .NET My Services in many different ways

An application developer can use .NET My Services in a variety of ways. Here are a few possibilities.

- An application running on a client machine might allow a user to access directly the information .NET My Services maintains. For example, software running on a

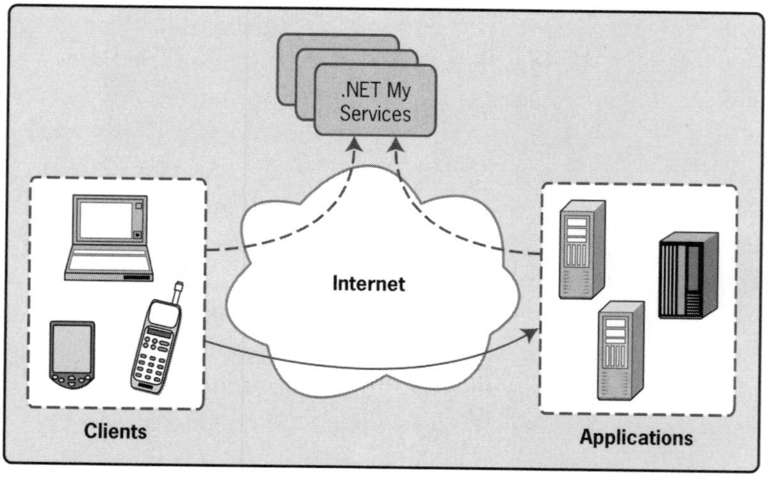

Figure 8-1   Both clients and servers can access .NET My Services across the Internet.

PDA might use the .NET Inbox service to allow a user to check his e-mail and then access .NET Contacts and .NET Calendar to synchronize information between his devices. Other examples include a user allowing her co-workers access to files stored in .NET Documents, thus providing shared access to these documents from any Internet-connected device or from an application that merges .NET Calendar information from multiple sources or multiple users into a single view, allowing better coordination of diverse schedules.

- An application running on a Web site and accessed via a browser might access .NET My Services information to learn about its user (with that user's permission, of course). For example, the application could first use .NET My Services's Passport service to authenticate the user. Once this was done, it could access the user's .NET Wallet service to acquire payment information and then use his .NET Calendar service to determine when to schedule delivery.

- An application could use .NET My Services to arrange other types of communication. For instance, a videoconferencing application might use services such as .NET Contacts, .NET Presence, and .NET Devices to arrange the videoconference and then use any appropriate protocol and data format for the conference itself.

- An application could expose one or more Web services, relying on .NET My Services to provide various foundation services. For example, a ticket booking application might expose a Web service that allows a user to book seats for a concert and then have notifications sent to a friend inviting him to attend. The application could use .NET My Services's Passport service for authentication, the .NET Alerts service to send asynchronous events, such as the invitation, and other services as needed.

Several organiza-
tions have shown
prototype
applications

Although it's early days for .NET My Services, a number of proto-type applications have been demonstrated. The Internet auction site eBay, for example, has demonstrated using Passport to authenticate to its service and then using .NET Alerts to inform a bidder when a higher bid has been received for an item of interest. American Express has shown a service that uses alerts to provide immediate information to the customer about potentially fraudulent use of his card, while the United States Postal Service has described an application that can examine a user's calendar through the .NET Calendar service and then determine when that user will be home to accept delivery of a package. The online travel agency Expedia has demonstrated a prototype that sends alerts to your wireless PDA, desktop computer, or mobile phone informing you that your outbound flight has been delayed.

.NET My Services
must attract appli-
cations to succeed

Applications are everything. For this technology to succeed, software developers must believe in .NET My Services and provide useful applications. Microsoft itself will surely provide some—look for options to use .NET My Services in a future release of Office, for instance—but as with any other application platform, one vendor isn't sufficient. Success requires a critical mass of applications. It's too soon to know how many developers .NET My Services will attract, but as just described, a number of organizations have shown early interest in exploiting this new technology.

Assuring Privacy

Data privacy is a
key issue for .NET
My Services

Relying on Microsoft to store personal information such as our calendar, our contacts list, and our credit card number immediately raises questions about the privacy of that information. Who owns it? Who can access it? Who can change it? Unless .NET My Services users feel comfortable with the answers to these questions, they won't use applications built on this technology.

Access to data is
controlled by the
user who owns that
data

According to Microsoft, the answer to all of these questions is very simple: All of a user's data is owned by that user, and nothing can be done to this data except with the user's permission. Microsoft promises not to access, modify, sell, or use any

.NET My Services as an Application Platform

Think about what it means to be a platform for applications. Most fundamentally, a platform must provide the services that developers need to support useful software. For example, every application platform must provide basic hardware services such as processing power, memory, and disk storage. A platform must also provide software services, including authentication, a way to store and retrieve files, and other services.

These services may be provided by a single machine. In this case, a developer relies on the operating system to authenticate users by making them prove their identity when they log in, to provide a file system, and to supply other services. With the advent of distributed computing, the notion of an application platform expanded to include a group of machines on a local area network. The basic services provided by the platform remain the same, but various machines in the network now provide those services. In a Windows 2000 domain, for example, authentication is provided by a machine acting as a domain controller, while file storage is provided by a machine acting as a file server. Both are available to any application running on any machine in the domain, and so both are part of the application platform.

The Internet is the next step in the evolution of application platforms. Many applications have been built on the Internet today, yet most of them treat the client as a relatively dumb device capable only of interacting with the user through a browser. Rather than functioning as a true application platform, the Internet today provides little more than support for remote terminals. To make this global network into an effective platform for applications, a set of core services must be made available to Internet-based applications. There could be a common way to authenticate Internet users, for example, just as there is today on a single machine or in a distributed environment such as a Windows 2000 domain. There could also be a common way to store information, allowing users to access it from anywhere in the network. Services like these, provided to any user on any device connected anywhere in the world, would transform the Internet from an environment supporting just dumb browsers into a global platform for applications.

.NET My Services provides these services. Just as application developers have exploited operating systems and distributed environments to build powerful applications, .NET My Services potentially allows them to create a new kind of application that exploits the Internet as a platform. For the most part, Microsoft doesn't position .NET My Services this way, choosing instead to focus on its data storage aspects. Yet .NET My Services surely can be thought of as a wholly new kind of application platform. The Internet has changed so much, why not expect it to change what we think of as an application platform?

of the data it stores in any other way without the user's explicit permission. (An exception to this rule is that to conform to legal requirements, information subpoenaed by authorized law enforcement agencies must be surrendered.) Furthermore, a user must always explicitly grant access to data for a particular application; that is, an opt-in model is always used. And any granted access can later be revoked by the user; it need not be permanent.

For .NET My Services to succeed, its benefits must outweigh the privacy risks

The key point here is that users, not application developers, will decide whether the advantages an application provides are worth the potential exposure of their personal information. For .NET My Services to succeed, software developers must create useful applications that solve real problems for their users. As always, the benefits must outweigh the costs.

The .NET My Services Business Model: Software as a Service
New technologies often beget new business models. The original Internet business model—advertising-supported free services—didn't work for most sites. The bursting of the dot-com bubble made clear that a different, more sustainable approach was required. And given that .NET My Services is accessed via Web services rather than browsers, advertising isn't an especially attractive option anyway.

How Can We Trust Microsoft with Our Personal Data?

Microsoft solemnly promises to keep all of the data we store in .NET My Services completely private. But why should we trust Microsoft to keep this promise? The temptation to make large sums of money from the data it holds might prove irresistible, since, if .NET My Services succeeds, it will hold a great deal of valuable information. Trusting Microsoft or any private organization to maintain the privacy of our personal information requires a leap of faith.

Yet if Microsoft breaks its promise, every .NET My Services customer will stop using the service, and .NET My Services will fail. In fact, business customers are likely to force Microsoft to sign contracts guaranteeing the privacy of their data, so selling this information would also expose Microsoft to large financial liabilities. Following through on its privacy promise is Microsoft's only chance to make .NET My Services succeed as a business. In a very real way, it's in Microsoft's interest to keep its word. If the company changes its mind or if the people at Microsoft promoting .NET My Services have lied to us, .NET My Services will replace Microsoft Bob as the company's most visible failure.

Even if Microsoft keeps its promise, however, there's another concern: What about the other organizations that we let access our data? If I grant access to my .NET Profile information to, say, an application running on some company's Web site, how can I be sure that company won't use my data in some way I don't approve of? It might sell my address or send me unwanted e-mail solicitations or barrage me with telemarketing calls at dinnertime. Although Microsoft has talked about requiring applications using .NET My Services to conform to some sort of privacy regulations, this will be challenging to enforce. More likely, it will be up to users to decide whether they trust an organization with the information they're allowing it to access.

Ultimately, it's customers who will decide. If they believe that the benefits of .NET My Services–based applications outweigh whatever loss to privacy those benefits bring with them, then .NET My Services will succeed. If they don't, .NET My Services will end up as just another evolutionary dead end in the technology ecosystem.

Organizations that build applications on .NET My Services will be charged an annual fee

Microsoft announced the preliminary business model for .NET My Services in late 2001. Under this plan, applications using .NET My Services would pay an annual fee ranging from just over a thousand dollars to a negotiated (and presumably higher) amount for very heavy users of the service. Most organizations that field .NET My Services applications should expect to pay not much more than $10,000 a year for use of those services, according to Microsoft.

End users will provide most of the revenue Microsoft derives from .NET My Services

The primary revenue source is intended to be end users, however, not organizations that deploy .NET My Services applications. Microsoft says that some services, such as Passport, will remain free, while others will likely have subscription fees. These subscriptions may be options available with other products, such as Microsoft Office, or they may be standalone services. Third-party developers who build applications using .NET My Services are free to charge their customers any way they like, including selling subscriptions and access-based pricing. In any case, the goal is to rely primarily on users, not on application developers, to pay for the cost of running the services and to provide the profits that Microsoft hopes to derive from them.

.NET My Services will eventually allow federation with other services

Microsoft has also stated that it will allow other organizations to host installations of .NET My Services, perhaps using Microsoft's software to do it. A third party such as a large Internet service provider might run its own installation of Passport, for instance, or its own .NET Documents service. All of these can be federated into a single unified system, allowing customers to choose the organization they'd like to work with. While this kind of federation may or may not be available in the first .NET My Services release, it appears to be a goal that Microsoft is committed to reaching.

Describing .NET My Services

.NET My Services includes Passport and a group of XML-based services

While they're all part of .NET My Services, it's useful to distinguish between the authentication service and the XML-based

Will Users Pay for Services on the Internet?

Up to now, the subscription model hasn't been especially successful on the Internet. Users have resisted paying when so much content is available for free. Yet the kinds of services that can be provided using .NET My Services are quite different from what has gone before. Large numbers of people are clearly willing to subscribe to services that they find valuable, such as cable TV, basic Internet access, and mobile telephony. To make .NET My Services's subscription-based business model work, Microsoft and application developers must provide services that people think are worth subscribing to. Users must be convinced of the value of the services they're getting.

This makes sense—new kinds of businesses require providing new value to users—and once again, it's a business issue. If Microsoft and independent software developers can't create applications that users are willing to pay for, .NET My Services will die. If they can, however, there's every reason to think that people will pay for "user experiences"—Microsoft's new term for applications—that make their lives better.

services. The information in Passport is not defined using XML, but the access protocol for this service is defined by Kerberos. All data in all other services is represented using XML, and those services are always accessed via SOAP. Accordingly, this section is divided into two parts, one for each of these categories.

The Authentication Service: Passport

Controlling which clients are allowed to access data requires knowing that a client is who it claims to be. Accordingly, authentication is at the heart of .NET My Services. Any client that wishes to access any of the .NET My Services relies on Passport to prove its identity. To do this, every .NET My Services user (that is, each principal) is assigned a Passport unique identifier (PUID). PUIDs are unique and unchanging, so once one is assigned, it will always identify the same principal. A PUID can

Every .NET My Services client authenticates with Passport

be assigned to a particular person, a group of people, or an application that uses .NET My Services.

Client identity has two parts

In .NET My Services, identity means more than just who a principal is. It's entirely plausible that you might wish to grant or deny access to information stored in .NET My Services based not only on who the principal is, but also on what application the principal is running. To allow this, each request carries the principal's PUID along with an indication of the application this principal is running. This allows things such as granting your broker access to your financial information when he's at the office running an approved application, but not when he's home at night using his own less secure personal computer.

As used by .NET My Services, Passport relies on Kerberos

As mentioned earlier, the .NET My Services Passport service relies on Kerberos. This well-understood protocol is also used in Windows 2000 domains and other environments, so it's a familiar solution to this important problem. Figure 8-2 shows a simplified picture of how Kerberos works.[2] When a user logs in, a request for a *ticket-granting ticket (TGT)* is sent to the Passport service (step 1). If the user has entered the correct password, the server returns the TGT (step 2), and the login succeeds. (It's important to note that the user's password is not transmitted across the network during this process.) Before the first access to any other service, whether it's one provided by .NET My Services or a service offered by a third-party application, the client presents the TGT to the Passport service and requests a *ticket* for this new service (step 3). The Passport service uses the TGT to verify the client's identity and, if all is well, returns a ticket to the requested service along with something called a *session key* (step 4). The client presents this ticket to the service being accessed (step 5), which verifies it,

---

2. This very short description omits many important aspects of the protocol, including how it actually provides its security services. For a more detailed discussion, see Chapter 3 of my earlier book *Understanding Microsoft Windows 2000 Distributed Services* (Microsoft Press, 2000).

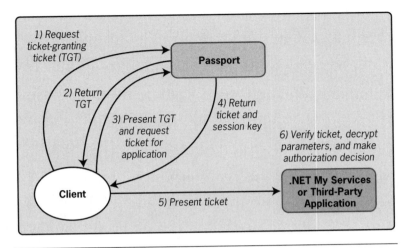

Figure 8-2   Kerberos uses tickets for authentication.

and then decides what access this user is allowed (step 6). The client might be a human being using a desktop computer or PDA, or it might be an application using .NET My Services. Both use tickets to prove their identity, and so both rely on the Passport service.

Along with authentication, Kerberos also provides data integrity and data privacy. To achieve these things, the session key returned in step 4 is used to encrypt information sent between the client and the software the client is accessing. When a client accesses .NET My Services, all user data sent on the request is encrypted with this key.

All .NET My Services user data is encrypted when sent across the network

XML-Based Services

With the exception of Passport, application developers see every service provided by .NET My Services as a collection of XML documents. Each service has an XML schema that describes the types of information it can contain. For example, the schema for the .NET Calendar service defines types such as event and reminder, while the schema for the .NET Profile service defines the type's name, address, emailAddress, telephoneNumber, picture,

Each XML-based service provided by .NET My Services has its own schema

Single Sign-on for the Internet

Users hate having multiple passwords. Single sign-on, the ability to log on once with one password and then access any number of systems on the Internet, could solve this problem. Making users' lives simpler in this way is a primary goal of Passport.

Yet single sign-on for the Internet also raises troubling questions. If only Microsoft provides the service, won't the company gain enormous control over what should be a multivendor network? One roadblock to this potential single-vendor dominance is that competitors are likely to appear, providing choices for both applications and end users about which authentication service they use. Another mitigating factor was mentioned earlier: Microsoft will allow federation of the .NET My Services Passport service. Using Kerberos, other organizations will be able to authenticate users without Microsoft's direct involvement. People who don't trust Microsoft to perform this function can turn to another authentication provider in the Passport federation.

While this dispersal of control might make customers feel more comfortable, it has the potential actually to make them less secure. In a federated Passport scheme, for instance, each Kerberos implementation needs to trust all of the others to authenticate users correctly. Is it safer to trust just one organization to do this correctly, or would you prefer to trust a potentially large group of organizations? Microsoft has talked about ranking different Kerberos providers in the federation according to how trustable they are, which might help. In any case, there are tradeoffs between security and control.

Even if no single vendor has total control, single sign-on for the Internet brings other concerns. For example, if I can log on just once to access many systems, doesn't this make the potential damage a successful attacker can do that much greater? If that attacker can somehow learn my password, he can now masquerade as me on many different sites.

Single sign-on is probably a mixed blessing. Some form of it is slowly working its way into the Internet, and .NET My Services looks likely to accelerate its growth. Like so many things, however, this rose is not without thorns.

and more. Schemas can also contain an *any* block, allowing an application to insert arbitrary information into a user's entry.

Storing Data

To understand what .NET My Services provides, it's useful to have a simple mental model of how the data it stores is organized. Conceptually, all of the XML-based services are implemented as data stored in some kind of database. To improve reliability and availability, the information in these services is replicated and stored at various .NET My Services data centers. The .NET My Services database is also partitioned, so the information in one user's .NET Calendar service might be stored in different physical locations than the information in another user's .NET Calendar service. This distribution isn't visible to applications, however—it's hidden by the .NET My Services infrastructure.

Data stored in .NET My Services is replicated

Each XML-based service is identified with a uniform resource identifier (URI). For example, the .NET Profile service might be named with the URI http://profile.microsoft.com/net. To access a service, an application specifies that service's name and then works with .NET My Services to locate the appropriate server. Along with naming a service, an application using an XML-based service must also specify which instance of the service it would like to access. In other words, the application must identify a particular user whose data it's interested in. To do this, the application supplies the PUID of the target user. As Figure 8-3 shows, .NET My Services can be thought of conceptually as a database of XML documents, organized by service, with PUIDs acting as the key for each. As the figure suggests, not all users will subscribe to all services, so each service has a document associated with a PUID only for its subscribers.

A client uses a PUID to identify an instance of the service it wishes to access

Accessing Data

Each XML-based service that .NET My Services provides is accessed through an XML Message Interface (XMI). .NET My Services is a new kind of application platform, one that exposes

The information in .NET My Services is accessed through XMIs

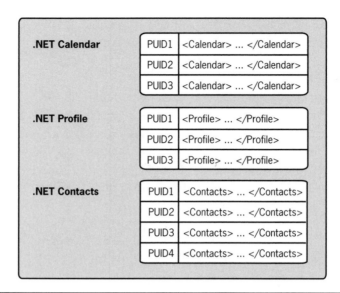

Figure 8-3   Each service can be viewed as a collection of XML documents indexed by PUIDs.

XMIs rather than conventional application programming interfaces (APIs). A .NET My Services application accesses the platform's services via these XMIs much as a conventional application accesses operating system services via APIs. Each XMI defines a set of XML messages that can be sent to and received from a particular service. And no matter what those messages are or what a service does, applications using any XML-based service always access it through SOAP.

The XML-based services each expose a group of methods

Each XML service exposes a common set of standard methods that include query, insert, delete, and update. Each of these methods does just what its name suggests to the data that service maintains. While the names of these methods are common across all of the services, the information sent as parameters and results is service-specific. Along with these standard methods, each service can also expose custom methods. For example, the .NET Inbox service provides the additional methods sendMessage, saveMessage, and copyMessage. The goal is to

The Risk of Committing to .NET My Services

Developers who create applications that depend on .NET My Services might feel that they're at Microsoft's mercy. Once they've committed to the platform, Microsoft could raise the price it charges for these services at any time. Microsoft is not a charity, so what stops the company from instituting outrageous fees for developers who can't easily move their applications elsewhere?

Well, what stops any vendor from raising its prices at will? The answer is simple: competitors. If this emerging market behaves like other markets, competition will keep Microsoft from being able to raise prices once developers become dependent on .NET My Services. If no competitors emerge, then it's likely .NET My Services itself won't be a success, since good ideas always attract others to a market. I'd also expect to see the creators of applications built on .NET My Services demand long-term contracts that lock in reasonable prices.

Microsoft certainly does have one big advantage over any potential competitors, however: It can bundle .NET My Services into Windows. Extending its reach from the desktop to the Internet is no doubt attractive to Microsoft (and to its shareholders). This idea is surely much less attractive to Microsoft's competitors, however. Whatever happens, don't expect this battle over Internet-based Web services to end anytime soon. Microsoft, and probably some of its competitors as well, looks to be in it for the long haul.

let each service expose common functions in a common way while still leaving the service's designer free to provide whatever is needed to meet that service's goals.

As Figure 8-4 illustrates, an application accessing .NET My Services data creates a SOAP request containing various pieces of information. Among other things, that information includes the name of the target service (such as .NET Contacts), the PUID of the user whose service instance should be accessed, the client's Kerberos ticket (which contains the client's PUID and other information), and a call to a method provided by that

Each request identifies a service, a target PUID, who the client is, and more

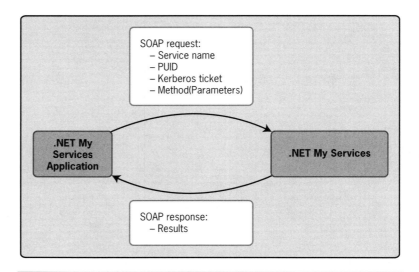

Figure 8-4   A client accesses .NET My Services via SOAP, with each request carrying a specific set of information.

service. Each query is an XPath expression, and any results are returned as XML-defined data.

.NET My Services uses several custom SOAP headers

As described in Chapter 2, SOAP itself is specified using XML, and it defines an envelope containing a body with an optional header. The body contains the parameters or results of a particular call, while the header can contain a variety of things. .NET My Services uses several headers that convey specific information about a particular call. The headers it uses are effectively those defined by Microsoft's Global XML Web Services Architecture (GXA). As described in Chapter 2, these headers provide a standard mechanism for conveying authorization information such as a Kerberos ticket, for relaying messages, and for carrying out other useful functions. Clients can access .NET My Services using either SOAP over HTTP, likely to be the most common approach, or the direct SOAP-to-TCP mapping called Direct Internet Message Encapsulation (DIME).

Controlling Access to Data

To fulfill its promise, .NET My Services will need to provide users with a very high level of control over how their data is made available. In .NET My Services, authorization—determining which clients can access which data—is based on the notion of *roles*. Each client can be assigned to a particular role, and a service's owner can use access control lists (ACLs) to determine which roles have which access rights. Different services can have different allowable roles, each allowing a particular kind of access and view of the data that service provides.

.NET My Services uses roles and ACLs to provide access control

For example, the .NET Calendar service includes (among others) roles with the following abilities:

Each service defines an appropriate group of roles

- Full access to all the information stored by a particular instance of this service. You would typically be in a role with this ability when accessing your own calendar.

- Access to only public data in the service. For example, an executive assistant may be able to manage work-related information in your calendar while having no access to your personal entries.

- Read-only access to the service's data. Your spouse might have this ability, allowing him or her to see what your plans are.

Other services have other roles, each providing a style of access appropriate for the various users that service is likely to have.

A .NET My Services Scenario

The best way to see how an application might use .NET My Services is to look at a scenario. Suppose, for example, that a theater Web site wishes to offer a Web services–based application. This application might let a customer book seats using a

How Can Microsoft Guarantee the Security of .NET My Services Data?

The .NET My Services servers and the information they contain will surely be tempting targets for hackers. Furthermore, Microsoft's history in building secure Web software is far from perfect, as the repeated problems with IIS have shown. How can the company guarantee that the data we place in .NET My Services will be secure?

I don't think it can. In fact, I don't believe Microsoft or any vendor can absolutely guarantee that its Internet-accessible servers will be hacker-proof. Once again, though, it's a business issue: If hackers are able to compromise the data .NET My Services contains, its customers will desert in droves, and .NET My Services will die. Guaranteeing complete security is probably impossible, but Microsoft certainly has a very strong incentive to protect its .NET My Services servers—it's life and death for this business.

It's also worth pointing out that every Internet-accessible Web service will face this problem. In fact, many of the issues that have been raised by .NET My Services are actually generic concerns that must be addressed by any organization that wishes to provide public Web services. .NET My Services is the first highly visible application of this idea, so it is the canary in the coal mine for public Web services. Other organizations that hope to mine this technology vein should pay close attention.

custom client and then send an invitation to one or more of his friends inviting them to join him for the show. Figure 8-5 shows how the application might use .NET My Services to accomplish this.

Applications can use .NET My Services in a variety of ways

Suppose that Mark wishes to book seats and have the application automatically invite Bob to join him. The process begins with Mark's system logging in from his home computer to Passport (step 1), and then requesting a ticket to the booking

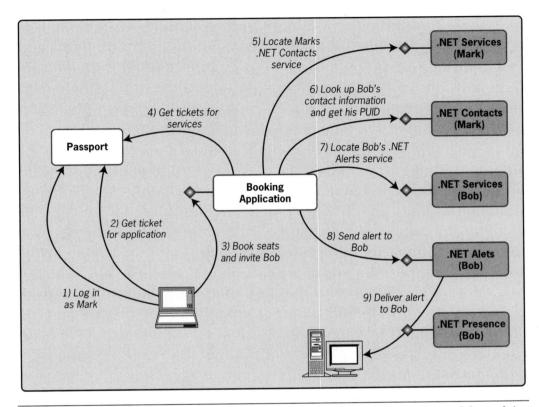

Figure 8-5   A Web services–based application that allows booking theater seats might exploit .NET My Services in many different ways.

application (step 2). Next, Mark uses Web services–based client software to convey his request to the booking application (step 3). This request includes Mark's Kerberos ticket, which the booking application uses to authenticate him and the application he's using. Mark also conveys to the booking application his wish to invite Bob to join him at the theater

Responding to Mark's request, the booking application reserves two seats and then uses .NET My Services to convey Mark's invitation to Bob. This process begins with the application acquiring tickets to the services it will access (step 4). It then uses

Mark's .NET Services data to locate and access Mark's .NET Contacts service (step 5). The booking application looks up Bob in Mark's contact list and extracts Bob's PUID, which is stored with his name (step 6). The application next accesses Bob's .NET Services data (step 7) to find Bob's .NET Alerts service and adds an alert message to Bob's .NET Alerts data (step 8) containing Mark's invitation.

Once this is done, .NET My Services uses Bob's .NET Presence information to locate a device Bob is near. In this case, that device is Bob's home computer, so the alert containing the invitation is sent there (step 9). How this alert appears to Bob depends on the software available on the device on which he receives it. In Windows XP, for instance, it can be delivered via a pop-up on the screen (sometimes referred to as *toast* because of the toaster-like way the message appears from the bottom of the screen).

This example could be significantly more complicated

Other services could also be used in this scenario. For example, the booking application could access Mark's .NET Wallet service to charge for the tickets, and it could also write the theater date into both Mark's and Bob's .NET Calendar service. The main thing to note in this example, however, is how much .NET My Services did on behalf of the booking application. First, this application used .NET My Services to authenticate Mark, its client. Then, once Mark had supplied Bob's name, the application relied on .NET My Services to locate Bob and send him the invitation. Providing these services independently, especially the location and asynchronous notification capabilities, would likely be a daunting task for the developers of the booking application. And if every application did these things for itself, the result would be an extraordinary duplication of effort. Just as with an operating system, having a common way to perform common tasks and store common information makes sense.

What's the Killer App for .NET My Services?

Nobody buys Windows for its own sake. Windows is a platform for applications, and it's those applications that make us choose it over another operating system. Similarly, .NET My Services is a platform. Without attractive applications, people won't pay for it. So what's the killer app for .NET My Services? What software built on this platform will be so valuable that a large number of customers will rush to sign up?

Nobody knows. Early tests have suggested that the ability to overlay the calendars of different individuals and organizations might be an attractive possibility. Imagine being able to display the free/busy days of every colleague you'd like to have at a particular meeting, or of every member of your family you'd like to join you on holidays, on one screen. Suppose your favorite sports team or the local symphony posted its schedule in a .NET Calendar, then let you overlay those dates with your own .NET Calendar.

Or, because more and more people have multiple client devices—computers at home and at work, mobile phones, PDAs, and others—perhaps using .NET My Services to synchronize address books and other information will be a service that people will pay for. Or maybe some new .NET My Services–based feature in a future version of Office will be a major driver for adoption. There's no shortage of possibilities.

But should we be surprised that the killer app for this new platform isn't yet obvious? No. The killer app for previous new platforms, the thing that really drove people to buy it, wasn't commonly obvious when the platform first shipped. Who knew that Lotus 1-2-3 would be so important to the future of IBM's personal computer or that desktop publishing would motivate the masses to buy a Macintosh? Both the creators of applications and their users take time to figure out which ones really matter. For .NET My Services to succeed, some very useful applications must appear. I'm not at all surprised that we don't yet know what these will be.

Conclusion

.NET My Services allows creating a new kind of application

A key goal of .NET My Services is to let end users access and share their own data from diverse software running on many different devices. More generally, though, .NET My Services's goal is to allow developers to create more powerful and more useful Web-based software. It's a new kind of platform for building a new kind of application. Because of this, it's likely to take some time for developers to understand what those applications should look like and how they should behave. Nevertheless, .NET My Services is an interesting and innovative idea, one with the potential to change our world significantly.

New ideas are the lifeblood of software

More than this, though, .NET My Services is a first-rate illustration of a fundamental principle in the field we work in: New technologies can create whole new kinds of applications. Not all of those applications succeed, but this in no way lessens the value of innovation. Microsoft's .NET initiative contains many new technologies, along with some reworkings of existing ideas, and it will spawn a host of new applications. Many will succeed, while others will surely fail. Yet whatever the fate of individual innovations, the core idea—moving forward into the unknown space of new technology—will remain the foundation of software development.

About the Author

David Chappell is principal of Chappell & Associates (www.davidchappell.com) in San Francisco, California. Through his keynotes, seminars, writing, and consulting, David helps information technology professionals around the world understand, use, market, and make better decisions about enterprise software technologies.

David has been the keynote speaker for conferences in the United States, Europe, Latin America, and the Middle East, and he's also delivered keynote addresses at many in-house events. His popular seminars have been attended by tens of thousands of developers and decision makers in more than two dozen countries, and his appearances have been covered in print and online publications in the United States, England, Israel, China, India, and other countries. David's books on enterprise software technologies have been translated into ten languages and are used in courses at MIT, ETH Zurich, and other schools. He is series editor for Addison-Wesley's *Independent Technology Guides*, and more than 100 of David's articles have appeared in various publications.

David also consults with a diverse group of companies each year, with Compaq, Microsoft, and Stanford University among his recent clients. His projects have included writing the standard technical presentation on a new technology for a software vendor's field organization, creating new product training material for an enterprise sales force, working with a software services firm to define a new practice area, and helping a software start-up create its marketing strategy.

David holds a B.S. in economics and an M.S. in computer science, both from the University of Wisconsin-Madison. He has also participated in executive education at the Wharton School of Business.

Index